From Bureaucracy to Hyperarchy in Netcentric and Quick Learning Organizations

Exploring Future Public Management Practice

a volume in
Research in Public Management

Series Editors:
Lawrence R. Jones and Nancy C. Roberts
Naval Postgraduate School

Research in Public Management

Lawrence R. Jones and Nancy C. Roberts, Series Editors

*Communicable Crises: Prevention, Response, and
Recovery in the Global* (2007)
edited by Deborah E. Gibbons

The Legacy of June Pallot: Public Sector Financial Management (2006)
edited by Susan Newberry

*How People Harness Their Collective Wisdom to
Create the Future* (2006)
by Alexander N. Christakis with Kenneth C. Bausch

*International Public Financial Management Reform
Progress, Contradictions, and Challenges* (2005)
edited by James Guthrie, Olov Olson,
Christopher Humphrey, and L. R. Jones

Budgeting and Financial Management for National Defense (2004)
by Jerry L. McCaffery and L. R. Jones

*Managing the Electronic Government:
From Vision to Practice* (2004)
by Kuno Schedler, Lukas Summermatter, and
Bernhard Schmidt

*Budgeting and Financial Management in
the Federal Government* (2001)
by Jerry L. McCaffery and L. R. Jones

From Bureaucracy to Hyperarchy in Netcentric and Quick Learning Organizations

Exploring Future Public Management Practice

by

Lawrence R. Jones
Naval Postgraduate School

and

Fred Thompson
Willamette University

INFORMATION AGE
PUBLISHING

Charlotte, North Carolina • www.infoagepub.com

Library of Congress Cataloging-in-Publication Data

Jones, L. R.
  From bureaucracy to hyperarchy in netcentric and quick learning organizations : exploring future public management practice / by Lawrence R. Jones and Fred Thompson.
     p. cm. -- (Research in public management)
  Includes bibliographical references and index.
  ISBN 978-1-59311-605-7 (pbk.) -- ISBN 978-1-59311-606-4 (hardcover) 1. Public administration. 2. Organizational learning. 3. Organizational change. I. Thompson, Fred, 1942 Oct. 29- II. Title.
  JF1351.J64 2007
  352.3--dc22

2006101882

ISBN 13: 978-1-59311-605-7 (pbk.)
         978-1-59311-606-4 (hardcover)
ISBN 10: 1-59311-605-5 (pbk.)
         1-59311-606-3 (hardcover)

Copyright © 2007 IAP–Information Age Publishing, Inc.

All rights reserved. No part of this publication may be reproduced, stored in a retrieval system, or transmitted, in any form or by any means, electronic, mechanical, photocopying, microfilming, recording or otherwise, without written permission from the publisher.

Printed in the United States of America

CONTENTS

Preface and Acknowledgments *vii*

1. Understanding Public Management as an International Academic Field *1*
2. The Evolution of Public Management Reform Practice *11*
3. Assessing Public Management Reform in an International Context: Performance Measurement, Managing for Results and Fiscal Devolution *23*
4. Phases of Organizational Transformation and Restructuring *97*
5. Changing Processes: What Works, What Does Not, and Why? *111*
6. Implementing the Continuous Learning Cycle to Improve Strategic Planning and Organizational Productivity *129*
7. Matching Institutional Structure to Strategic Planning and Positioning *147*
8. Creating the Quick Learning Organization in Government *185*
9. Moving From Bureaucracy to Hyperarchy and Netcentricity: Enabling the Quick Learning Organization Using IT and Modern Technology *231*

References *261*

PREFACE AND ACKNOWLEDGMENTS

This book focuses on the inherent contradiction between bureaucracy, hierarchy, and the vision inspired by the architecture of modern information technology of a more egalitarian culture in public organizations. We agree with Evans and Wurster (1997, pp. 71-82) and others who have argued that, in the future, knowledge-based productive relationships will be designed around fluid, team-based collaborative communities, either within organizations (i.e., deconstructed value chains), or in collaborative alliances such as those with "amorphous and permeable corporate boundaries characteristic of companies in the Silicon Valley" that is, deconstructed supply chains (pp. 71-82). In such relationships everyone can communicate richly with everyone else on the basis of shared standards and, like the Internet itself, these relationships will eliminate the need to channel information, thereby eliminating the trade-off between information bandwidth and connectivity. "The possibility (or the threat) of random access and information symmetry," they conclude, "will destroy all hierarchies, whether of logic or power" (pp. 71-82)

To develop this theme and argument we first ground our discussion in our conceptions of the field of public management, of governance, and of government—characterized as it is by highly bureaucratic organizational design. We endeavor first to define the nature of the beast we are attempting to change and then indicate why and how it should be reformed. In this regard we may observe that the outline and to some extent the framework of a theory of public management and reform has been developed over the past several decades. However, the practice of reform is still open for examination interpretation. This is part of the reason for writing this book. Our initial objective in the book is to define contemporary public management as an international disciplinary field. The definition provided is intended to contribute to a better understanding of how the field should be viewed and how public management differs from private sector management and traditional public administration. The second objective is to define and delineate some important terms used to describe and direct change in public organizations. The third objective is to explore recent reform trends in public management in an international context, with emphasis on Asia in particular, and to a lesser extent New Zealand and Australia. The fourth is to demonstrate, in our view, how public organizations ought to be reformed to make them more productive using methods that are useful in both the public and private sectors in selected contexts. Chapters 1 and 2 are intended to address our first and second objectives. Chapter 3 is aimed at satisfying our third objective and includes case studies and examples from a number of Asian nations (including Cambodia, China, Indonesia, Mongolia, the Philippines, and Thailand) to illustrate reform initiatives in practice in the region and of fiscal devolution as a Asian reform agenda in particular. The remaining six chapters are offered to meet our fourth objective to indicate a methodology for public sector management reform practice in transition from bureaucracy to hyperarchical, quick learning, and netcentric organizations.

So much has been written about public management and administrative reform in the past decade that in developing the approach for this book we wondered whether there was anything new to say. As is the case for most professionals working in our field, we recognize that the topic of new public management has been worked over very thoroughly. New public management is no longer "new" and, therefore, we believe in the future it is better to use the words public management change or innovation when speaking and writing about emerging initiatives in the public sector. And, as most in our field also understand, the topics receiving significant attention at present are networking and a set of issues related to what is termed "governance." Research on networking has been ongoing since at least the 1970s. Many issues related to networks and networking remain unresolved so that continued dialogue in this area is constructive. Renewed attention to governance (versus government) appears to have emerged in the public management dialogue and literature in the past 5 years or so.

What do those who focus on the need for renewed emphasis on governance issues mean when they exhort the field to think about this topic? While no claim is made that we capture all of what is intended, it seems to us that a renewed interest in governance concentrates on five issue clusters, each with its own set of imperatives: (a) improved understanding of linkages between politics and administration, (b) the need for improved analysis of stakeholder positioning and preferences in formulating public policy and management execution strategy, (c) analysis to better define network relationships among stakeholders internal and external to government, (d) the necessity for addressing potential and real abridgements of public participation rights and basic principles of democracy, and (d) finding remedies to address the absence of government responsiveness to citizens in policy formation and execution. Furthermore, the governance movement may be viewed as a response to a perceived absence of sufficient attention given to these five issue areas in the drive to devise and implement New Public Management (NPM) or neo-managerialism in government over the past several decades.

While defenders of NPM may argue that the intent of managerial reform was to improve efficiency and effectiveness within government, thereby making government more responsive to citizen service preferences, few would argue that these objectives have been achieved as a result of world-wide adoption of many of the management policies, procedures, and methods advocated by NPM proponents. Proponents of NPM often argue that not enough time has elapsed to thoroughly evaluate NPM implementation. From our view, this is more the truth in some settings than in others. Experience with NPM in New Zealand, for example, is mature enough so that many of the consequences of implementation are relatively well understood. However, in Switzerland it is clear that more time is needed to assess the impact of NPM-oriented reform. In the United States, there probably is enough evidence to pursue such evaluation but, as of yet, satisfactory empirical analysis has not been presented. However, beyond the issue of evaluation, few defenders of NPM would argue that those who assert the need for improved governance are wrong or misguided in directing attention to problems in this area. One thing that we have learned quite clearly from evaluation of NPM is that little reform takes place beyond reengineering in public organizations (which in most cases has been positive in and of itself) unless political policymakers become interested and take on as part of their mandate a consistent push to put the concepts and practices of NPM into place, and then to monitor and steer its implementation. Thus, the need for improved governance is evident to both supporters and critics of past public management reform.

Given these understandings, our instincts and synthesis of current events in the field of public management indicate that the area most neglected and in need of greater academic and practitioner attention is the issue of strategy, whether viewed from the perspective of management reform implementation, strategic planning, results-oriented management, or performance management. Thus, the framework and the works represented in this book address the dimensions of strategy in public management reform from different perspectives including increased demands for accountability, decentralization, devolution, application of information technology, management control, anticorruption initiatives, and performance assessment and management. Most of the works employ case study methodology as part of their efforts to investigate the presence or absence of strategic intent and approach, and the relative success of various strategies, in venues where reform has been sought as an explicit goal of governments, elected officials and public managers.

We believe the organization of this volume and the content presented offer a valuable perspective on the dynamics of reform in a variety of venues. Our aim is modest in this regard. We hope to contribute to the continuing dialogue over strategy, objectives, management practice, implementation, and evaluation of consequences that characterizes research in the field of international public management.

One observation related to this last point is that, as far as we can tell, over the past decade a new subdiscipline has emerged—international public management. With respect to issues deemed worthy of attention in this subdisciplinary area, there is little or no difference between what is of interest to those who conduct research on domestic reform versus comparative or international reform. What distinguishes the new subdiscipline is its explicit emphasis on international and comparative research, that is, a wider content within which to investigate issues of relevance to reform.

What often signals the emergence of new subdisciplines is the appearance of new outlets for publication. Over the past decade a number of new journals have begun publication of research on or related to management reform in an international and comparative context. Further, a number of existing high-visibility journals are publishing articles that may be viewed to contribute to the relatively new field. *The International Public Management Network* and its *International Public Management Journal* and *International Public Management Review* may have contributed to the emergence of this subdiscipline in some, but this represent only a small part of a very evident trend across the world landscape. The Chinese blessing "May you live in interesting times" seems to have been realized for many of us who work in the field of international public management. Indeed, never before has there been so much data available from so many contexts upon which to base research on change in public sector management and governance.

In conclusion we wish to acknowledge the contribution a number of colleagues to this book. First, Donald Kettl is coauthor of chapter 3 which includes material from an article published by L. R. Jones and Donald F.

Kettl in the *International Public Management Review* (2003, pp. 1-19). Clay Wescott also contributed to this chapter. Gil Reschenthaler contributed to chapter 8. Some of the content in chapter 9 was published in *Digital State at the Leading Edge*, edited by Sandford Borins et al. (Thompson, 2006). Also, some of the material in this book draws on our 1999 book *Public Management: Institutional Reform for the Twenty-First Century* (Jones & Thompson, 1999).

We wish to thank our colleague Michael Barzelay for his critical thinking and writing that stimulated us in working on this book. Additionally, many colleagues helped us formulate our conception of organizations, the field of public management, and our understanding of the dynamics of reform, notably Robert Biller, Robert Behn, Barry Bozeman, Sandford Borins, Geert Bouckhaert, Phillip Candreva, Christopher Hood, Steven Kelman, Todd LaPorte, Irvine Lapsley, Charles Levine, Riccardo Mussari, Frieder Naschold, Mark Nissen, June Pallot, Christopher Pollitt, Kuno Schedler, W. T. Stanbury, John Wanna, Clay Wescott, Aaron Wildavsky, Jiannan Wu, and William Zumeta. We thank them all for their creativity, attention, and contributive work to the field of public management, much of which is cited in this book.

Finally, this book could not have been written without support from the Program Executive Office, C4I and Space Systems Command in the form of sponsorship of the George F. A. Wagner Chair in Public Management at the Naval Postgraduate School, the Naval Pacific Air Command, the Asian Development Bank and Willamette University through its sponsorship of the Grace and Elmer Goudy Chair in Public Management and Policy in the Atkinson Graduate School of Management and, last, the International Public Management Network.

L. R. Jones
Monterey, California

Fred Thompson,
Salem, Oregon

CHAPTER 1

UNDERSTANDING PUBLIC MANAGEMENT AS AN INTERNATIONAL ACADEMIC FIELD

Public management has evolved as a distinct subdiscipline within the larger discipline of management over the past several decades. Public management is different from what is often referred to as "traditional public administration" in that the former focuses more on what happens within governments and on the operation of the line functions of government while public management pays more attention to the operation of government organizations from the perspective of their interaction with the environments in which they operate. Public management tends to conceive of governments and governance systems similar to the ways that organizational theorists focus on strategic behavior in response to contingency in the environment. Public management views organizations that provide services to the public as adaptive systems influenced by critical variables in their surroundings. Additionally, public management incorporates an economics perspective on the value of competition between organizations in markets, and also business/marketing thinking about

---

From Bureaucracy to Hyperarchy in Netcentric and Quick Learning Organizations: Exploring Future Public Management Practice, 1–9
Copyright © 2007 by Information Age Publishing
All rights of reproduction in any form reserved.

strategic positioning of products/services and product/service lines relative to the attributes of consumer preferences and market demand.

Public management as a field has become increasingly international. Contributions to the field have been made by scholars from nations around the world, reflecting the understanding that what may be learned from the experience in a broad range of nations may be relevant in specific national contexts and in other public sector settings within nations. The internationalization of the dialogue on public sector reform and change recognizes the importance of studying and comparing institutional arrangements and management methods between nations and among sets of nations to contribute to knowledge about what works, what does not, and why in a variety of contexts.

The differences between public management and public administration also may be understood by comparing the influence of Luther Gulick (1937) and the Gulick and Urwick POSDCORB model that stipulated the tasks of public administration to consist of planning, organizing, staffing, developing (the organization culture), controlling, operating, reporting, and budgeting. This may be contrasted with the perspective of organizational theorist James D. Thompson (1967) and his conception of the study of complex organizations as adaptive systems. Public management places emphasis on the role of the manager as an active and motivating agent whereas public administration tends to view administrators as those who more passively execute the will of their political masters. To illustrate this point further it is useful to contrast the Gulick and Urwick model with the view of renown management scholar Peter Drucker in his explanation of the role of the manager (1953, pp. 343-344): "A manager sets objectives ... organizes, motivates and communicates ... and develops people." Drucker's words also resonate with a major tenet of public management scholarship—creating circumstances in organizations that "let managers manage" (See also Drucker, 1969, 1993, 1994).

Even when public management scholars look inside organizations they tend to be influenced more by the perspectives of sociologists including Peter Blau, Chris Argyris, Charles Perrow, and others, political scientists including Aaron Wildavsky (e.g., on political dynamics in budgeting), and economists and public choice theorists rather than the public administration functionalists perspective that rests on the PODSCORP model and on more mechanistic views of organizations represented in the work of Frederick Taylor and "Taylorism."

Additionally, when public management scholars look inside organizations they tend to focus on the incentives and disincentives that produce specific types of behavior, relationships, and decisions rather than the rules and forms that prescribe how personnel, civil service, budget, and other functions are guided and operated. Public management focuses on the operation of management systems and the use of management techniques, technology and control systems, that is, the performance of entire systems evaluated by performance criteria versus the tendency to concentrate on how the individual parts of the government operate and evaluate these based on workload and similar measures.

In this regard, public management also tends to focus on the outcomes of systems more than on the factor inputs to production. Public management shares much with the benefit/cost and risk/benefit perspectives and methodologies familiar to scholars who work in the field of public policy analysis, and in this way scholars in both public management and policy approach analysis and problems solving in ways that are different from the methods of traditional public administration that tend to look at hierarchy and bureaucratic rules and procedures.

Public management shares with public administration the methods of interview and survey, participant observation and case analysis. However, in public management we tend to push these methods beyond the ways that public administrationists or political scientists often use them. For example, public administration researchers often try to gauge the power of a government agency by the strength of its ties to powerful elected officials and also to voter preferences. Public management researchers want to use surveys of citizen satisfaction with services in much the same way that private sector marketer researchers do, based on a desire to shape service provision policy to the patterns of citizen needs and preferences, and to determine appropriate service delivery methods, differential pricing alternatives, and different institutional arrangements for the provision of services—including provision by the private and not-for-profit sectors.

Public management research is concerned with the operation of agents, agencies, agent relationships, and government entities as they operate within networks and with stakeholders inside and outside of government. Public management research accepts the premise that individual agents, agencies and governments cannot solve problems by unilateral action. Rather, if problems are to be resolved at all, the pathways to progress will lie in cooperation or some other forms of relationship between a number of entities (i.e., stakeholders) in the problem environment.

Public management research tends to conceive of "resolving" problems and moving on to new ones that have to be dealt with continuously as the relationships between methods and the nature of problems evolve as dynamic systems operating within unpredictable and contingent environments.

Public management has taken on methodological concepts and tools from the private sector, for example, reengineering, reinvention, new technologies, citizen/consumer market analysis, differential pricing to influence patterns of demand.

Public management scholarship tends to focus on incentives and disincentives, as noted, on the input side to government and governance, and on the results or outputs and outcomes of what networks of government agencies and other entities produce. The application of what is termed the production function model (input > production/workload measures > output and output measures > outcomes and outcomes measures in a feedback loop) is prevalent in public management as a product of business-type thinking.

Public management research has attempted to assess performance of public entities and to devise measures to evaluate performance over time. The purpose of evaluation is, in the end, to find ways to deliver services more effectively and efficiently to citizens. The improvement of an administrative system that might be judged as successful from the public administration perspective using measures of workload appear to public management scholars to focus on the wrong measures of success. Improvement of a payroll system may, for example, satisfy internal budget and administrative criteria for success. However, unless services are better supplied to citizens as a result, public management success criteria will not be satisfied. Accomplishment of the tasks of performance measurement, performance management, reengineering, and realignment are not ends in themselves for public management scholars. The goals of system change from the perspective of public management are oriented toward reduced cycle time, increased quality, and reducing costs for citizens.

Much published public management scholarship argues for delegation of management authority and responsibility to managers (as individuals) and for holding managers accountable for the performance of the entities they manage. The dictum of public management, noted above, is to "let managers manage" but this must also acknowledge that managers also must be held more closely accountable for the successes and failures of the units they manage. Public administrationists, in contrast, tend to want to place responsibility and accountability more on entire entities such as government agencies or departments. Public management scholars tend to view this as placing the authority and responsibility where accountability cannot be obtained effectively. Rather, where this is practiced, predictable "bureaucratic" pattern of behavior emerge. Bureaucrats and elected officials, from the public management perspective, tend to take credit for successes but to avoid association with failures—or even risk and ambiguity. On the other hand, public managers are expected to cope with risk and uncertainty and be held accountable for how they manage under such conditions.

Public management scholarship in the past decade has placed great emphasis on the concept of value, for example, on management changes that increase or reduce value to citizens, government entities, agencies, mangers, and employees. The concept of value creation is essential in assessing management processes, performance, and reform. Public management scholarship tends to look at value production from the perspective of value chain analysis and similar approaches. The concept of cutting rules, procedures and process that do not add value to the production of the outputs/outcomes that satisfy the mission of the organization or government is central to the public management paradigm.

Much public management scholarship de-emphasizes the differences between management in the public and private sector. "Good management is good management regardless of sector" is a phrase that represents this view in essence. This does not presume that the objectives of government and business are identical. However, many objectives do not appear to differ much, that is, organizations and managers in both sectors are interested and motivated to "increase value" in their organizations and outputs. Additionally, public management research tends to assume that work condition attributes and incentives that produce employee satisfaction in one sector are roughly the same as those of the other sector. An example is the widely shared assumption in the field that employees are not motivated solely by money. Survey research has demonstrated that employees want to feel as though what they do matters in terms of contributing to the satisfaction of the mission of the organization, and they want to know how what they do specifically contributes value in this effort. People want to get up in the morning and look forward to going to work rather than dreading the experience. These factors do not seem to differ between the public and private sectors. Consequently, public management seeks the flexibility to manage people with the same degree if flexibility as employers in the private sector, although this flexibility has been reduced to a considerable extent in business over the past several decades. Civil service rules and procedures and labor unions tend to resist changes to personnel systems that move further toward performance management and away from seniority and protection of the rights of workers. Public management advocates do not deny the need to protect civil servants from the abuses of political systems, patronage, fraud, waste, and abuse of privilege. However, public management scholarship tends to view the costs of the operation of the controls and control systems (command and control) in personnel management, budgeting and other areas of government as often more costly that the costs of abuse under properly designed and implemented management control systems.

The conception of the learning organization that constantly restructures, reengineers, reinvents, realigns, and rethinks its methods and policies is central to the vision of much public management thinking. From this perspective, organizations that learn to move through the observation, orientation, decision, and action loop more quickly learn faster from their actions relative to key attributed in their environments so as to be more likely to survive and thrive than organizations that do not act and learn as quickly.

Public management is recognized as a highly interdisciplinary field of study. Substantial contributions to the development of public management have been made by scholars whose primary fields of research include (a) those of the traditional social sciences—including political science, economics, sociology, psychology, philosophy, cultural anthropology, (b) the biological and physical sciences—biology, mathematics/statistics, physics, chemistry, and (c) applied fields of study including law, public administration, policy analysis, program evaluation, organizational theory and behavior, business management, operations research and systems analysis, computer and management information systems, accounting, corporate and municipal finance, program, education, medicine, and others.

The scholarly output of researchers in the field of public management, reflecting the case study method in many instances, that has emerged over the past several decades has been published in a broad range of journals. Among these journals are the *Journal of Public Policy Analysis and Management, Governance, Management Science, the Academy of Management Journal*, the *Academy of Management Review, Administrative Science Quarterly, Public Choice, Public Management Review, Harvard Business Review, Sloan Management Review,* the *International Public Management Journal,* the *International Public Management Review, Financial Accountability and Management, Administration and Society, Policy Sciences, Public Administration Review, Public Productivity and Management Review, IEEE Engineering Management Review, Risk Analysis,* the *Journal of Public Administration Research and Theory, Public Interest,* and others. In addition, hundreds of books on public management have been published in the past 2 decades, indicative of the high level of dialogue among scholars in the field.

To illustrate the nature of the interdisciplinary influence on the evolution of this relatively new field, work in public management comprehends that research in the areas of electoral politics, voter behavior, theories of governance, the dynamics of political systems and other subdisciplines in political science, including public administration and public policy, are highly relevant to an understanding of policy making, its relationship to implementation, political leadership, resource competition, and allocation decision making. Public management research methodology is influenced by public choice and new institutional economics—as well as by sociology and organizational theory, mathematics/statistics, psychology, and so forth. The emphasis that public management scholars give to the environments in which management systems, organizations, governments, governance systems, nonprofit organizations, and other public entities operate has been influenced directly and indirectly by foundation work in economics, political science, sociology, anthropology, philosophy, and biology as well as that in business (especially marketing) and law. Public management scholarship conceives of public sector organizational change organically, as "evolutionary" and "adaptive" to environmental contingency almost as if organizations were living systems. Public management scholarship searches for the presence of sufficient inputs (political, economic, social, cultural) to form a "critical mass" of elements necessary to support management change and reform, using the term much as physicists and chemist do in their fields of research. Public management scholarship investigates policy and organizational networks under many of the assumptions familiar to biologists and ecologists. Public management analyzes the cultural characteristics of organizations and their environments in ways learned one way or another from anthropologists, sociologists, biologists, and even physicists and chemists. In empirical case analysis, public management scholarship formulates tests of hypotheses and applies statistical methods in same ways in which the scientific method is employed in the physical and biological sciences. In summary, public management is highly interdisciplinary—and the degree to which this is the case has increased over the past decade.

CONCLUSIONS

The distinguishing characteristics of public management may be understood as follows:

1. A focus on management functions and the impact on production and service delivery of dysfunctions in the organizational context, for example, coping with contingency in the environment;
2. A focus on understanding the behavior of organizations and organizational units from the perspective of stakeholders (external) rather than on bureaucratic line functions and processes (internal and more typical of public administration);
3. A focus on the components and performance of management including leadership, strategic planning, human resource management, financial management (including accounting and budgeting), acquisition and contracting, transportation, logistics, supply chain management, information technology, marketing,

and an emphasis on the application of economic theory and logic in assessment of management performance;
4. A focus on economy, efficiency and the responsiveness of public sector organizations;
5. An emphasis on quality, cost, and cycle time in improving the delivery of services to the public;
6. An emphasis on citizen driven definition of services demand versus bureaucratic definition and of responding to public demands and preferences;
7. A focus on executive leadership and the delegated roles of midlevel managers and service providers, that is, "letting managers manage" and providing the requisite skills to do so effectively;
8. Consideration of management as generic, minimizing the differences between public and private sectors, with a strong philosophical link to the evolution of management thinking in the private sector, but with some linkages to public administration and political science, sociology, psychology, and economics;
9. An acceptance that political analysis is inherently parochial, whereas managerialist analysis may be more ecumenical, and that the field's primary common denominators show best where its discourse is focused on transition;
10. In comparison with political science, public management is more applied and oriented toward prescription (making suggestions for how to improve the performance of public organizations), as opposed to mere explanation and analysis of problems from a theoretical viewpoint. In comparison with policy analysis, public management is more concerned with implementation—what actually has to happen inside the organization for good ideas to turn into reality—as opposed simply to making abstract prescriptions about good policy. In comparison with public administration, public management is oriented more toward strategic actions by organizational leaders, in particular in interacting with the political system as opposed to an emphasis on lower levels within organizations and line functions;
11. 11. A focus on value added in analysis of public management change and reform (see for example Moore, 1995);
12. Case analysis is used extensively in public management research. In addition, public management as a field has become increasingly international. Contributions to the field have been made by scholars from nations around the world, reflecting the under-

standing that what may be learned from the experience in a broad range of nations may be relevant in specific national contexts and in other public sector settings within nations.

In the next chapter we chronicle the rise, maturation, and status of the public management reform movement with emphasis on and examples from Asian nations.

CHAPTER 2

THE EVOLUTION OF PUBLIC MANAGEMENT REFORM PRACTICE

The conduct of the public's business is undergoing wide-sweeping change. This is a worldwide phenomenon—not merely with respect to the fact of change, but in its content as well. The components of the public management reform paradigm include: a commitment to providing high quality services that citizens value; giving public sector managers increased autonomy to acquire and manage resources; rewarding them for meeting demanding operating targets; providing the resources, human and technological, they need to meet those targets; and, "a receptiveness to competition and an open minded attitude about which activities should be performed by the public sector as opposed to the private sector" (Borins, 1997, p. 49).

The prominence of the public management reform in the United States is initially due to some extent to the efforts of David Osborne, a journalist, and Ted Gaebler, a former city manager, who wrote the widely read book *Reinventing Government: How the Entrepreneurial Spirit is Transforming the Public Sector From Schoolhouse to Statehouse, City Hall to the Pentagon*" (Osborne & Gaebler, 1992). Publication of *The Gore Report on*

Reinventing Government: From Red Tape to Results, Creating a Government that Works Better and Costs Less, Report of the National Performance Review further heightened interest in public management reform practice. These critics of bureaucratic rigidity and others called for inventing, "a government that puts people first," by creating a clear sense of mission, by steering more and rowing less, by delegating authority, by replacing rules and regulations with incentives, by developing budgets based upon results, by exposing government operations to competition, by searching for market rather than administrative solutions, and, whenever possible, by measuring the success of government's actions in terms of customer satisfaction (Gore, 1993; Jones & Thompson, 1999).

Reforming government is part of a much larger movement, one that is now worldwide. Public management reformers are to be found at most if not all levels of government in nations as diverse as the United Kingdom, Sweden, the Netherlands, Canada, Switzerland, Germany, Italy, Denmark, Finland, the United States of America, Argentina, Brazil, Singapore, China and Hong Kong, Mongolia, Thailand, Cambodia, Indonesia, the Philippines, and, of course, New Zealand and Australia. Also noteworthy is that public sector managerial reform now is widely practiced in lesser developed nations, although the human and institutional infrastructure and capacity in these nations must be present before reforms can move very far (Schick, 1998; Wescott & Jones, 2006).

Reformers wish to foster decentralization of authority, replacing rules and regulations with incentives, development of budgets based upon results, exposing government operations to competition, searching for market rather than administrative solutions, and, whenever possible, measuring the success of government in terms of customer satisfaction. Barzelay (1992, 2001) writes about an emerging postbureaucratic paradigm in nearly identical terms, as do Schwartz (1994) in his examination of state reorganization in Australia, Denmark, Zealand, and Sweden in the 1980s, and Kuno Schedler (1995, 2001, 2003; Schedler & Proeller, 2006) in description of the Swiss model.

The World Bank has shifted its attention to providing institutional design assistance. It too likes incentives, competition, and market solutions. However, in one respect its approach differs from most of the postbureaucratic literature. The World Bank's conclusions about the benefits of privatization and market-like mechanisms are based on extensive data and careful case studies. Most of the of the other writings on the topic are wholly convincing only so far as they claim that something new has been tried and seems to make sense; the World Bank actually shows that divestiture works and that poorly designed market-like mechanisms do not perform as intended.

The terminology used most widely to label the changes now occurring in the conduct of the public's business is "managerialism" which Christopher Pollitt (1993, p. 180) described as:

1. A bold use of market-like mechanisms for those parts of the public sector that cannot be transferred directly into private ownership;
2. Intensified organizational and spatial decentralization of the management and delivery of services;
3. A constant rhetorical emphasis on the need to improve service quality;
4. An equally relentless emphasis on customer satisfaction.

Indeed, these elements, especially the stress on quality and customer satisfaction, are found in every treatment of public management reform from Barzelay to the World Bank. However, the new public management (NPM) is no longer, having been practiced since at least the 1980s. Thus, in this book the term public management reform is used instead of NPM. Given this perspective, what is different in public management versus traditional public administration? As Lynn (1996) explains in review of the literature on public management, there is little that is new about the use of market-like mechanisms, privatization, decentralization, an emphasis on quality or even a customer orientation (see also Juran, 1944; Shewhart & Deming, 1945).

Because public management reform logically implies a difference from traditional public administration, the best place to begin to answer to these questions is with the traditional public administration. According to David Garson and Sam Overman (1983), there are six differences between public management and public administration. These are:

1. A focus on management functions rather than social values and conflicts between bureaucracy and democracy;
2. A focus on economy and efficiency in lieu of equity, responsiveness, or political salience;
3. A focus on midlevel managers in lieu of political or policy elites;
4. A tendency to consider management generic, or at least minimize the differences between public and private sectors in lieu of accentuating focus on the organization in lieu of a focus on laws, institutions, and political-bureaucratic processes;
5. A strong philosophical link with management study in lieu of close ties to political science or sociology.

None of the literature on recent public management reform reviewed, with the possible exception of Pollitt's *Managerialism and the Public Services* (Pollitt, 2003), focuses on social values, equity, responsiveness, or political salience, political or policy elites, or laws, and none shows close ties to political science or sociology, although all give more or less attention to the political feasibility of reform. Instead, they tend to focus on economy and efficiency, to minimize the differences between public and private sectors, and to show close ties to management study. For example, business and organizaional theory gurus such as Peter Drucker, Theodore Levitt, W. E. Deming, Thomas Peters, Michael Hammer, Chris Argyris, D. A. Schon, Joseph Bower, Robert Anthony, Karl Weick, James March, Robert Kaplan and Robin Cooper, Henry Mintzberg, Michael Porter, Alfred Chandler, C. K. Prahaladad and Gary Hamel, and Peter Senge are positively and frequently cited in the literature—they are cited far more often than are the giants of public administration. Clearly, public management reform practice has a lot in common with the traditional public administration, but there are differences and these are arguably crucial.

In the first place, public management reform places emphasis on processes, missions, and deemphasizes functions, activities, and tasks. The building blocks of the old public management were bureaucracy and hierarchy. Bureaucracy involves breaking tasks down into their simplest component parts and recombining them into organizational units, based usually on function and geography. It rests on the presumption that the exercise of judgment should be passed up managerial ranks, activities simplified, standardized, and controlled from above, and administrative functions delegated to staff specialists. Under this approach, organizational processes move like relay races, with one group of functional specialists passing the baton to the next.

The basic building block of public organizational reform is the multidisciplinary team whose members work together from start of a job to its completion. Public management reform practice holds that jobs should be designed around an objective or outcome instead of a single function, in part because functional specialization and sequential execution are inherently inimical to expeditious processing. Besides, the use of modern object-oriented data bases, expert systems, and networked information systems have rendered administrative centralization and specialization of staff functions such as reporting, accounting, personnel, purchasing, or quality assurance largely obsolete. Computers make it possible to capture information once—at the source—and to coordinate parallel activities during their performance—not after they are completed.

In the second place, public management reform practice emphasizes holds that decision-making authority must be delegated to the teams that do an organization's work and control built into job designs. Again, modern information technology makes it efficient to push the exercise of judgment down into the organization, to wherever it is needed. This implies a commitment to decentralization; the corollary of which is flattening organizational structures by eliminating layers middle managers and staff specialists, who in the old management gathered and processed quantities of data for top management to use to coordinate activities, allocate resources, and set strategy.

Of course, business pioneered all of these notions. As Zuboff explained (1988, p. 204), efficient operations in the modern workplace call for a more equal distribution of knowledge, authority, and responsibility—to create value from information, members of the organization must be given the opportunity to know more and do more. This means, quoting Jack Welch (2001) about his reform initiatives at General Electric, "dismantling the very same managerial hierarchy that once brought greatness" (p. 46) One of the most dramatic organizational alternatives to hierarchy and bureaucracy was the virtual proximity system used first by IBM at its facility in Dallas, Texas in the early 1990s. It is designed to mimic a market-like, self-organizing system. Everyone in the organization plays the part of "customer" or "provider," depending on the transaction, and the entire plant was transformed into a network of dyads and exchanges. Each exchange became a closed loop involving four distinct steps: request from a customer and offer from a provider, negotiation of the task to be performed and the definition of success, performance, and customer acceptance. Until this last step is completed, the task remains unfinished. Each closed loop of workflow is further broken down into subloops.

Under this system, even simple tasks give rise to dozens of loops and interconnecting lines; more complex tasks, such as modifying a major product, to hundreds; and managing the entire Austin plant to thousands (obviously computers are needed to keep track of all of these loops and lines). However, the effect was to break down departmental boundaries, eliminate bottlenecks, empower employees to take initiatives and coordinate actions themselves, and give IBM insight into the integrity, trust, and morale of employees.

Perhaps, even more dramatic, however, is the U.S. Army's Joint Tactical Information Distribution System, which ties specialized military units and maneuver elements into a single, real-time, spatially structured information system that is supposed to permit activities to be coordinated as they are carried out. Combat is the classic example of reciprocal task interdependence, a condition that has always justified tight centralization and detailed staff planning. The U.S. Army has experimented with and is reorganizing itself using an approach to the coordination of parallel activities that is very similar to that used by IBM. Like IBM, the Army uses computers to chart all activities and operational flows within a given theater of operations, to keep track of progress made at each stage of each transaction, and to prod tardy participants into action. The U.S. Army probably understands that complete implementation of this system would lead to a much flatter, less hierarchical, less bureaucratic organizational structure, although high ranking officers and officials in the Department of Defense do not wish to acknowledge this fact because it would lead to fewer commands and fewer promotions. The same is true for other branches of the military in the United States and abroad.

In the third place, public management reform practice defines economy and efficiency entirely in terms of customer satisfaction. Indeed, they are preoccupied with the problem of identifying customers, assessing their wants, developing products to satisfy those wants, and, where possible, ensuring accountability by having customers fund providers on a fee for service basis. This definition of efficiency is, of course, the gospel taught in every management school on earth.

In the fourth place, public management reform practice is less interested in organizations per se than in institutional design and choice. Public management reform practice seeks to privatize services that can be privatized, contract out (or in) support services, establish bottom-line bureaus governed by performance contracts, management contracts, or regulatory contracts as appropriate, take advantage of competition where possible, and restrict direct bureaucratic provision to core public services. These concerns are evident to a far greater extent in the non-American than in the American reinvention literature, perhaps because elsewhere so much more needs to be privatized or deregulated and because contracting/tendering is still a lot rarer.

And last, in addition to strong link to management study, public management reform practice has close ties to economics, especially the economics of organization and public choice. For examples, Tom Borcherding, Harold Demsetz, Victor Goldberg, Michael Jensen, Paul Milgrom and John Roberts, William Niskanen, Roger Noll, Gordon Tullock, Oliver Williamson, and Ronald Coase are frequently cited in the literature, usually positively. Again, public management reform practice ties to economics are more evident in the non-American than in the American reinvention literature, perhaps because elsewhere institutional choice has greater salience.

OTHER DIFFERENCES BETWEEN PUBLIC MANAGEMENT REFORM PRACTICE AND TRADITIONAL PUBLIC ADMINISTRATION

There are two other themes found in the non-American literature on public management reform practice that are largely missing from the American public administration literature. The first has to do with the devolution of authority from the central government to lower levels of government, especially municipalities. This is an especially important theme of the European literature on public management. It is not of much interest to Americans, in part because the American literature on the topic of federalism is already overwhelming. The second has to do with responsibility budgeting and accounting. It should be of considerable interest to Americans as we explain in chapter 7.

Pollitt (1993, pp. 52-58) has traced what he terms "managerialism" in the United Kingdom back to the Thatcher government, especially its Financial Management Initiative, which was announced May 17, 1982. The Financial Management Initiative called for a radical change in the internal structure and operations of government agencies. Objectives were to be assigned to "responsibility centers," within which costs would be systematically identified to enable those responsible for meeting particular objectives to be held responsible for the cost of the resources they were consuming. Costs were to be measured on an accrual basis (i.e., matching resources consumed to services delivered) and include not only the direct costs of service delivery but apportioned overheads as well.

Again, of course, the Financial Management Initiative was inspired by private sector practices. In the private sector, operating budgets are primarily a means of motivating managers to serve the policies and purposes of the organizations to which they belong. Budgets convert an organization's commitments into terms that correspond to the sphere of responsibility of administrative units and their managers and provide a basis for monitoring operations, evaluating performance, and rewarding managers. As explained some time ago (Thompson & Jones, 1986), the greatest difference between budgeting in most governments and standard practices in well run firms is that operating budgets in government tend to be highly-detailed spending or resource-acquisition plans, which must be scrupulously executed just as they were approved; in contrast, operating budgets in the private sector are usually sparing of detail, often consisting of no more than a handful of quantitative performance standards.

This difference reflects the efforts made by many firms to delegate authority and responsibility down into their organizations. As the Organisation for Economic Co-operation and Development (OECD) report (1995), *Budgeting for Results: Perspectives on Public Expenditure Management*, explains, delegation of authority means giving agency managers the maximum feasible authority needed to make their units productive—or, in the alternative, subjecting them to a minimum of constraints. Hence, delegation of authority requires operating budgets to be stripped to the minimum needed to motivate and inspire subordinates. Ideally the operating budget of an organization would contain a single number or performance target, for example, a production quota, a unit cost standard, or a profit or return-on-investment target for each administrative unit.

Responsibility budgeting is merely the most common approach to operational budgeting used by well-managed private organizations. The fundamental construct of responsibility budgeting is an account structure oriented toward responsibility centers, that is, an administrative unit headed by a manager who is responsible for its actions. Responsibility centers are usually classified according to two dimensions:

1. The integration dimension—that is, the relationship between the responsibility center's objectives and the overall purposes and policies of the organization;
2. The decentralization dimension—that is, the amount of authority delegated to responsibility managers, measured in terms of their discretion to acquire and use assets.

On the first dimension, a responsibility center can be either a mission center or a support center. The output of a mission center contributes directly to the organization's objectives. The output of a support center is an input to another responsibility center in the organization, either another support center or a mission center. On the decentralization dimension, discretionary expense centers, the bureaucratic norm, are found at one extreme and profit and investment centers at the other. A support center may be either an expense center or a profit center. If it is the latter, its profit is the difference between its expenses and "revenue" from "selling" its services to other responsibility centers. Both profit and investment centers are usually free to borrow, and investment centers are also free to make decisions about plant and equipment, products, and other issues that are significant to the long-run performance of the organization. In the context of responsibility budgeting and accounting, control means monitoring a responsibility center's performance in terms of the target specified and rewarding its manager accordingly. Responsibility centers coordinate their activities via a process of mutual accommodation. Following the launch of the Financial Management Initiative in Great Britain and the reforms in New Zealand, other governments including Australia, Canada, Denmark, Finland, Sweden, and Switzerland have adopted responsibility budgeting and accounting. A more in-depth analysis of the methodology of responsibility accounting and budgeting is provided in chapter 7.

WHY INVEST IN PUBLIC MANAGEMENT REFORM?

Pollitt has viewed public sector "managerialism" primarily as a manifestation of the triumph of right-wing politics. However, this explanation dies not hold because public management reform of the type described here has been implemented by governments from the right and left wings of politics for more than a decade. Further, the view that bureaucracy is the problem, not the solution, is by not confined to the United Kingdom and the United States. Nevertheless, it is also true that public management reform practice was introduced and zealously implemented by left-of-center governments in Australia, Denmark, New Zealand, and Sweden (Schwartz, 1994). Moreover, even in the United Kingdom, where the Labor Party was often skeptical of privatization and contracting out and vigorously opposed the elimination of the Civil Service Department, it fully supported the introduction of responsibility budgeting and accounting, the Thatcher government's main managerial reform, and continued to do so under Prime Ministers Major and Blair. One does not have to be a right winger to believe that government performance is not all that it might be or even that the citizenry's abilities to control its elected agents would be materially enhanced if their attentions and responsibilities could be suitably focused on fundamental issues involving a core public sector, instead of the details of administration.

Others (Schedler, 1995; Schwartz, 1994) attribute the rise of public management reform primarily to economic crisis—recession combined with increased international competition. Again, there is undoubtedly some truth to this view. Crisis is a catalyst for government reform. Many public management reforms were adopted by governments that were under a great deal of economic and fiscal pressure—New Zealand, Australia, Great Britain, Sweden, Canada, even Switzerland. However, pressure does not explain the content of these reforms. In the second half of the nineteenth and the first half of the twentieth centuries, increased international competitiveness and depression seemed inevitably to lead to more government, more bureaucracy, and greater reliance on hierarchy. Nor is scarcity a new discovery. Fiscal pressure has justified nearly every American administrative reform from the creation of the executive budget in 1921 onwards (McCaffery & Jones, 2001).

Both the rise of government and bureaucracy in the first half of this century and their decline in the second can be explained as rational responses to changing circumstances, which have created opportunities as well as threats. In the United States, the progressives created a professional bureaucracy to manage the public functions of the early twentieth century city. Streets had to be paved, harbors deepened, electric lighting systems, street railways, sewage disposal plants, water supplies, and fire departments had to be installed or drastically improved. Moreover, establishing a professional bureaucracy at the municipal level led directly to higher levels of investment in infrastructure and significant increases in economic growth (Rauch, 1995). Clearly, in the first half of our century, direct government provision and regulation worked fairly well when compared to the alternatives—private monopoly, contracting out, and so forth. Indeed, in that era "postalization" (e.g., state provision of communications, transportation, and power infrastructure) played about the same role as "privatization" in this one—and for much the same reasons.

Administrative efficiency once implied the Weberian bureaucratic paradigm (Barzelay, 1992). Large bureaucracies were justified by economies of scale and scope. Scale economies are produced by spreading fixed expenses, especially investments in plant and equipment and the organization of production lines, over larger volumes of output, thereby reducing unit costs. Scope economies are produced by exploiting the division of labor—sequentially combining highly specialized functional units in multifarious ways to produce a variety of products. In turn large bureaucracies were made possible by nineteenth and early twentieth century innovations in organizational design and administrative control.

It may be argued that the driving forces behind public management reform are similar to those that produced the bureaucratic revolution of the early twentieth century. As indicated later in this book, reductions in information costs have produced four major shifts in the comparative advantage of alternative institutional arrangements. These are:

1. The efficacy of the market has increased relative to government provision and control, which has had the effect of increasing the payoffs to free markets, secure property rights, and minimal government intervention;

2. The efficacy of the market and other self-organizing systems has increased relative to hierarchically coordinated systems, which has had the effect of decreasing the payoff to hierarchy and vertical The efficacy of decentralized allocation of resources and ex-post control has increased relative to centralized allocation and ex-ante control, which has had the effect of decreasing the payoff to scale; and

3. The efficacy of process-oriented structures has increased relative to functional structures, which has had the effect of decreasing the payoff to scope.

These shifts are hardly surprising. As Coase (1937) and Williamson (1975) have demonstrated, the comparative advantage of any institutional arrangement boils down to a question of information or transaction costs. Changes in information costs should dramatically alter the relative advantage of alternative and institutional designs.

For example, the computer and the use of the World Wide Web are rapidly eroding economies of scale in administration, production, and marketing (although not brand development, at least not so far) and, thereby, the comparative advantage of hierarchy and bureaucracy. Today, any organization that can afford a computer workstation and software can have first-class administrative systems, ranging from purchasing and inventory control to human resources management to financial planning and capital budgeting to marketing and logistics. Twenty years ago these systems were available only to giants. Moreover, computerized production now permits organizations to produce customized services at mass-production prices.

CONCLUSIONS

As a result of the declining importance of economies of scale, the average size of the workplace has been falling throughout the industrialized world for the last 20 years. Large companies are mimicking their smaller competitors by shrinking their head offices, removing layers of bureaucracy and breaking themselves up into constellations of profit centers, concentrating on their core businesses and contracting everything else out, putting a computer on every desk, and giving power to frontline workers (Jones & Thompson, 1999).

Market evolution is fundamentally a Darwinian process while organizational change fundamentally market driven and certainly nonlinear. Markets motivate learning; organizations facilitate it. Williamson's (1975) dictum that the choice between markets and hierarchies can be resolved to a question of minimizing transactions costs (i.e., minimizing search, bargaining, and enforcement costs) can, therefore, be reformulated as a question of which is contextually harder, motivating people to perform or teaching them to perform. Bureaucracy is a brilliant system for perpetuating and even refining existing information; it is, however, a slow and cumbersome mechanism for acquiring knowledge. The organizational forms (e.g., multidisciplinary teams, located close to the customer) rely on information technology to supply read-only memory (i.e., to maintain existing information), and focus on the acquisition of knowledge. That is, they are primarily learning organizations. Businesses, for example, used to believe that access to capital was their most valuable asset and that the chief task of top-management was allocating it to productive uses; now most believe that knowledge is their most precious resource and that management's most important job is ensuring that knowledge is generated widely and used efficiently. As Jack Welch, chairman of General Electric explained, centralized bureaucratic procedures it once used were, "right for the 1970s, a growing handicap in the 1980s, and would have been a ticket to the bone yard in the 1990s" (See Anthony & Govindarajan, 1995, p. 30)

Under this interpretation, public management reform practice is a world-wide phenomenon because it is a manifestation of a fundamental transformation and de-bureaucratization affecting nearly every corner of the globe. To the extent that this interpretation is valid, the only real impediments to its triumph are the capacities of a jurisdiction to insulate itself from the world economy and its propensity to policy gridlock. Neither of these forms of behavior would be advocated by political leaders and public sector managers in the developed or developing world. As we explain in the chapter that follows, fundamental change has taken place in public management practice throughout the world.

CHAPTER 3

ASSESSING PUBLIC MANAGEMENT REFORM IN AN INTERNATIONAL CONTEXT

Performance Measurement, Managing for Results, and Fiscal Devolution

Over the past 3 decades a number of criticisms about government performance have surfaced across the world from all points of the political spectrum. Critics have alleged that governments are inefficient, ineffective, too large, too costly, overly bureaucratic, overburdened by unnecessary rules, unresponsive to public wants and needs, secretive, undemocratic, invasive into the private rights of citizens, self-serving, and failing in the provision of either the quantity or quality of services deserved by the taxpaying public (See, for example, Barzelay & Armajani, 1992; Guthrie et al., 2005; Jones & Thompson, 1999; Osborne & Gaebler, 1992; Pollitt & Bouckhaert, 2000, 2004). Fiscal stress has also plagued many governments and has increased the cry for less costly or less expansive government, for greater efficiency, and for increased responsiveness. High profile members of the business community, financial institutions, the

---

From Bureaucracy to Hyperarchy in Netcentric and Quick Learning Organizations: Exploring Future Public Management Practice, 23–95
Copyright © 2007 by Information Age Publishing
All rights of reproduction in any form reserved.

media, management consultants, academic scholars, and the general public all have pressured politicians and public managers to reform. So too have many supranational organizations, including the Organisation for Economic Co-operation and Development (OECD), the World Bank, and the European Commission. Accompanying the demand and many of the recommendations for change has been support for the application of market-based logic and private sector management methods to government. (See, for example, Harr & Godfrey, 1991; Milgrom & Roberts, 1992; Moe, 1984; Olson, Guthrie, & Humphrey, 1998a; Jones & Thompson, 1999) Application of market-driven solutions and business techniques to the public sector has undoubtedly been encouraged by the growing ranks of public sector managers and analysts educated in business schools and public management programs (Pusey, 1991).

Driving the managerial reform movement has been a notion that the public sector builds on the wrong principles and needs significant change (Barzelay & Armajani, 1992; Osborne & Gaebler, 1992; Jones & Thompson, 1999). Strategies have recommended include caps on public spending, tax cuts, selling off of public assets, contracting out of many services previously provided by government, development and use of performance measurement and management, output and outcomes-based budgeting, and business-type accounting. The reforms produced all sorts of promises: a smaller, less interventionist, and more decentralized government; improved public sector efficiency and effectiveness; greater public service responsiveness and accountability to citizens; increased choice between public and private providers of public services; an "entrepreneurial" public sector more willing and able to work with business; and better economic performance, among others.

The potential has lured many elected officials into announcing highly ambitious agendas for change. However, academic observers, citizens, and public managers alike have wondered how many of these promises are likely to produce genuine results—and how long any such results will endure. Some principles have already well established themselves. Many financial management and accounting reforms have already proven successful. So, too, is the notion that public organizations should be better managed, more responsive, and held more accountable for results. Almost everything else about public management, reform however is open for debate.

In both practice and study, reform is an international phenomenon (see, for example, Borins, 1997; Gray & Jenkins, 1995; Guthrie et al, 2005; Hood, 1995; Hood, 2000; Jones & Schedler, 1997; Jones & Thompson, 1999; Kettl, 2000a; Olsen & Peters, 1996). The OECD continues to monitor reform developments across a range of countries (OECD, 1997; OECD, 1999), and researchers have reported on developments in particular countries, especially New Zealand, that have drawn international attention (e.g., Boston, Martin, Pallot, & Walsh, 1996; Jones & Schedler, 1997; Guthrie & Parker, 1998; Pallot, 1998) In its early days in the 1980s, new managerial reform (or what Hood (1991) termed new public management) was mostly strongly associated with right-leaning governments, such as Thatcher in the United Kingdom, Reagan in the United States, and Hawke in Australia. Since then, however, it has lost its ideological stripes. Left-leaning governments like Clinton in the United States and Blair in the United Kingdom have embraced it as well, along with a democratic Swedish parliament, a conservative British parliament, (Olson, Guthrie, & Humphrey, 1998b) and conservative U.S. President George W. Bush.

The rapid spread of reforms in various shapes and sizes, has produced wide diversity in practice, even across countries widely regarded as active reformers. If financial management and accounting changes have been perhaps the most universal reforms, there has been little detailed analysis of the practical application and results of these techniques (Hood, 1995; March & Olsen, 1995; Olson et al., 1998b; Guthrie, Olson, & Humphrey, 1999; Guthrie et al., 2005). Indeed, analysts have found that the public financial management has not been so much a uniform, global movement as a "reforming spirit" focused on instilling private sector financial practices into public sector decision making. It has emphasized new standards in financial reporting, accrual accounting, debt and surplus management, and capital investment strategy that had previously been missing from much government decision making. It there has been broad application of these techniques, however, there has been little research about what results these strategies are likely to produce.

Attempts to understand the global public management reform movement suggest two general implications for research. First, there is a glaring need to understand the short and longer-term outcomes of the reforms where they have been implemented. Second, despite the importance of conducting this research, doing so is almost impossible in the short term and exceedingly difficult in the long term. It is hard enough simply to keep pace with management changes in each nation. It is even harder to make sound multicountry comparisons. Efforts to solve this problem sometimes led researchers to use a particular nation's reforms—often New Zealand's—as a benchmark, but the particular problems facing each nation weaken the value of such comparisons (see, for example, Riley & Watling, 1999; Olson, Humphrey, & Guthrie, 2000: Guthrie, Humphrey, Jones, & Olson, 2005). The paucity of "results about reforms" and the need to assess whether management reforms have helped each nation solve its particular problems should motivate researchers to press ahead.

In the first part of this chapter we provide an analysis of the performance measurement and managing for results agenda for reform, and then delve into selected initiatives and outcomes discernible in the Asia and Pacific region and, by implication, for the developing world. We then document and summarize some of the lessons learned in the period 1990 to the early 2000s (and in some cases from the 1980s and into the mid-2000s) concentrating on Asia, with notes added about New Zealand and to a lesser extent Australia. We then turn to the example of the United States, drawing conclusions for other nations, especially developing countries.

With respect to New Zealand and Australia, we concentrate primarily on the period 1990-2000 because most of the highly visible *grand* public management reform initiatives in these nations were launched during this time. Since then it is much more difficult to discern trends so we have not attempted to address this challenge. We would characterize the period 2000 to 2007 in New Zealand and Australia as one of consolidation or in some case refutation of the *grand* public management reforms of the previous several decades. Also, we do not review reform in Europe, nor the United Kingdom. We refer readers who seek a more contemporary set of examples and extrapolation of results on Europe to the works of Pollitt and Bouckhaert (2000, 2004).

PERFORMANCE MEASUREMENT AND MANAGING FOR RESULTS

The international development community is increasingly focused on ensuring that financial and human resources are used to achieve intended results. Development practitioners have long strived to improve performance in developing nations, for example, in GDP (gross domestic product) per capita, literacy rates, nutrition levels, and many other aspects of country performance. However, in recent years many developing countries are choosing to follow patterns that have emerged in developed countries over the last several decades of establishing results-oriented monitoring frameworks that report on progress against strategic plans, budgets, and sector strategies (Bhatta, 2006; Schiavo-Campo & Tommasi, 1999). This results orientation builds on participatory approaches to strengthen and take advantage of citizen and other stakeholder perspectives on how to improve public services. Under a results-oriented approach initiatives are taken to track a manageable set of indicators, and to provide accurate, timely and transparent information on which to base comprehensive reports to all stakeholders. Development partners are reinforcing these trends in various ways, including a global effort to achieve "Millennium Development Goals" by 2015, and efforts to harmonize the work of aid agencies to reduce the burden of aid administration on developing country governments (OECD, 2005). This section of the chapter addresses five key elements of this new orientation: (i) clarifying the language of performance, (ii) defining indicative performance indicators, (iii) exploring tools for performance measurement, (iv) making changes to improve performance, and (v) creating the performance and knowledge culture in organizations. It then gives examples of these elements from Asia.

Performance in public agencies is the consequence of response to public actions that express demand for goods and services, and may be defined in terms of both results and effort. Most recent attention has been on the former, and the sequence of events leading to results. This process may be viewed in the form of a production function model: inputs, work planning, and activity leads to outputs and ultimately outcomes or I + WPA – > OP – > OC. This sequence starts with expression of stakeholder demands for a service or a set of results. Governments respond by allocating resource inputs to meet demands, and these resources are then used so as to contribute to production of results that may be measured as outputs and outcomes. A set of processes or activities are employed to acquire and transform inputs into results including, inter alia, strategic planning, policy and program decision making, and implementation through workload definition, budget formulation and execution, procurement, performance monitoring and, finally, accounting, auditing, and policy and program evaluation (Moynihan & Ingraham, 2003). The production function model implies some degree of efficiency in transforming inputs to results. However, in practice, various public sector rules, regulations and processes instituted for diverse reasons including control, accountability, transparency, affirmative action, regional balance and, not the least, the politics of compromise among elected leaders, often work against achievement of efficiency and effectiveness in transforming inputs into results (Jones & Thompson, 1999).

After inputs and workload, outputs are the most identifiable link in the results production chain: the physical goods, services, institutional and/or behavioral changes that are created by work using various inputs. Outcomes follow from production of outputs. Outcomes are, ideally, the correct responses to public service demands, that is, purposes achieved. Outcomes typically are achieved over a longer period of time than outputs and are thus more difficult to measure with any degree of confidence in the short term. Outcomes may be positive, neutral or negative (benefits – costs = net benefits or outcomes). Further, the impact of multiple outcomes goes beyond that of any single outcome, that is, higher-level results to which multiple outcomes contribute. Outcomes may be quite different from what was intended. And even if the intended outcome is achieved, there may be unanticipated factors that affect eventual results. For example, in the United States, the federal government response to Hurricane Katrina and the resultant disaster for the city of New Orleans succeeded in achieving its intended output of assistance to residents of the city and region. However, the length of time that it took for the government to respond created all kinds of negative and unanticipated consequences. The eventual results of federal government assistance to New Orleans and the area affected by the hurricane remain uncertain in terms of net benefit. If the intended initial result was lives saved through rapid evacuation, provision of immediate medical aid and maintenance of social stability in the crisis aftermath, then the actual result was not what was expected by residents of the area and the American public.

An alternative and more traditional way to assess performance is based on level of effort (workload). Measuring effort often is much easier than measuring outputs and outcomes. Measuring and recognizing effort often is important for morale. Still, there are many reasons why hard work, even if it can be measured accurately, may not translate into expected results, including the difficulty of tasks and multiple agent coordination, and the influence of unexpected and uncontrollable external events. In addition, hardworking individuals and teams may find that even though they followed rules, regulations, and procedures in using inputs, and delivering outputs in the proper manner, the resulting outputs and outcomes are less than desired. To address such problems, many public managers in recent years have found innovative ways to deliver expected outputs, in hope that desired outcomes will be achieved. Such public managers view their agencies as adaptive systems that respond to demands of citizens and other stakeholders and to contingency in the environment. And increasingly, under new institutional governance arrangements including outsourcing and privatization, managers may tend to view their agencies as involved in competition with other service providers to deliver the best value for money to their citizen/customers. Under such circumstances, they tend to think like businessmen about strategic positioning of their product and service lines in conformance with consumer preferences and market demand (Jones, 2005).

Performance Indicators

Since it is often the case in public organizations that "What gets measured, gets done," (Peters, 1986; see also 1987) it is important to selectively measure events in the results chain. Input/workload/output indicators include measurement of work performed and productivity ratios, time targets, utilization rates, and unit-cost indicators. Workload and productivity ratios measure the quantity of work performed, such as number of cases handled, number of patients treated, number of students taught, number of new recruits signed up per week, or number of driving licenses processed per day. Time targets measure the time expended for completion of a given task such as processing an income tax return, or uploading completed census questionnaires into a computer, that is, cycle time. Utilization rates measure the extent to which a service is used, such as number of visitors at a national park, or number of officials completing a training course. Unit-cost measurement ties performance measures to resources consumed in production, that is, the average or marginal cost of delivering a defined unit of service, such as the cost of providing schooling for a third grader for 1 day or 1 school year or the cost of performing a specific type of medical procedure. Unit cost measurement requires both careful specification of units of service and direct and indirect costs of service production.

Performance indicators should meet five criteria. They should be:

Clear: Precise and unambiguous (not necessarily quantitative);
Relevant: Appropriate to the objective at hand (and not used simply because they are readily available);
Economic: The data required should be available at reasonable cost;
Adequate: By themselves or in combination with others, the measures must provide a sufficient basis for the assessment of performance;
Monitorable: In addition to clarity and availability of information, the indicators must be amenable to independent scrutiny (Schiavo-Campo & Tommasi, 1999, p. 334).

If an indicator does not meet all five criteria, it should not be used. For example, the input/output indicators noted above are best for measuring standard services such as clerical tasks, and routine teaching and health care. They may not be adequate for measuring complex education and health services, econometric, political, or legal work. As one moves up the results chain from inputs through to outcome and impact, it becomes even more difficult to find indicators that meet all the criteria. For example, public perception surveys are often used to measure process, outcome, and impact of public services. Such surveys, although useful for anecdotal evidence, are fraught with methodological problems. Corruption perception surveys, for example, may reveal an *increase* in perceived corruption when anticorruption agencies become more active and their work is reported in the media, even though the more effective policing may actually be reducing corruption.

Performance Measurement

Once appropriate indicators are selected, performance measures may be determined based on suitable criteria. Targets may be set based on applicable standards or benchmarks. Thus, a health care agency may benchmark itself against counterparts in other parts of the country, or in other countries. Agencies responsible for road maintenance may use a standardized tool for budget and work planning to ensure that timely maintenance is carried out. Although public agencies often find they lack data to enable accurate measurement of performance, realization that this contributes to the drive to improve data element definition and collection so as to enable eventual measurement.

For aid dependent countries, standards or benchmarks may be suggested by donor agencies. For example, the World Bank and Asian Development Bank (ADB) use a common set of 16 economic and governance indicators and a much larger number of subindicators for monitoring annual performance to determine eligibility for concessional financing. Each subindicator is graded on a scale of 1 to 6 by donor agency staff, in consultation with partner governments. Scores are made public each year to encourage transparency, and civic pressure on governments to improve their ratings. Such standards also may be set by intergovernmental bodies such as the Financial Action Task Force (FATF), which combats money laundering and terrorist financing. The FATF monitors country implementation of necessary measures, reviews money laundering and terrorist financing techniques, and countermeasures, and promotes the adoption and implementation of appropriate measures globally. Countries judged not to measure up to basic standards can be severely sanctioned (FAFT, n.d).

Changes to Improve Performance

Once performance can be measured and performance shortfalls are identified, many actions may be taken to address shortfalls. Two broad types of actions are suggested here: strengthening individual performance appraisal and incentives, and adopting one or more organizational changes.

To determine the proper mix of each type of action, capacity assessments are often required (Wescott, 2004b). Competitive pay and incentives are necessary, but not sufficient, conditions for building capacity to effectively perform critical tasks. Improving the performance of a task needs to begin with mapping the organizations involved in performing it (Hilderbrand & Grindle, 1995). The organizational map is the picture of the task network: the organizations with primary responsibility for carrying out the task, those that are less central but still play a role, and those that provide various kinds of support to the performance of the task. The description of interactions between these organizations is important, as is analysis of whether the interactions among the institutions are effective or are an area of capacity weakness. Questions of relationships and coordination among organizations are important here. All the dimensions of capacity need to be viewed from the perspective of the performance of the task.

The second step involves looking outward from the task network. What contextual factors play a significant role regarding the capacity to perform these tasks, and how do they affect how—and how well—the tasks are performed? At the level just above the task network, the impact of the institutions of the public sector needs to be considered, along with variables in the broader economic, political and social environment.

The third step focuses on each organization and its human resources. These are closely interwoven, with the human resources a principal component of organizational capacity, but only as brought together, structured, and utilized by the organization. A profile of the human resource dimension should focus on the recruitment, training, education and retention of skilled managerial, professionals, and technical personnel. Questions to be addressed about performance include: what impact does the organization's human resource profile have on its ability to perform its assigned tasks and reach its goals? What are the organization's human resource strengths and weaknesses? Whereas the human resource profile of an organization is very important, whether those skilled personnel are effectively utilized is frequently the key to an organization's level of capacity to perform its assigned tasks and reach its goals. This focuses analysis on the organizational level, where such factors as the structure of work and authority relations, appraisal and incentive systems, formal and informal behavioral norms, management practices, and leadership influence whether skilled personnel are able and willing to contribute fully to performing tasks.

In addition, there are a number of other human resource related capacity issues. Does the organization possess and allocate adequate financial and physical resources to function effectively? Is it organized to use resources effectively and efficiently to reach its goals? Is it able to interact with other organizations, clients, and other stakeholders in networking and problem solving? Capacity strengthening is most effective when it is designed based on a thorough assessment relative to the issues noted above.

Evaluations of ADB and other donor agency support to capacity strengthening show that such assessments are often not carried out, and thus the assistance is less effective that desired (ADB, 1997). To address these concerns, ADB contributed to an extensive capacity assessment in 2003 of elected commune councils in Cambodia, and key organizations they work with at national, provincial, and commune levels prior to making investments in capacity building. Elected commune councils have relatively little decision-making power, and are subject to bureaucratic control from their governor, and from central ministries. Although citizen participation is minimal in commune affairs, survey results suggest that citizens have a favorable impression of their performance. Since commune council members are mainly elderly, conservative men with relatively low levels of education, most have limited capacity for absorbing training. However, commune clerks need enhanced skills to deal with complex programming requirements (ADB, 2003). Training also is needed to support civil registration of 95% of Cambodia's citizens not presently registered. This exercise requires close coordination with commune council chiefs, provincial and district staff, and the Office of Civil Registration and Department of Local Administration (DOLA) of the Ministry of Interior. A separate assessment for DOLA outlined the following priority steps for building capacity: competitive staff incentives, clear strategic direction, new organizational structure aligned with this, and a professional human resource function. Without these initiatives, any training provided will mainly contribute to the personal development of staff, not to the achievement of organizational goals (ADB, 2004a).

One element of capacity strengthening deserves special mention. For reforms to take hold there need to be change agents strategically located in key functional areas to spread new ways of working throughout the public administration system. These agents need to be carefully selected, positioned at an appropriate level, and provided with good working facilities, flexible procedures, and other incentives. They need to be good at teaching others on-the-job, about how to network across organizations. Such agents of change and their organizational units are different from the project implementation offices typically set up by donor agencies. The latter are intended to be insulated from mainstream administrative systems on the assumption that this is the best way to prevent corruption and ensure effective delivery of donor support. In contrast, agents of change emerge within existing structures and work to change them from within, then spreading innovations across government.

For example, the Hyderabad (India) Metropolitan Water Supply and Sewerage Board uses its Single Window Cell (SWC) to reduce corruption for new connections. Previously, applications were made to one of 120 section offices, and then forwarded to 14 other staff before approval, each requiring "speed payments." Under the SWC, the application process is centralized in one, public place, with applications recorded on computers that are difficult for corrupt officials to alter. Staffs become motivated to provide good service with distinctive uniforms, modern offices and individual computer terminals. Their service improvement has been praised extensively in the media, which further improves staff motivation (Davis, 2004, p. 63).

Another element of strengthen performance has to do with appropriate monitoring and control system design and use of controls that are compatible with performance management goals. The dilemma in the use of management control in public organizations boils down to a matter of emphasis. The emphasis of control systems can be on management *control* or on *management* control, the former used to enforce rules while the primary use of the latter approach is to motivate employees to work productively.

Due to this distinction, the design and operation of control systems can profoundly influence governmental performance. Legal strictures and sanctions exist to prevent fraud, waste and misuse of funds, but they are not enough. By their very nature, they emphasize what not to do, not what to do. Without appropriate performance standards, managers cannot be held accountable for performance. Consequently, central agency control systems are not designed to optimize the quality, quantity, and price of goods and services purchased with public money, but to enforce accountability oriented rules (Anthony & Young, 1988).

The choice of whom to subject to controls and when to execute controls is not as easy. The control system designer has a number of options given the possibilities for combining the following variables. First, the subject may be either an organization or an individual. Second, controls may be executed before or after the subject acts. The former may be identified as *ex ante* and the latter as *ex post* controls (Demski & Feltham, 1976). *Ex ante* controls are intended to prevent subjects from doing wrong things or to compel them to behave legally. Necessarily, they take the form of authoritative commands or rules that specify what the subject must do, may do, and must not do. Subjects are held responsible for complying with these commands, and the controller attempts to monitor and enforce compliance. In contrast, *ex post* controls are executed after the subject decides on and carries out a course of action and after some of the consequences of the subject's decisions are known. Since bad decisions cannot be undone after they are carried out, *ex post* controls are intended to motivate subjects to make good decisions. Subjects are held responsible for the consequences of decisions, and the controller attempts to monitor consequences and rewards or sanctions accordingly.

This synopsis of control system design and use is intended to indicate that *ex post* controls designed to motivate good performance are superior instruments in terms of compatibility with performance management. This is not intended to imply that *ex ante* controls will cease to be employed. To the contrary, rules to prevent illegal behavior are absolutely necessary and must be sustained and used diligently. However, when it comes to the selection of control methodology as part of a performance management system, much greater emphasis is needed in progressive public organizations on *ex post* controls accompanied by economic and other types of evaluation after the fact to define how management performance can best be improved. The emphasis of use of the *ex post* approach is to guide, coach and steer rather than to exercise direct control, per se. To reiterate, the purpose of management control systems should be to motivate good performance through the use of incentives rather than punitive sanctions (Thompson & Jones, 1986).

Ingraham, Selden, and Moynihan (2000) provide additional perspective on individual and organizational performance incentives. They explain that building human capital should be regarded as an investment and not simply as a cost to the organization to sustain productivity. "Members of the public service are ... government's most important resource. Failure to understand and value that resource will inevitably be linked to lack of capacity and performance" (Ingraham et al., 2000, p. 56) They also point out the difference between providing rule-based versus goal or performance based managerial flexibility. As Kettl, Ingraham, Sanders, & Horner (1996) discovered, the former does not contribute to increased value creation while the later is more likely to produce the alleged benefits of "letting managers manage" (p. 25). Ingraham et al. (2000) also cite the importance of leadership commitment, "Leaders are part of the organization's culture, its reward structure, and as such define the clarity of goals and objectives. If leaders abdicate this responsibility, the performance effort is moot." They emphasize that leaders and managers, "should be rewarded for high employee and organizational performance" (p. 57) They also point out the importance of organizational partnering and networking out of recognition that few, if any, complex socioeconomic problems can be solved unilaterally by government agencies, NGOs (nongovernmental organizations) or other entities. Finally, they note that, "Performance is the driver.... Performance rewards and incentives must actually contribute to performance" (Ingraham et al., 2000, p. 58)

Some public sector organizations have tried to boost performance by allocating financial bonuses to their best performing staff, as is the case in many private businesses. However, there is little evidence that such bonuses in the public sector help to improve performance for many reasons. First, because public sector jobs are diverse and multidimensional, it is almost impossible to compare the accomplishments of staff to one another by a common metric. Second, in the public sector tasks tend to be performed by teams and not by an individual. The award of bonus to one individual within a team is likely to occasion considerable resentment amongst other team members. Third, public sector employees are importantly motivated by the values of their organization as well as by their financial compensation. For public officials focused on financial gain, a significant portion may come after they leave public sector employment, and parlay their expertise and contacts for the benefit of the private sector. Bonuses received during public sector employment are typically too small to motivate performance, and risk causing damage to teamwork and the feeling of making a valuable public service contribution (Behn, 2004; Klitgaard & Light, 2005, pp. 23, 39, 309; O'Donnell, 2000). The financial incentives that tend to work best during public sector employment are associated with merit-based promotions. Bonuses may also be effective when they are offered to staff doing a very similar job, such as Navy recruiters (Asch, 1990a).

Increased information technology (IT) support is another of the many changes needed to improve performance and employee productivity. Other elements of change to enhance productivity may include altering the nature of markets within which organizations operate. Alternative institutional arrangements for the provision of services may lead to productivity enhancement—including devolution of authority and responsibility to subnational jurisdictions, outsourcing to the private and not-for-profit sectors, and privatization of service delivery. Cohen and Peterson (1999) point out the need for a broadening of institutions producing and providing needed goods and services to the public at more efficient costs, wherever they are located and whether they are public, quasi-public or private (p. 61). The use of differential pricing systems under such arrangements may increase productivity by rationing services more equitably. Enhancing market competition in provision of services to the public may result in a plurality of agencies, public and private, operating at different scales of jurisdiction, providing potentially duplicative services. This circumstance gives rise to debate about the consequences of such overlap in terms of economic efficiency, the longer term consequences of increased public agency and market competition, problems of clarity of accountability where mandates are devolved to create overlap of roles and responsibilities, and the fiscal effects on subordinate governments of multiple source service provision.

Key to longer term improvement of performance in public organizations is creation of a knowledge culture that encourages self-assessment and learning, quick analysis and innovation, and knowledge creation investment in human resources and technology (Jones & Thompson, 1999). In countries that were developing in the nineteenth and first half of the twentieth centuries, progressive leadership backed by a populist following created a professional bureaucracy to manage the public functions of the early twentieth century city. Streets had to be paved, harbors deepened, electric lighting systems, street railways, sewage disposal plants, water supplies, and fire departments had to be installed or drastically improved. And, in fact, developing nations face similar challenges presently. As Rauch (1995) has pointed out, establishing a professional bureaucracy at the municipal level in what are now developed nations led directly to higher levels of investment in infrastructure and significant increases in economic growth. Clearly, in the first half of the twentieth century in what are now developed nations, direct government provision, and regulation worked fairly well when compared to the alternatives—private monopoly, contracting out, and so forth. Indeed, in this era "postalization" (e.g., state provision of communications, transportation, and power infrastructure) played about the same role as "privatization" does today—and for much the same reasons. In twenty-first century, it is evident that developing nations face the need to establish and promote effective civil service systems. However, the corollary question that arises is whether this movement should be accompanied by creation of large, centralized bureaucratic organizations as a means of guiding development, or does the better path lie with devolution of authority and responsibility to local jurisdictions similar to those that were successful in building infrastructure in nations in the past? We think the latter is the best way. For more on this theme see chapter 9.

The lessons for developing nations would seem to be that they do not need to repeat the experience of developed nations to benefit from better approaches to knowledge creation, human resource motivation, productive use of new information technologies, devising organizational designs to best advantage, and testing of new types of institutional arrangements for production and delivery of services to the public. The lessons from both government and the private sector in developed nations indicate that new institutional forms and a greater market orientation, along with enhanced devolution of fiscal rights and responsibilities to local governments, plus experimentation with competition in service delivery should be combined with traditional measures such as developing a highly competent civil service system operated according to the rule of law and merit principles as the way of the future. According to the arguments advanced here, creating the knowledge culture requires a combination of practices, old and new, some associated with the design of better governance systems, others taking advantage of competitive market dynamics, and increasing the trend toward fiscal and policy devolution where human resource capacity has been created in developing nations so as to permit them to manage effectively and less centrally.

PERFORMANCE MANAGEMENT AND KNOWLEDGE CREATION IN ASIA

While more examples of performance management and knowledge creation in the public sector may be found in the developed world, it is clear that advances in these areas also are underway in Asia. As explained in this chapter, there are a number of ways to approach strengthening performance management in public sector. China is a prime example of a developing nation that is experimenting with market solutions to public service supply within a system that evidences a high degree of fiscal and policy devolution. This pathway is pursued under the authority of a highly centralized national political and governance framework, but one that permits a high degree of provincial and local economic experimentation and innovation. Performance is enhanced through a combination of hierarchy, given the nation's well-developed civil service system, and performance rewards associated with nonbureaucratic approaches, for example, individual leadership and managerial rewards in terms of career enhancement opportunity for successful teamwork and organizational goal achievement.

The Chinese experience with reform of various types has been difficult to assess until recently due to the absence of information, and especially that published in English or other Western languages. However, more recently some research has begun to emerge to shed more light on the Chinese experience, particularly in the areas of fiscal policy and performance management (see, for example, Junsheng, 2006; Wong, 2005; Xiang & Lou, 2004). A summary review of this work reveals that over the past 15 years the government has experimented with a variety of budgetary reforms including implementation of Program Based Budgeting (PBB) by the Ministry of Finance, and that the latest reform is departmental/ministerial budgeting (D/MB). By and large the changes made in the fiscal policy system have led to increased devolution of budgetary management horizontally across the national government and vertically to provincial and other subnational governments. Further, the government and some academic observers are presently engaged in a dialogue on establishment of a performance management system (PMS) at the national level of government that would, in theory, support experimentation with performance assessment and integration of performance measures into budgeting (Junsheng, 2006). However, this is an ambitious step in a system that currently has many flaws. As Junsheng (2006) observes:

> Since 1978, China took a series of transformation reforms with the fiscal system and the former highly centralized fiscal system was gradually broken. In

1994 China launched a large-scale campaign to further the reform whereby a big leap forward of fiscal system was made. But generally speaking, the reform of the fiscal system in China in the past years has made achievements mainly in the area of government revenue. In expenditure, especially in expenditure budgetary drafting and managing system, however, the reform has remained weak. The budgetary system still adopts the traditional input-oriented method. The input-oriented budgetary system exist many problems, the budget drafting method is unscientific and there are not enough details available, the distribution and application of the budgetary fund is not transparent enough and the legal restricting force on the budget is lowered. Such a budget is not only difficult for the legislative institutions to carry out any budget examination, but it is also harmful to the standardized implementation and legal supervision of the budget. As a result, the present governmental expenditure efficiency is in any case not satisfying. Shortcomings of the current budgetary system include: a cost-benefit estimate system [that] is almost blank; overstaffed offices, financial profusion, even corruption exist more or less; [it] cannot allocate resources according to priorities and objectives; [it] cannot identify results from expenditure. (p. 2)

It is further noteworthy that the ADB continues to provide assistance and encouragement to China to support reform that would lead to adoption of results based management in the form of management for development results (MfDR) (ADB, 2005a, 2005b, 2005c).

In the Philippines, a major initiative has been undertaken to develop results-based budgets. A proposal to adopt this approach is underway and is to be submitted to Congress in 2005. In addition, ADB and the World Bank recently issued a report on decentraliztion in the Philippines that states, "Measuring and managing LGU [local government unit] performance assume special importance in the context of the issues examined in this report" (ADB & World Bank, 2005, p. 43). The report notes that performance management has advanced at two levels in the Philippines, national government and partner organizations have shown, "interest in nationally standardized tools that could be used to assess LGU performance and provide incentives to high performing units and capacity building to others. The result is that a wide array of such tools is in use" (p. 43). Some measures apply to measurement of cash management of revenues and expenditures while others are applied to evaluate LGU performance on specific normative criteria and also permit comparison between local governments. Some of the measures are directed at rule compliance while others measure "development outcomes." The report also notes that some of the performance tools are used by the LGUs themselves "to measure costs and ongoing performance" (ADB & World Bank, 2005, p. 43). At the same time, a highly visible initiative has continued to be used by the Department of the Interior and Local Government

(DILG) in the form of a Local Productivity and Performance Measurement System (LPPMS). LPPMS was initiated in the 1980s for monitoring of LGU service delivery and with the legal enactment of LGUs in 1991 it has proven useful to monitor the substantial devolution of powers and functions authorized in law. More recently, the LPPMS has been employed as more than a central agency monitoring instrument; it is now used as a management mechanism by some LGUs to measure and assess their own performance, for example, in planning and budgeting. Other national government departments have developed LGU performance monitoring systems. For example, the Bureau of Local Government Finance, with assistance from the U.S. Agency for International Development, has created and maintains an online database of 126 distinct features of LGU finance and the idea of linking this data into the LPPMS is under consideration. Other government national agencies have databases that might be similarly linked, for example, the Department of Budget and Management, the Commission on Audit, and the Civil Service Commission.

In addition, a Citizen Satisfaction Index System (CSIS) is in place in the Philippines to score and evaluate a variety of areas of devolved service delivery responsibility and to increase citizen participation and influence in local governance, for example, agriculture, health, social services, the environment, and natural resources. In augmentation of these efforts an Internet based Local Development Watch (DevWatch) system also has been deployed to evaluate the level of development in LGUs and to focus on and make more visible highest priority needs in underserved local governments.

One evident question about the orientation of these monitoring systems is: for what purposes are they used? Monitoring often leads to control, which in the case of the Philippines, given the degree of devolution established in the law in 1991, could result in excessive influence of central agencies over LGUs. On the other hand, good monitoring systems can be used to steer resources to highest areas of need both in terms of location and sector.

In selected other nations, as reported by ADB in 2004, different elements of results-based management (RBM) have been put into practice to enhance performance. The ADB report states,

> RBM involves ensuring the desired outputs and outcomes are defined as results, that resources are adequate and timely to deliver these results, that the organization has clear accountability and authority for performance and that processes in place support the conversion of resources into results. (ADB, 2004b)

As part of its reform agenda in mid-2003 ADB adopted management for development results (MfDR) as a management approach to focus on outcomes that matter to developing member nations (DMCs). MfDR is intended to increase "attention to the value generated from resources invested and to incorporate lessons from ongoing operations to improve the design and implementation of development interventions" (ADB, 2005b) ADB is attempting to mainstream MfDR in support of poverty reduction in Asia. The long term goal is to strengthen DMC capacity to implement results-oriented poverty reduction initiatives on a sustainable basis. Examples of recent adoption of the approach in South Asia are found in introduction of results based (RB) Country Strategy and Programs (CSPs) in Nepal, Bhutan, and Bangladesh. In addition, there are two ADB sponsored technical assistance projects under development with the National Planning Commission in Nepal, one assistance program in Maldives to assist with the development of a results oriented seventh National Development Plan, and in the Pakistan ADB resident mission is working closely with the government to develop an IT based project performance monitoring system now under pilot testing. The South-Asia Regional Department (SARD) has been instrumental in support of these initiatives in the region.[1]

About the MfDR initiative an ADB official observed:

> The development results are on the ground in the developing countries. Therefore, the developing countries ownership, leadership, incentives and capacity in MfDR are key important. The establishment of MfDR country systems such as results-based M&E system at the national level (in Vietnam, Tajikistan, Nepal, Bangladesh and China), and at the project level (in China) is the basic MfDR infrastructure on the ground. This is a time consuming and political sensitive process in developing countries, but doable .... MfDR incentive may be more important, relevant and urgent than the MfDR capacity in developing countries. The MfDR incentives can come from parliament, civil societies and development partners. It is also possible from the government itself—this is especially true in the decentralization process in many developing countries. (ADB, 2006)

A number of other initiatives are in progress in South Asia to strengthen public sector performance including development of national poverty reduction strategies, adoption of medium term expenditure frameworks, improving intergovernmental fiscal relations including fiscal decentralization and devolution (Wescott, 2005), poverty monitoring, civil service reforms, anticorruption initiatives, use of improved information technology in financial management, accounting, and other areas, and use of public scorecards on performance (ADB, 2005c).

Mongolian and Cambodian Finance and Education Initiatives

Additional examples of adoption of performance and results-oriented management in Asia are initiatives in progress, in Mongolia and Cambodia. The following initiatives are reported in the education sector in these nations (ADB, 2004b).

Mongolia uses performance agreements to set out what education results are to be achieved by political and administrative units at central, provincial, and local government level. Mongolia has proposed a set of new measures for measuring performance and results in education. Cambodia has set national targets for school performance and teacher assessment and Mongolia provides for individual school target setting. Gender target setting and planning to achieve a more equitable gender balance is a targeted result in both Cambodia and Mongolia. In Cambodia, girls are underrepresented and in Mongolia boys are underrepresented. Cambodia has instituted a program to raise gender performance targets. Raising student enrollment rates is targeted in Cambodia but barriers include discretionary fees by schools that poor families cannot afford. Cambodia has tackled this problem with an innovative program. To avoid the delays and barriers of the usual budget funding practices, they came up with a series of program budgets that moved funds directly to schools and made schools accountable for this funding.

Mongolia is concerned about monitoring quality of education outputs and outcomes and seeks solutions to enable such initiatives. In Mongolia there also is concern over getting greater results from kindergartens—especially achieving greater coverage achieving greater coverage and more equitable access. Some performance measures and possible solutions have been suggested.

Provincial demand forecasting is used in Cambodia by provincial education leaders in attempt to sustain adequate service supply over the medium term. Forecasting demand and supply is used to gain sufficient time to initiate remedial action in building or acquiring facilities and training and redeploying teachers. The Cambodian case study demonstrates how forecasting reveals trends that promote timely decisions to avoid future crisis.

Ministry-Donor partnership. In many countries efforts to improve education take place with little coordination between donors and the ministry under pressure to implement initiatives advocated by each donor. Case studies of Cambodia and Mongolia show that these problems are avoided to ensure that results and resources are aligned.

Achieving results is the job of the Education ministry but control over resources rests with Ministries of Finance. Often there is a lack of cooperation and understanding between these two ministries with the result that education initiatives are frustrated. Cambodia has recognized the results-based management benefits in close cooperation between finance and education ministries. Cambodia has improved communication by establishing a joint committee to promote understanding and cooperation.

RBM relies upon clear statements and chains of accountability. Job holders must know what is to be achieved, how they will be measured and to whom they are accountable. In Mongolia, performance agreements have been developed between political appointees, minister to governors, and also between the minister and the department and provincial and district units. Education involves many people at all levels from schools to central ministry. With so many involved, it is important that there are effective means of building an RBM culture that includes developing and communicating plans and targets and reviewing past results. Cambodia does this through convening an annual education congress.

A major challenge for education officials is how to measure education quality and ensure that provincial educational units have the capacity to advise upon and assess quality performance. Mongolia is developing its capacity to evaluate education delivery quality. Mongolia is attempting to improve effective communications using IT networking. With education delivered through many schools, districts, and provinces, good communication systems are vital. IT systems allow information, plans, performance and knowledge to be shared. Barriers to good communications include lack of electricity, few computers, and absence of computer communication skills. Education in Cambodia has adopted internal auditing to build confidence in the government and among donors in educational governance, to demonstrate the appropriateness in use of funds and the reliability of its reported performance data. Cambodia provides means for resolving disputes in the complex task of delivering education. Key issues pursued include how communities can make their grievances on education results, resources and processes known so as to have them resolved. In Mongolia, a "good practice" school performance agreement sets out expected results to indicate how school performance should be judged and who can be held accountable for what.

ADB also provides all its member nations with process and procedural guidelines and a framework for developing results based country strategies and programs that indicate how to achieve alignment of country and development goals, how to approach specification of how to define outcomes and outcome indicators, how to effectively mobilize country teams, the method for conducting performance of country assessment program evaluations, implementation and results monitoring instructions, and sector roadmaps for use of RBM (ADB, 2005b; ADB, 2005d). It should be noted that the Organisation for Economic Co-operation and Development (OECD), the United Nations Development Programme (UNDP), the Inter-American Development Bank (IADB), the United States Agency for International Development (USAID), and the World Bank also provide documents to assist nations in adopting results-based management approaches.[2]

More broadly it may be observed that many Asian nations have worked energetically to reform their governments and public management systems, but understanding and comparing results by external observers has been handicapped by a number of factors including the relatively small collection of studies of reform undertaken and the paucity of evaluative work published in English. Even the banks that lend money to nations in the region find it difficult to evaluate the results of management reform initiatives, particularly in the short-term, for example, the Asian Development Bank and the World Bank. Moreover, since many of these reforms have occurred in developing nations, they present very different issues and require a different kind of analysis. Wescott (2001, 2004b; see also Wescott & Jones, 2006) has posed a number of important questions concerning the conditions necessary to promote Asian management reforms. Is it possible, he asks, to measure the quality of overall governance in developing Asian countries? Are present measures robust enough to allow the ranking of countries along a continuum from well-governed to poorly-governed? Should these rankings be used by donor agencies and private investors in making investment decisions? Wescott reflects on these questions and concludes that, despite the complexity and diversity of approaches of governance systems, qualitative and quantitative tools are being used reasonably well in reform in many nations in the region and that real progress is taking place to improve government accountability, transparency and poverty reduction initiatives. However, he also warns that wide-spread corruption threatens such progress in the region.

In Hong Kong, for example, Kevin Yuk-fai Au, Ilan Vertinsky, and Denis Yu-long Wang (2001) declared that by 2000 a paradigm shift had taken place through implementation of new public management. They argued that reform had its roots in the late 1960s and early 1970s, with periods of lull and renewal characterized by shifting powers and expectations among stakeholders. Early reforms, especially in the colonial period, sought social legitimacy. The transfer to sovereignty, adjustment of both the economy and society, and diffusion of new ideas into public management all shaped Hong Kong's reform. The authors investigated the conditions that shaped the reform process in each of Hong Kong's key episodes, the triggers that accelerated it, and the forces that emerged to dampen it. They conclude that, as with many nations, it is simply too early to determine whether reforms now under implementation will be successful. This is particularly the case by the mid-2000s given that the central Chinese government has taken control of management in Hong Kong through the Communist Party and that the government of Hong Kong is caught in a political battle with Beijing over political control and authority. Thus, the fate of reform in Hong Kong remains in doubt at least until the degree of political freedom to be afforded this special part of China is resolved and the next phase of development is fully accepted as legitimate and in their interest by the people of Hong Kong.

Yu-Ying Kuo explored public management reform in Taiwan in the 1990s. The apex of the movement was government reinvention. In 1998, then Premier Vincent C. Siew announced, "the Executive Yuan is energetically planning for and promoting the national development plan for entering the next century, of which the Asia-Pacific Regional Operations Center (APROC) plan and the Taiwan Technology Island Initiative comprise the core." Yu-Ying Kuo (2001) argued that new public management (NPM) developments were likely to determine the direction of Taiwan's government modernization over the next several decades. The government launched an across-the-board reinvention to create a new, flexible, and adaptable government and to raise national competitiveness. However, similar to Hong Kong, politics has overtaken management reform. The government of President Chen Shui-bian has pushed independence of Taiwan from China since 2002 as a means of attracting and sustaining political support. By the mid-2000s this government was caught up in a scandal related to allegations of fraud in gaining reelection and there was significant public debate and unrest about whether the future of Taiwan would be best served by moving closer to China as opposed to pushing for independence. At this point there is no way to tell what the Taiwanese government in power presently or an opposition government more inclined to seek closer ties with China will do in terms of management reform or where political developments may lead. Both the Taiwan and Hong Kong cases demonstrate again the critical importance of politics with respect to management reform. Without stable political support, no real reform is likely to occur.

To support this point even more dramatically we may refer to Roberts's work on the strategies that public officials used to cope with "wicked problems" in Afghanistan in the 1990s—notably previous to the attack on the United States of 9/11/06 and the subsequent war against the Taliban government and then al Qaeda led terrorists that followed this attack. Three coping strategies—authoritative, competitive, and collaborative—were found to be important by Roberts. These strategies were derived from a model based on the level of conflict present in the problem solving process, the distribution of power among the stakeholders, and the degree to which power is contested. Collaborative strategies, she believed, offered the most promise, as illustrated in her case study of the relief and recovery efforts in Afghanistan in the late 1990s. From this case Roberts foresaw implications for using collaborative strategies to deal with wicked problems around the world. Whether such an approach proves to be successful, for example, in Western efforts to negotiate with Iran over its nuclear ambitions or with North Korea by a five nation coalition including South Korea, the United States, China, Russia, and Japan (or bilateral efforts by South Korea and the United States), remains to be seen (Roberts, 2001).

David Shand (2001), a senior official at the World Bank who has worked extensively in the East Asian region, examined World Bank experience in public sector management reform in Asia. Shand found that the imperatives of management reform have deeply affected the institutions working with Asian nations as well as the nations themselves. He argued that public sector management reform had stimulated a "new wave" of activity in the World Bank since the 1970s. Many of the World Bank's strategies to reinvigorate state institutions began in the 1990s to reflect more directly the thinking of the new institutional economics—the importance of structures, incentives, rules and restraints, norms, and best practices. Public sector reform of this type has been encouraged by the World Bank in the "East Asia five"—Thailand, Indonesia, the Philippines, South Korea, and Malaysia—and in smaller Asian countries including Cambodia and Laos. The World Bank also has made preliminary efforts to influence management reform in the transition economies of China, Mongolia and Vietnam with varying success. Shand concluded that fiscal crises and economic competition in Asia have created pressures for public sector management reform, particularly where such change can be argued to contribute to greater competitiveness. Less clear, however, is how the broader lessons of the Asian experience add up. Research has been scanty and far less systematic than the work on the New Zealand and Australian reforms, and reform elsewhere in the world. Moreover, the experiences of developing Asian nations are bound to be different from highly developed governments with different administrative norm and traditions. As we have noted, unless managerial and administrative capacity is strong in developing nations it is unlikely that any postmodern reform will take hold successfully.

FISCAL DEVOLUTION IN ASIA

Another area of reform in Asia is devolution of fiscal authority within nations, under the principle that increased devolution may be effect means for moving decision-making and financing capacity to lower levels of government closer to the public service demands and preferences of ordinary citizens. In this section we examine fiscal devolution in East Asia, providing examples from five nations.[3] First we address the Asian context for fiscal and managerial devolution of authority and responsibility.

In almost all countries of the Asia Pacific region, devolution has appeared an attractive policy option for national governments at one point or another in recent history. In mildest form, devolution policies are advocated on the grounds that increased public participation in planning and implementing nationally sanctioned development policies and priorities will be further facilitated. By moving decisions to the subordinate levels, policy deliberation and decisions may better address local needs and result in greater efficiency and effectiveness. On the other hand, devolution also may increase the risk of moral hazard that could eliminate efficiency gains and, in extreme cases, undermine macroeconomic stability (Rodden, Eskeland, & Litvack, 2003).

The country case studies examine to varying degrees the relationships between fiscal devolution and trends as influenced by (i) historical experience and country governance evolution and context, (ii) modification over time in national constitutions, laws, and rules, (iii) actual fiscal policy change versus what is merely authorized in constitutions and law, (iv) subnational government capacity, (v) efficiency and effectiveness measures, and (vi) citizen participation in local fiscal policy deliberations and decision making. At the outset it may be observed that all hypothetical (and especially positive) associations between fiscal devolution and positive socioeconomic and other outcomes are somewhat speculative because effects are so difficult to measure (Gooptu, 2005, p. 54). This is evident in examination of fiscal devolution in other contexts and time periods, for example, as a result of Tanzanian policies in the 1970s, and centralized planning under Marcos, and then under in the Philippines. With respect to East Asia, in official government and policy pronouncements, devolution often is tied to the twin imperatives of reducing poverty and stimulating economic growth. Whether the association between fiscal devolution rhetoric and actual results are as robust as hoped relative to these aspirations is debatable and the subject of much dialogue and debate in the region, which to some extent mirrors international dialogue on this issue.

The Asia-Pacific region's comparative success over the last several decades in promoting economic growth and poverty reduction is noteworthy. While this success has varied between and within individual countries, the region overall has dramatically changed. As Quibria (2002) notes, "the dramatic improvement in the quality of life that accompanied this miraculous economic transformation has virtually abolished extreme poverty in these societies" (p. 1). Accompanying this growth has been significant progress in poverty reduction. In the early 1970s, more than half the population of the Asia Pacific region was poor, average life expectancy was 48 years, and only 40% of the adult population was literate. Over time the percentage of poor people has decreased and life expectancy has increased significantly, and more of the population is literate. Devolution may have contributed to this overall record of success in some East Asian countries, and might further contribute in the future.

FISCAL DEVOLUTION IN FIVE ASIAN NATIONS

This section describes and analyzes the experience of five East Asian nations in which experiments with fiscal devolution are significant: Cambodia, Indonesia, China, the Philippines, and Thailand. At the end of the country case studies some observations are offered about progress in these nations, which types of initiatives have been successful and what remains to be accomplished.

Cambodia

Cambodia's government signaled its commitment to a mild form of fiscal devolution with the passage of key legislation in 2001 and the election of commune councils in February 2002. However, until systems and procedures for decentralized planning, financing, and service delivery are promulgated in full, and extended across the more than 1,600 communes in the country, it is fair to characterize Cambodian practice as a limited form of fiscal deconcentration.[4] Certain expenditures made by provincial and district branches of central ministries are paid through provincial treasuries, subject to tight, preaudit controls from the Ministry of Finance. This said, there has been some success on a pilot basis with greater degrees of fiscal deconcentration at province level, and the delegation of powers, functions, and resources to commune authorities emulating various kinds of devolution.

Any analysis of Cambodia needs to viewed in the light of its tragic recent history, including the deaths of more than 1 million people either killed or starved to death during the period 1975-79 (Chandler, 1993). Although the Khmer Rouge was formally removed from power in 1979, factional fighting continued sporadically until October 23, 1991 when the four main political factions signed the peace accords in Paris. This laid the groundwork for general elections in 1993 and the development of a liberal, multiparty system, and a market economy. One of the provisions of the accords was a commitment to democratically elected local government, a pledge that was fulfilled on February 3, 2002.

Because of the tragic events in Cambodia, statistics on economic growth and poverty reduction in the period 1980-1992 are not available. Based on the available data, it can be determined that Cambodia achieved an average per capita growth in real GDP from 1992-1996 of nearly 7%, and from 1996-2000 of 4%, a figure exceeded on average by 1 to 2 percentage points from 2000 through 2005. There has been modest success in addressing poverty during this period, with a reduction of poor households as measured by a head count index from 39% in 1993/94 to 36% in 1997, and further reduced from this time through 2005. Analysts attribute this success to improvements in security, improved macrofiscal management, large aid flows, and growth in new businesses, especially in the garment industry for export and in tourism, which has increased markedly in the period 2002-2007. Government poverty reduction policy priorities are to some extent linked into the national budget, although there is need for better alignment to direct additional resources to the agricultural sector and to rural development to reduce poverty, increase service delivery, and promote local economic development.

The situation and challenges for fiscal devolution should be understood in the wider context of ongoing, improvements in fiscal management. As a result of implementing the Public Financial Management (PFM) reform program, supported by ADB and other partners, the government has strengthened revenue administration, with overall revenue collection meeting its target during 2004, and for the first 6 months of 2005 reached 60% of its annual target. A pilot, merit-based pay initiative in the Ministry of Economy and Finance is being introduced, drawing from an initial design prepared by ADB. The initiative is giving higher wages and clear responsibilities for selected officials to spearhead the reform process. Other tangible outcomes of the PFM reform program include smooth budget implementation in 2005, substantial reduction in outstanding debts by national treasury to a record low, and the release of more funds for spending in priority sectors. Following the adoption of the audit law (which was supported by ADB) and subsequent establishment of the National Audit Authority (NAA) in 2002, ADB provided institutional support including training for the NAA's staff until September 2004. Also, ADB has supported the preparation of the internal audit subdecree (approved by the Council of Ministers in April 2005), the creation of internal audit department in the Ministry of Economy and Finance (MEF), and training for internal audit and inspection staff.

However, the remaining challenges are sizable. In Cambodia there is an extreme shortage of qualified and competent public finance specialists and line managers. While a small but dedicated group of specialists has been able to bring down the fiscal deficit, they have yet to achieve transparent and accountable fiscal operations to ensure budget execution is in accordance with budget allocation. Programs to raise social welfare through improved health, education, and welfare services are among the least effective as a result of major institutional problems in program design, resourcing, delivery, and evaluation. Although a reasonable legal framework is in place for budget management, governance structures at the provincial and local levels tend to exacerbate the misallocation of resources, and waste and abuse of public monies.

Despite these reform challenges and limited capacity, the government has been able to make some progress on fiscal deconcentration and some degree of devolution on a pilot basis. Most government expenditures at any level are subject to preaudit control of spending. Ministries must seek MEF approval for spending requests including a commitment visa from MEF, Department of Budget, Finance and Accounting (DBFA) (up to 10 signatures are needed and this can take months), and a payment order from MEF, leading to payment by national treasury (or donor funded account of National Budget Committee (NBC)), via provincial treasury, in cash. The advantage of the present system is that it maintains tight control of spending, clearly defines roles, ensures that basic financial reporting is carried out, and provides severe sanctions for incorrect behavior. The disadvantages of the present system include slow budget execution and absence of public administration capacity to administer and monitor budget execution and results. Recent moves to multiple steps may have strengthened control, but also may have diminished accountability; many pre-audit signatures are perfunctory and add no value to final decisions. Budget expenditures are uneven and tend to surge in November and December. Finally, there is absence of formal mechanisms for citizen participation in planning or monitoring from villages/communes/districts.

To address these problems, three alternative systems have been tried on a pilot basis. The Accelerated District Development system, introduced in 1996, was tested in 27 districts, consisting of 5% of health expenditures. Funds were allocated on a postaudit basis direct to the district level. There continues more to be more flexible reallocation of funds between categories in pilot implementation. A problem with this approach is the need to collect cash in Phnom Penh (since checks cannot be cashed outside of major centers), and a limit of 500,000 Riels (about U.S.$125) per spending request

Priority Action Programs (PAP) were introduced in 2000 in education and health, and there are plans for introducing them in agriculture and rural development in the future. Under PAP, funds are made available at the provincial level on a postaudit basis, budgeted funds are protected. Provincial departments of health and education spend and account for funds through budget management committees, and payments are made by the national treasury (or donor funded account of National Bank of

Cambodia), via provincial treasuries. In 2001, 25 billion Riels of the education budget (14%) and around 40 billion Riels of the health budget were disbursed through this system.

A third system is the government's Seila Program to promote rural development through decentralized planning, financing, and management of investments in basic services and infrastructures. Seila, introduced in 1996, is the most ambitious devolution initiative implemented to date, resulting in the creation of commune development committees in six provinces encompassing over 1,000 villages and 100 communes. Key features of devolution policy and laws, as noted below, reflect the Seila experience. Over 5 years, the government committed to expanding the Seila Program to all provinces and communes. Under the Seila Program funds were made available at the provincial level on a postaudit basis. Provincial Rural Development Committees (PRDC) set priorities based on consultations at provincial and local level. An executive committee of the PRDC spends and accounts for funds. Withdrawals from the treasury account require the governor's signature; from donor accounts, one or two signatories depending on account, and payment is by national treasury (or donor funded account of NBC), via provincial treasury. In 2000, 2.1 billion Riels of government funds were disbursed through this system, plus donor funds of about U.S.$8.5 million, rising to 5 billion Riels of government funds in 2001.

While there is evidence that these pilot exercises improved disbursement and effective targeting of public expenditures in rural areas, and that they made positive contributions to citizen participation in governance, devolution in Cambodia is in its infancy. Beginning on February 3, 2002, for the first time in its history, Cambodia elected local government corporate entities. With over 1,600 newly created rural and urban commune councils, with over 12,000 local councilors, the task of establishing and internalizing appropriate legal, administrative, fiscal, and supervision mechanisms has been immense, particularly in view of the known weaknesses in skills and institutional capacity throughout the public sector. There also is a need to house and equip the councils, build communication networks, and review commune boundaries. Government officials responsible for the devolution process have been hopeful of creating a substantial program of medium-term support to complement the mainly short-term aid inputs provided earlier.

The government decision to hold local council elections in 2002 was an authentically national initiative. Although the government received much less external support for the commune elections than it received for the national elections in 1998 (and vastly less than for the process organized by the United Nation Transitional Authority for Cambodia in 1993), it financed the voter-registration process and preparatory work from its own resources. However, limited powers and capacities for commune councils were provided in the early years. Still, the decision to elect local councils was an important step toward deepening the concept of democracy and popular understanding of democratic rights and freedoms in a country that—until the last decades—had known only autocratic rule. Although the direct service role of elected local councils has been modest to date, they offer great opportunity for increasing local voice and representation in issues such as land-use rights, common property and natural resource use, and the efficiency of government service delivery. Increased transparency and accountability over resource use will help to promote investment and reduce vulnerabilities in addition to the intrinsic value of democratic systems in promoting participation and social inclusion.

To underwrite devolution, the national assembly and senate passed two major pieces of legislation. The Law of Commune Administrative Management broadly defines the nature, functions, and powers of the commune councils and defines a modest form of devolution of responsibilities and resources to elected commune councils. The Commune Election Law regulates commune elections. A policy of deconcentration of powers and functions to the provincial and district levels remains under consideration within the framework of the National Program for Administration Reforms, presented to the aid community at the consultative group meeting of February 1999 in Tokyo. Government policy recognizes the essential complementarity and the need for a parallel implementation of devolution reforms.

Devolution of government to the communes will only work if supporting functions also are deconcentrated to the provinces and districts. The Seila Program, mentioned above, was planned to cover all rural provinces by 2005. Under the Seila Program, commune development committees (CDCs), chaired by a commune chief and including representatives from all villages, are responsible for the development of the commune. After the elections, commune councils are to progressively replace the CDCs. The commune councils have 4-8 elected representatives with a 5-year mandate. For at least the first year, planning and priority setting mechanisms in place for the CDCs is to be carried forward by the commune councils including the local planning process, commune development plans, and commune investment plans and budgets.

Yet outside of Seila communes, fiscal devolution to commune councils is limited. For many, the only revenue sources they control are one time civil registration fees, at U.S.$0.10 per registration. These and the small funds received from the national budget are managed by provincial or municipal treasuries, deconcentrated arms of the Ministry of Economics and Finance (MEF), with the help of commune clerks, employed by MOI.

Thus, most commune councils have little involvement in financial decision making (Blunt & Turner, 2005).

The Cambodian government has, as of 2005, a policy objective to improve community involvement in rural development initiatives. Devolution practices have evolved to enhance opportunities for communities to participate in the planning, budgeting, and monitoring processes of local governments. The Council of Ministers recently approved a Strategic Framework for Decentralization and Deconcentration Reforms. However, despite the fact that this framework has been approved, funding for the initiative is limited. Community participation in local government policy and planning dialogue and action, and at all levels of government, remains far lower than desired. This demonstrates that although government policy encourages increased participation to accompany fiscal devolution, community capacity to meet expectations must match opportunity. In turn, this reveals deeper problems in the social infrastructure that relate to capability to participate, for example, access to and availability of education services of reasonable quality.

Indonesia

Given its large and diverse population and geographical spread, international experience would suggest Indonesia's governance structure would be decentralized and involve considerable fiscal devolution (Buentjen, 2000). However, when Soeharto stepped down, Indonesia was highly centralized, with subnational expenditures only 10% of national expenditures. The Soeharto government regularly postponed any major reforms in fiscal devolution. Although Law No. 5/74 on regional government was drafted in the late 1980s, adoption required the revision of Law No. 32/1956 on fiscal balance, and a political deadlock prevented this from happening. Yet in the late 1990s, pressures were mounting for action, not least motivated by claims for secession by West Papua, Aceh, Riau, East Kalimantan, and certain districts in Maluku. Given the lack of legitimate institutions, the manner in which concerns were raised was frequently not very orderly. Although there were frequent demonstrations, sometimes violent, against the existing political system down to the village level, precise concepts of an alternative system were largely missing. Devolution thinking did not play a major role until the more recent unitarism/federalism debate. This makes it more difficult to identify the major proponents of Indonesian devolution reform.

What seems clear from this period is that provincial interest groups used the atmosphere of reform following the downfall of Soeharto to raise their demands for improved human rights and sharing of national wealth. Discussions took place behind the scenes and were not transparent to the general public. In November, 1998 a People's Consultative Assembly, the legislature legislature (Majelis Permusyawaratan Rakyat or MPR) decision was delivered which provided the political mandate for the then new administration to reform the devolution framework—and it seemed to have been influenced by the provinces. The MPR is the highest state institution. It usually meets once every 5 years. It consists of approximately 1,000 representatives, including the 500 representatives from the Parliament, and 500 others nominated by the provinces or appointed by the president as representative of various groups in the society.

Since 1998, three important new laws have been enacted:

- Law No. 22/1999 on Regional Government (UU Pemda/Undang-undang Nomor 22 tentang Pemerintahan Daerah) replaces Law No. 5/74 on Regional Government and Law No. 5/1979 on Village Administration. The law revised the assignment of functions and redefined the roles of institutions at all levels of government including the villages;
- Law No. 25 on Fiscal Balance (UU PKPD/Undang-undang Nomor 25 Tahun 1999 tentang Perimbangan Keuangan antara Pemerintah Pusat dan Daerah) replaced Law No. 32/1956 on the Fiscal Balance between the central level and the regions. The essence of this law was definition of sources of finance for devolved, deconcentrated, and coadministered functions;
- Law No. 34/2000 on Regional Taxes and Regional Levies, amending Law No. 18/1997 (See Table 3.1).

Box 1 summarizes the major changes in administrative and political devolution stipulated in Law No. 22/1999 on Regional Government. Law No. 34/2000 introduced new regional taxes and regional levies, and specified allocation amounts for each jurisdiction. Previously, Law No. 18/1997 on regional taxes and levies had limited the number of provincial taxes to three, and the number of district taxes to six. In addition, the number of provincial and districts levies was limited to 30. Earlier studies showed that the revenues of the more than 200 regional taxes and charges that were abolished by Law No. 18/1997 did not contribute meaningfully to regional revenues. Yet, the large number of taxes and levies contributed to a lack of transparency and thus greatly facilitated corruption at regional level by violating a basic rule of tax administration (Bird, 2004) to "keep it simple."

Although Law No. 34/2000 potentially allows for new taxes and levies, the results are not yet clear. Competition among the regions for limited investment resources, and a working political process is likely to moderate the eagerness to tax over time, but in the short run, excesses may occur.

Table 3.1: Box 1: Major Changes From Law 22/1999

- The principle that all functions that are not specifically assigned to central and provincial level automatically belong to the districts was introduced. However, the functional assignment to the central level and the provinces was vague and open to interpretation, thus depending on implementing regulations.
- Regions were given more control over their finances, planning process, civil service organizations and cooperative bodies.
- Central ministries in general were no longer to be allowed to maintain independent deconcentrated offices in the Provinces or in the rural and urban districts for purposes of executing central level projects/programs. The deconcentrated offices were to be absorbed into regional organizations.
- Rural and urban district heads are fully autonomous and no longer report hierarchically to provinces. They function solely as the head of the autonomous local government and are directly and solely responsible to the local parliament.
- The regional executive arm is to be more accountable to the regional legislature, particularly at the district/city level where the regional parliament elects the head of the district/city and their deputies with no interference from the center.
- A 2-year implementation time frame was foreseen in the laws; subsidiary legal instruments were to be ready by May 2000 and field implementation realized by May 2001.

Source: Wescott and Porter, 2002, p. 29.

Beyond taxes, charges and user fees can become a fertile ground for raising more revenues. While increasing fees and levies may be good policy to reduce (implicit) subsidies that burden the budget, they could also deprive the poor of the services they need to help themselves. Therefore, any revenue mobilization strategy that relies heavily on user charges must be accompanied by measures that protect the poor.

The regulatory framework for revenue sharing (natural resource revenues and land and building taxes, general-purpose grants (dana alokasi umum/DAU) and specific-purpose grants (dana aloksasi khusus, or DAK) were provided by Law No. 25 of 1999 and government regulation 104 passed into law on November 10, 2000. The precise provincial and Kabupaten allocations of the DAU for 2001 were authorized by presidential decree (KEPPRES 181) on December 23, 2000 (Lewis & Umum, 2001). The first allocations of the general-purpose transfers were made in 2001. Although the amounts actually required by regional governments to finance the delivery of decentralized services are not known with any degree of certainty, according to first studies (Lewis & Umum, 2001) these amounts appeared at that time to be sufficient to fund both provincial and kabupaten requirements in the aggregate. This observation is made with somewhat less confidence regarding the provinces than the kabupaten. In fact, it appears that only 80% of the DAU were allocated based on the formula which was designed with an equalization effect in mind. Since the devolution program was launched on January 1, 2001, achievements have included (i) regulations drafted by majority of regions concerning authority, organization, and personnel; (ii) regulatory frameworks finalized by most departments and other units in accordance with law 22 (e.g., forestry, mining); (iii) 11 departments and agencies completed initial development of minimum service standard guidelines; (iv) fiscal allocation criteria were changed to address fairness and sufficiency concerns, based on recommendations from an independent, academic evaluation; (iv) ongoing work to revise and update Law 2 (Ministry of Home Affairs, 2001). The 2002 budget for subnational expenditure as a percentage of total public expenditure was 32%, up from 17% in 2000 (World Bank 2002, 2003a, p. 2; World Bank, 2005, Table 5.1, p. 86). Two surveys were undertaken focusing implementation of the new laws at the district/municipalities level. The first phase of the Indonesia Rapid Decentralization Appraisal (IRDA), a project supported by the Asia Foundation and funded by USAID, was conducted in 13 districts and municipalities between December, 2001 and January, 2002. The latest (fifth) phase added 39 districts/municipalities. The Governance and Decentralization Survey (World Bank, 2002), administered in the period, then supplemented by the Public Expenditure Review (World Bank, 2003b), provides extensive additional data and analysis of the success of these initiatives.

In the period 2002-2005, two key challenges have emerged: (i) the legal framework still needs more clarity and a more coordinated approach; and (ii) there is a need for greater balance between the standards that are set for public services and the resources that are allocated. To address these challenges, important revisions have been prepared the Law on Regional Governance (Law 32/2004, previously Law 22/1999) and the Law on Regional Autonomy (Law 33/2004, previously Law 25/1999). Under the latter, there is greater clarity in revenue assignment. The government is also amending the Law on Local Taxes and Levies to address multiple taxes and levies (ADB, 2005d).

Two additional findings on fiscal devolution are notable. First, the transfer of large numbers of civil servants to the regions resulted in high portions of the budget spent on salaries, squeezing the available funds for service delivery and capacity building. Second, although largely dependent on central government transfers, local governments have sought ways to increase their own sources of income in the form of taxes and levies. In some instances local governments have imposed local taxes and levies that have become a burden to citizens and business. However, much work remains to be done since subnational revenue is only 3% of total national revenue. Citizens are demanding more open dialogue and consultations about changes in revenue generation methods (and rates) and budget allocations.

People's Republic of China (PRC)

China has achieved one of the fastest growth rates of any country, with an average per capita growth of real GDP of 7.5% from 1981-90, 9.2% from 1991-1999 (World Bank, 2001, 2002), and approximately 9% on average from 1999 to 2007. However, in 2006 growth exceeded this figure by more than 1.5% in several quarters, leading the China's central bank to ratchet up interest rates to slow down growth under evidence of real inflation and in anticipation of further increases in prices. In September, 2006 the International Herald Tribune (IMF) projected growth for China in 2007 at approximately 10% ("IMF Raises World Growth Outlook," 2006a). There was corresponding success in addressing poverty during this period, with a reduction of poor households to an estimated 18.5% of the population (or about 250 million people) surviving on U.S.$1 per day or less (UNDP, 2001, p. 149). The official poverty line in at this time China placed about 4.6% of the population (or about 60 million people) in poverty. In 2006 the official number was reported to have dropped to 30 million. PRC achieved its rapid growth and poverty reduction from the 1980s to the 2000s for many of the same reasons as other countries in the region, including sharp increases in labor intensive exports, market-friendly policies, large inflows of foreign capital, rapid development of physical and social infrastructure, and improvements in service delivery.

Although the PRC is a unitary state, there are four subnational levels of government, 31 provinces (excluding Hong Kong), 333 prefectures, 2,148 counties, and 48,697 townships, towns, and city districts (Lin & Zhiqiang, 2000; Rao, 2001). Each level devolves functions to the next most subordinate level. Prior to the 1980s, no subnational jurisdiction had a separate budget: the central government collected all revenues, and prepared a consolidated budget for all subnational tiers. State owned enterprises (SOEs) remitted all surpluses to the central government, which in turn covered all their expenditures by fiscal appropriation.

At the national level China's Ministry of Finance has traditionally exercised strong central fiscal power and control but lower governments have ways to get around such control. As Wanna explains:

> In the People's Republic of China, under the Central Committee of the Communist Party, the Ministry of Finance is regarded as exercising an almost dictatorial authority over the annual budget round. Few other agencies are involved in the process and very few of the people's representatives ever have the chance to see the brief summary of budget proposals, often as little as eight pages of tables. Secrecy and exclusivity are imposed as political techniques. But the regions of China notoriously play games and attempt to disguise incomes, while maximising their claims on the central budget. The

Finance ministry does not necessarily have its way, and regions can achieve 'wins' despite the centralised rules and procedures. (Wanna, 2004, p. 3)

Despite this degree of central government fiscal policy control, beginning with the market-oriented reforms in 1979 the fiscal system became increasingly decentralized, where revenues were increasingly shared by the central and provincial governments, and by successive tiers. There were three main reasons for the changes. First, the growth of township and village enterprises, joint ventures, and private firms had lessened the importance of SOEs. As SOE losses mounted, the government was forced to look for alternative revenue sources. Second, the economic reforms shifted the balance of political power toward local autonomy. Third, the new awareness of the importance of markets and incentives was an impetus to provide local governments with incentives to step up revenue collections.

As with other reforms, fiscal reform started as an experiment. As early as 1977, Jiangsu province was chosen to try out an alternative fiscal arrangement with the central government. The province was contracted to remit a share of its total revenues each year to the central government. In 1980, broader revenue sharing arrangements were adopted. Revenues were classified by source and divided into central fixed revenues (e.g., customs duties and revenues remitted by centrally-owned SOEs), local fixed revenues (e.g., salt taxes, agricultural taxes, industrial and commercial income taxes, and revenues remitted by locally-owned SOEs), and central-local shared revenues (e.g., profits of large-scale enterprises under dual ownership, industrial and commercial taxes, or turnover taxes).

In 1985, the tax system was again reformed, including a change calling for income taxes from SOEs rather than profit remittances. Although revenues were still divided into the same three categories, the new categories were related to type of tax collected rather than on ownership (e.g., of SOEs). Fourteen provinces, including three municipalities, were contracted to remit a specific share of their local fixed and shared revenues. Five provinces received lump sum transfers from the central government, while the remaining ones received central subsidies. Under this new system, shared revenues were by far the largest of the three categories. Thus, central government relied on local governments to increase total revenues, and local governments had an incentive to boost their revenue collection (since they could retain some of the shared revenues).

The tax system changed again in 1994 due to a sharp fall in the ratio of revenues to GNP (35% in 1978 to 12% in 1996), caused by the falling profitability of SOEs and the inability of the tax system to capture the expanding tax base arising from economic prosperity. There were also disincentives to subnational authorities to generate revenues and transfer them to the center. The differential sharing mechanism introduced in the 1980s served to enhance the powers of more affluent provinces, and reduced the central share in revenues. This reduced the ability of the center to undertake redistribution and stabilization functions effectively. It encouraged the center to push expenditure responsibilities down to adjust to lower revenues, and encouraged the use of extrabudgetary financing, with correspondingly diminished transparency and accountability. Another consequence was tax competition among jurisdictions, both through tax incentives, and varying levels of public services (Bao, 2003).

The 1994 reforms included introduction of the value added tax, changes in the distribution of shared revenues, establishment of separate tax administrations for national and subnational governments, and earmarked transfer schemes. Yet despite these reforms, the budget still is not comprehensive, with large extrabudgetary financing and spending. This problem is greatest for subnational levels where revenues were recentralized, but expenditure functions have continued. The result has been both under provision of services and extra budgetary financing, both of which having adverse consequences on accountability, efficiency, and equity in spending. Tax sharing also does not address the problem that more affluent provinces get to keep more revenue than the poorer provinces. The central government has provided hundreds of types of earmarked grants as offsets, but they are allocated in an arbitrary and opaque manner, and thus do not adequately address the problem. Local governments have addressed budgetary shortfalls through a combination of extrabudgetary financing, internal and external borrowings, tax preferences, and other measures risking fiscal discipline (Jin & Zou, 2003; Zhang & Zou, 1998).

An estimated 69% of public expenditure takes place, and over 64% of revenue is raised at the subnational level in PRC (IMF, 2005; Wong, 2005, p. 86), the highest proportion of any country covered in this study of five nations. Analysts have tried to estimate the consequences of this series of devolution initiatives on economic growth, with mixed results. Zhang and Zou (1998) estimated that fiscal devolution has lowered economic growth in provinces with the greatest degree of delegated spending. Lin and Liu (2000), using a different measure of fiscal devolution, find that it has promoted economic growth at the county level, but has had an insignificant effect at the province level. Clearly, more analysis of the effects of fiscal devolution in the PRC is necessary to determine net effects with any level of confidence.

The Philippines

The Local Government Code (LGC) of 1991 affected 77 provinces, 72 cities, 1,548 municipalities, and more than 42,000 villages (barangays). Between 1991and 1994, 61% of the field personnel of concerned agencies were devolved to local government units (LGUs). Regular elections were required for local officials and legislatures. Although devolution has affected particularly the health, agriculture, social welfare, and natural resources sectors, all aspects of public service delivery were affected in some way (Bauer, 1998).

The Autonomous Region in Muslim Mindanao (ARMM) has a separate Local Government Code of Muslim Mindanao, enacted in 1993. The ARMM code, while similar to the national LGC, includes guidelines relating to Muslim institutions and organizational structures in ARMM. In practice, the regional ARMM government and its agencies maintain direct control and supervision of all devolved functions.

A Devolution Master Plan (1993-98) was formulated to further implement the devolution process. The LGC was amended to abolish unfunded sectoral mandates, improve LGU financial resources, and rationalize LGU and national government agency (NGA) functions based on the principle of subsidiarity, with the extension to LGUs of responsibilities for national roads and power generation and transmission, administrative reorganization, reform of personnel functions, bottom-up planning, and electoral reforms. Implementation of the LGC led to more integrated services delivery, more focused on local priorities, and more cost effectiveness. LGUs are interested in providing more investment and maintenance support for projects they themselves have formulated and implemented. They are also more actively looking for cost-sharing arrangements with the private sector and NGOs, as well as fees or user charges for services provided.

In agriculture, pre-LGC delivery of extension services was viewed as nonstandardized, poorly managed, and often not adapted to local realities. Staffs were unfamiliar with local conditions. With devolution, a rationalization of personnel took place, resulting in more area-specific programs and more productive fieldwork. However, there are serious concerns from LGUs that the Department of Agriculture (DA) is continuing to execute national projects, and is reluctant to provide LGUs access to technical assistance. LGUs have limited control over planning, implementation, monitoring and evaluation of projects funded from the national budget and from official development assistance. As a result, LGUs typically source their own technical assistance outside the DA structure. Unlike the DA, the Department of Agrarian Reform, whose functions are less devolved, cooperates closely with LGUs to implement their projects and helps build governance capacity at the local level.

In the health sector, LGUs have assumed more than 60% of the Department of Health staff and approximately 40% of its budget, including 12,560 rural health units, municipal health centers and barangay health stations, and 595 hospitals. Devolution in the health sector has resulted in (i) significant improvement in the timely procurement of medicines and supplies, (ii) a reorientation toward more flexible basic health programs, (iii) more innovative mechanisms for revenue generation, and (iv) more integrated and client relevant area-focused planning and services delivery. On the negative side, funding shortfalls and increasing inequity between richer and poorer jurisdictions endure as major concerns. Less developed LGUs often find it difficult to maintain quality of health standards due to lack of funds.

Distinct from agriculture and health, the devolution of social welfare functions is perceived in most respects as successful. The four reasons for smooth devolution are (i) the Department of Social Welfare Development (DSWD) carefully managed the devolution of its personnel into local organizational structures, (ii) along with the devolution of responsibilities, the DSWD devolved substantial funding to LGUs, and provided further opportunities to access external funds, (iii) DSWD personnel were equipped to immediately work at the local and field level, and (iv) LGUs (often together with NGOs) expanded the demand for social services. The implementation of the Minimum Basic Needs data system and the thrust given to poverty reduction under the localized social reform agenda further accelerated the process of sound devolution.

Environmental and natural resources management offers the greatest continuing challenge for LGUs. There is (i) a growing concern over the effectiveness of the Department of Environment and Natural Resources to carry out its functions, and over the lack of LGU involvement in planning and management of national programs, (ii) increased interest of LGUs in exercising greater authority over solving environmental programs, (iii) a growing awareness at the LGU level that environmental management skills are lacking, and (iv) a rapid rise in ad hoc efforts addressing multisectoral environmental issues at the local levels.

Another aspect to devolution in the Philippines, as in other countries, has been its catalytic effect on innovations in administration and governance. For example, Naga City is internationally recognized for a range of governance innovations. An extensive e-government system, for example, goes beyond that in many other jurisdictions to inform citizens on budgets, bidding documents, legislation, and procedures. Since many citizens do not have access to the Internet, the city also provides a hard copy of the Naga City Citizen Charter that contains essential information that is also on the Web site on how to access city services (Wescott, 2004a).

Sources of LGU financing are the internal revenue allotments (IRA), local taxes and revenues, loans and grants from donors, and borrowing. The LGUs are classified according to their income levels. Although the LGC provides for the allocation of significant national revenues to LGUs, a large unfinished agenda remains to insure the real autonomy of LGUs. For example, officials most involved in LGU financial management remain appointed by national agencies. While the LGC limits the control of central agencies over the local planning process and tax policy, it does not eliminate it.

The major source of LGU finance has been the IRA. LGUs have received 40% or a slightly greater amount more recently (up from 11% in 1991) of the IRA based on total collections of the third fiscal year preceding the current fiscal year. However, an approximate 40% share still is less than 15% of total public expenditures. There have been moves to increase the IRA to 60%, and to change the calculation procedures to be based on the current year collections. The IRA is allocated among different levels of LGUs, giving 2% each to provinces and cities, 34% to municipalities, and 20% to barangays. Each LGU level gets its share based on population (50%), area (25%), and equal sharing (25%). The criteria favor cities, as well as municipalities with small populations and large land areas. In addition to the IRA, LGUs receive a 40% share of the cross collection derived from mining taxes, forestry charges, and others.

While the IRA remains the main source of LGU revenue, selected LGUs have been increasingly tapping their own sources, including the issuing of municipal bonds. However, the IRA has become a more important share of LGU income under devolution. Whereas the share of locally generated resources declined from 49% of total LGU income to 37% in 1994, the IRA share increased in the same years from 37 to 61% In less developed LGUs, the IRA share reach 95% of the total. More recent data suggests that roughly the same pattern persists to 2005. In addition, some cities have taken loans from government finance institutions. However, LGUs receive less than one fourth of their estimated capital requirements from this source, with poorer LGUs getting much less.

The LGC provided LGUs with the authority to access private capital markets. Build-Operate-Transfer (BOT) and Build-Operate-Own arrangements have been used. In 1997, the BOT center in the Department of Finance had identified 79 potential local BOT projects. More recent data was not obtained by the time this study was written. Although LGUs can legally borrow from donors such as the ADB, they cannot access these funds directly unless the national government gives its sovereign guarantee. Whereas a number of functions have been devolved to

LGUs, the funds often remain at the national level. Particularly in health and agriculture, LGUs have the devolved staff, but central agencies still control the funds.

To summarize, devolution appears to have improved the capacities of LGUs to carry out new functions, including intergovernmental cooperation. However, there are still major concerns regarding LGU capacity to (i) prepare comprehensive urban development plans, (ii) effectively link the local planning exercise with public investment plans and expenditure surveys, (iii) join into more efficient economic planning units, (iv) organize effective participatory consultation and (v) reengineer local bureaucracies and develop quantitative indicators to measure the efficiency and effectiveness of local institutions.

A proposal that may be viewed as one type or stage of devolution has gained increasing attention recently. Establishment of the Philippines as a federalist state has been promoted by various entities including the Citizen's Movement for a Federal Philippines (CMFP) and the Coalition for Charter Change Now (CCCN) (Brillantes, Montes, & Sonco, 2005; Go, 2005). Under federalism proposals the president of the nation would have reduced powers with the election of a prime minister by the Parliament. The prime minister would have responsibility for establishing government policy and the management roles and responsibilities of national ministries, assisted by a cabinet selected from members of Parliament. Congressional district seats in Parliament would be increased from the present number of 220 to approximately 300 with members elected under proportional representation (moving away from the existing system of "reserved" seats) as envisioned by the 1987 Constitution. The 79 existing provinces would be merged into 10 or 11 states (regions also merged), thus creating new legal governance entities positioned between local and national governments. As noted, the existing Philippine political system provides little real power to LGUs and preserves the dominance of the president and national government.

The proposed state government political structure would feature elected assemblies, each of which would draft its own constitution, consistent with the federal constitution, as in other federalist systems. Members of state assemblies would be elected by provinces under the state's jurisdiction, with members elected as representatives of political parties as under the current system. The position and authority of provincial governors under the current system would be abolished. States would administer their elections in replacement of the existing election system now operated centrally by an often criticized Commission on Elections. State assemblies would elect state governors to serve as the executive of state government.

Advocates argue that the new governance arrangement would encourage healthy competition for political and socioeconomic representation within and among states, especially if revenue and expenditure rights were passed to states from the national government as intended under federalism proposals. Devolution of taxing powers and development of effective administrative, tax and budgetary systems in states and, through further devolution, in LGUs would be critical to the effectiveness and capacity of both levels of government to respond appropriately to citizen and interest group demands for improved services. In theory, enhanced power under federalism would better enable local economic development and productivity because, unlike the present system, revenues generated in states would be available for allocation to highest state and local government policy and program priorities, for example, health, education, infrastructure investment. Further, it is argued that federalism would create incentives to stimulate more ethical, responsible, and transparent behavior of elected an appointed officials and government managers, and would lead to increased managerial capacity and accountability in both state and local governments. These changes could, under optimistic assumptions, reestablish and reinforce similar norms and behavior at the federal government level in Parliament, the office of the prime minister and in government ministries.

Additionally, economic development successes at the local and state levels would contribute to national goals of poverty reduction, improved social service system design and delivery, increased competitiveness in world markets and socioeconomic and political stability. It is advanced that under federalism state governments would become positioned to work more effectively than the national government does presently with LGUs, the private and nongovernment sectors to create competitive economic incentives that would, over time, stimulate overall Philippine economic growth, resulting in a higher per capita GDP and more equitable distribution of employment opportunity, income. and wealth. Advocates point to success under federalism in nations including Australia, Switzerland, Germany, Austria, the United States of America, and Canada as examples of what could be achieved under this system for the Philippines.

Advocates of federalism concede that recreation of the Philippine political system cannot and should be attempted rapidly. Rather, federalism proposals should be widely vetted to stimulate dialogue about the relative merits of the new system compared to the existing system of national governance. Advocates point out that a variety of local entities and interests successfully adapted to changes brought by the 1991 Local Government Code as evidence that adjustment to a federal system could be accommodated within the Philippine political culture. Still, they caution that any attempt to impose federalism increases the risk of anarchical responses that would imperil Philippine political and socioeconomic progress (Brillantes, Montes, & Sonco, 2005). However, it may be observed that as was the case in New Zealand, Australia and other nations in the 1980s and 1900s, absence of market competitiveness and slow economic growth (resulting in national fiscal stress) may, eventually, increase the attention of Philippine citizens and leaders in business and government sectors to consider federalism along with other less ambitious devolution alternatives. The experience of these two nations provides contrasting examples for the Philippines as Australia governs under a federal system while New Zealand has remained a national state.

Thailand

Thailand is divided into 76 provinces (*changwat*). Bangkok has an elected governor, while the Ministry of Interior appoints governors for the other provinces. Provinces are subdivided into 811 districts (*amphoe*), each administered by a chief district officer appointed by the Ministry of Interior. The districts are further divided into 7,409 subdistricts (*tambon*), which are broken down into approximately 67,581 villages (*muban*), both traditionally headed by local chiefs and village headmen. In addition, a number of special municipal or local authorities operate semiautonomously. Policy making and major policy implementation functions are centralized in Bangkok, but some responsibilities are decentralized to local governments. Some functions are the joint responsibility of the central government and local governments, while others are either provided by the central government or are monitored and controlled by the central government (Nelson, 2000). Local governments are allowed to obtain revenues from a limited number of sources, primarily property taxes.

Provincial governors, their deputies, and assistants are appointed from the staff of the Department of Local Administration of the Ministry of Interior. Tambon councils are made up of village headmen, departmental officials, and local notables. Scott (1996) points out that the councils have the symbolic power of bringing together key figures in a forum that appears to have authoritative status; but they generally have little income or real power. Since the councils are dominated by centrally appointed officials, they help to strengthen central control, and maintain national unity.

Thailand achieved its rapid growth and poverty reduction in the 1980s and 1990s for many of the same reasons as other countries in the region including sharp increases in labor-intensive exports, market-friendly policies, large inflows of foreign capital, rapid development of physical and social infrastructure, and improvements in service delivery. These improvements were achieved in a highly centralized administrative and fiscal structure. Yet despite the gains, there has been a growing public desire for political change and democratic government, widely characterized as "turning government by the politicians to government by the people" (Bowornsak & Burns, 1998, p. 241; Klein, 1998). Following the military takeover and violence of 1992, consensus crystallized in support of fundamental reforms of the political system to halt the 60-year cycle of military coups overthrowing elected governments. In 1993 the House of Representatives set up the Constitutional Reform Committee which in 1995 presented a reform constitution, eventually approved by parliament in 1997.

Several unique features of the 1997 constitution set it apart from its predecessors, including strengthening the rule of law and human rights; enhancing accountability mechanisms and enforcing much stronger conflict of interest standards; and improving transparency, participation, and devolution. The constitution also provides one of Asia's most liberal codes of individual freedom, including both political rights (freedom of speech, religion, association, and assembly) and social rights (the right to receive health care and 12 years of education at the state's expense).

The constitution embraced devolution while leaving vague many specifics that were to be addressed through separate legislation and administrative actions. It sought to end the practice of guided democracy at the local level by specifying that most local government bodies would be elected. This contrasted with previous practice, whereby many local employees were appointed from Bangkok and owed their allegiance to individual ministries. In the past, the only elected officials were councillors in the municipalities of Bangkok and Pattaya. Under the revised arrangements, each of Thailand's 7,951 appointed local councils were replaced by elected ones when their terms expired. The power to transfer, promote, increase salaries, and punish local officials was vested with local governments, although the approval of a local officials committee was required. This committee consisted of an equal number of representatives of relevant government agencies and LGOs. Public services such as health, education, and police were placed under local control. Local governments were also made responsible for conserving local arts, customs, knowledge, and culture, and for managing and preserving natural resources and the environment.

The National Decentralization Act (NDC) came into effect on November 18, 1999. This act defined the role of the NDC as responsible for preparing the devolution framework. NDC has 36 members and is chaired by the prime minister and deputy prime minister. The NDC recommended procedures for decentralizing administrative power to local administrations in an action plan. Once the cabinet approved the plan it was submitted to Parliament for consideration and was announced in the *Government Gazette*. Once it was signed into law, it became legally binding in terms of agency operations. To comply with the NDC, the government proposed gradually increasing the budgetary allocations to and the responsibilities of LGOs in three phases as follows:

- *Phase 1, FY 2001.* During this period the Bureau of Budget ensured that LGOs had the equivalent of 20% of national revenues (approximately B160 billion) to finance local activities. National revenues exclude revenues raised by LGOs, administrative fees charged by the Revenue Department to collect taxes, and government borrowing. Of this amount, LGOs managed B40 billion under the Procurement Management Regulation, whereby the central government provides local governments with training in estimating future budgets. This phase was completed. Although the targets were largely met in terms of spending at the local level most budget implementation was fully controlled by central ministries, as had been the case in the past.
- *Phase 2, FY 2002–FY 2004.* During this period local governments were required to respond to the increased budgetary allocations by providing strategic plans and the manpower to manage them. During this period the Bureau of Budget ensured that LGOs had the equivalent of 25% of national revenues.
- *Phase 3, FY 2005–FY 2009.* During this period all activities are to be decentralized and transferred to local governments. The Bureau of Budget is to ensure that LGOs have the equivalent of 35% of national revenues by the end of the 9th Plan period in 2006. If these budgetary allocations are met, Lao-Araya (2001) points out potential risks to macroeconomic stability, and the need for increased revenues. Yet, as indicated above, these risks could also be addressed by having central ministries continue to retain control over budget implementation at the local level.

Overall, DOLA estimated that as of early 2000, less than 10% of total governmental spending in Thailand was executed at the municipal level compared to 14% for all local governments. If Bangkok is excluded from the calculation, municipalities are responsible for only about 2% of total government spending. Approximately 60% of municipal spending is dedicated to recurrent purposes, with salaries and supplies accounting for almost two-thirds of this amount, or approximately 40% of the municipal budget. The remaining 40% of municipal budgets are used for public works spending. However, since most local expenditures are not linked with a specific revenue source, municipalities tend to finance a large portion of their capital projects from recurrent revenues in a "pay-as-you-go" fashion. While municipal expenditures as a percentage of total government spending has increased since 2000, it remains low and its distribution is roughly the same, and long-standing inequities remain.

In general, central and local governments have overlapping expenditure functions and responsibilities, which usually result in central government dominated administration. Due to these overlapping functions and responsibilities of central government ministries and local governments, the central government usually assumes responsibility for most large expenditures. The NDC supports mandates for assigning more direct responsibility to local governments for specific, well-defined expenditures. These expenditure assignments should result in minimal administrative overlap of responsibility among central and local governments.

Fiscal devolution in Thailand remains in an early phase—but this phase seems to have lasted too long relative to the progress of other nations in the region. Whether the measures that have been proposed are implemented effectively is critical to local government ability to contribute to economic growth and poverty reduction. Results depend, in part, on how implementation proceeds with respect to six issues: local revenue authority, central government transfers, local expenditure, citizen participation, civil service and personnel system reforms, and public auditing of local accounts, and borrowing.

The larger issue with respect to increased fiscal devolution in Thailand appears not to be the absence of a constitutional and legal framework to enable it. Rather, the essential problem seems to be failure to implement fiscal devolution governance arrangements for local governments consistent with the intent of constitutional law and other decisions already made by the national government, as explained above in this case study. As Smoke (2005) notes, "the country needs further legal and regulatory instruments to define the subnational system more fully" (p. 29) Local government capacity weaknesses may explain to some extent the lack of confidence in the national government that full implementation of governance arrangements is desirable at this point. However, the absence of national level political will to further enable local governance appears to be an important factor in explaining the lack of progress in Thailand. Whether any of this will change as a result of the military coup that replaced the corrupt government of first former Prima Minister Thaksin Shinawatra with military rule which then moved through the transition to a new government in late 2006 and 2007 is impossible to forecast. It is clear that little real progress was made under Thaksin despite the fact that his primary populist appeal and support was from rural constituents.

The problems noted above are not unique to Thailand in the Asia region. While the World Bank study (Smoke, 2005) cites the Philippines as having achieved more effective fiscal decentralization than other nations, Thailand in particular, the case study research findings in this chapter on the Philippines suggests this is more illusion than reality. While the constitutional, legal, and regulatory frameworks are in place in the Philippines, the policy and fiscal dominance of the national government over subnational governments has a direct consequence in limiting the distribution of real power and authority to provide these governments both revenue and expenditure rights consistent with a fully implemented system of fiscal devolution as defined in this chapter. This broader conclusion leads to the assessment of the overall East Asian experience with fiscal devolution provided in the section that follows.

OBSERVATIONS ON THE ASIAN EXPERIENCE WITH DEVOLUTION

In terms of revenue raising and expenditure powers, governments of developing countries are generally less decentralized countries of the OECD group for example, but the gap has closed in the past decade East Asian nations, in particular, have a history of strong central rule although it is also true that the roots of local government and decentralized arrangements in some cases reach back to the early periods of state formation. It is certainly the case that some nations, such as Vietnam, have maintained long-standing arrangements for fiscal equalization across a highly diverse national terrain and in some of the most difficult political and economic environments imaginable (Porter, 1995 and Wescott, 2003). Whether the devolutions applied in East Asia have positive or negative results for citizen participation, let alone at the ambitious reach of "economic growth" and "poverty reduction" is uncertain. Devolution policies, and the variety of forms policy they assume in practice, are adopted for range of (at times incompatible) reasons. Some underpinnings to policy echo past experiments (e.g., Cheema & Rondinelli, 1983). Others clearly reflect recent global pressures on the nation state that are played out in changing state-society relations in East Asia in particular, and in country specific ways (Kerkvliet & Porter, 1995). The recent upsurge in interest in intensifying these arrangements seems to have occurred in the case study countries for a combination of four main reasons.

First is the particular experience of East Asian nations undergoing the expansion of democratic models of governance, an emerging middle class and the consensus that decision-making should be located closer to the people. The increasing prominence of democratic movements, for example, in Indonesia, Philippines, Taipei (China), Thailand, South Korea, and elsewhere, has affected the progress of devolution in the region. Initially in most countries, central governments attempted to cope with these pressures through consultative forums rather than elected or empowered local governments. Where there were elected local officials, they were usually supporters of the central regime. In recent years, this pattern has started to change in some countries. In Taipei (China), for example, an opposition party received 41% of the vote in mayoral and country magistrate elections of 1993; 6 years before, the country had been under martial law and ruled by a single party. The 1991 Local Government Code in the Philippines promised to increase democratization, and would probably not have been passed under the Marcos regime. In the Cambodia case, the 1991 UN peace accords included a provision for elected local government (first realized in 2002), as a step in Cambodia's transition to become a liberal market oriented democratic country. And the PRC and Thailand, while almost polar opposites in terms of extent of fiscal devolution, have made constitutional changes, passed laws and issued regulations intended to foster increased fiscal devolution.

A second trigger for devolution has been a belief that assignment of functions to subordinate levels—smaller administrative units (e.g., provinces, districts, and municipalities)—will bring efficiency gains, thus benefiting both service delivery and cash strapped central government budgets. There are typically two aspects to this assumption. The first is the economic efficiency argument, where it is claimed that shifting to local government decisions on the level and mix of taxes and expenditures will ensure that people get more of what they want, that they will pay taxes against value received, and services will be provided more efficiently. Second and closely connected to the first assumption, the revenue mobilization argument is that a decentralized tax structure will lead to an increase in the overall rate of revenue mobilization. In the PRC for example, fiscal devolution was prompted starting in the 1980s by market reforms, and the growth of township and village enterprises as sources of revenue. This development was so "successful" for some prosperous provinces that the share of revenue passed on to the central government needed to be renegotiated upward in the 1990s.

Devolution, for other states, was prompted by changing international economic conditions, including structural adjustment programs that lead to serious fiscal difficulties for central governments and the often rather desperate need to pass on service obligations to local governments. The disappointing performance of some centralized systems has directed attention to both the untapped fiscal and other local resources that allegedly can be exploited through greater disbursal of state power. More positively, it is believed that devolution will foster greater responsiveness to local needs in ways superior to what may be expected from decision makers in a distant capital. Related technical arguments also extend to the devolution of authority, which is presumed to increase accountability, participation, and to result in improved performance, including allocative and financial efficiency. Allowing local governments to raise funds through taxation or borrowing makes them more accountable for the fiscal and financial consequences of their policies. And when obliged to compete among themselves for access to financial resources, it is presumed they experience fully the costs of any unsound economic policies or decisions in ways that affect future decisions.

Third, there are many examples in the region where government agencies at all levels have delegated authority to private firms, NGOs, and development agency funded implementation units. This includes a variety of public-private partnership arrangements to provide water, electricity, communications, refuse collection, municipal markets, toll roads, urban transport, airports, and shipping ports among many others. There are also many partnership arrangements in rural areas, and in many countries NGOs manage and directly finance a large share of public services, including health and education, farmer extension, environmental protection, and natural resource management initiatives. Some countries have delegated to professional associations responsibility to license, regulate, and supervise their members. Urban resident groups are delegated tasks of implementing sites-and-service housing schemes. These contractual arrangements are made based on the belief that government units lack sufficient managerial and technical capacity or equipment to effectively provide such services, are overly hampered by bureaucratic politics and practices, and that nongovernment agencies have access to sources of funds, and legitimacy not available to government. Private businesses and NGOs are thought often to be able to provide services more effectively and efficiently than government, since they are not as hampered by these and other constraints. Such contractual arrangements usually include user charges, although governments must often provide hefty subsidies to ensure quality and sufficiency of services. It is presumed that service provision to the public under some forms of competition among public, private, national, regional, and local providers provides incentives for good performance (Jones & Thompson, 1999)

Fourth, aside from electoral pressures and arguments on technical grounds, there has been an increased articulation of demands from subnational groups for autonomy, and here we see devolution promoted for reasons related to central regime stability. There are cases where certain geographical areas of countries have become more closely linked economically to the markets of other countries than to the national market, thus leading to calls for greater devolution of authority. Contrarily, it is a fact of contemporary geopolitics that not all areas are equally well connected and favored by regional economic growth or endowed with public services available elsewhere in the country. The demands of certain regions for greater autonomy, backed by ongoing civil conflict (e.g., Mindanao Philippines, Aceh Indonesia, Bougainville, Solomon Islands) have pressured central regimes to adopt or think more seriously about developing various types of devolution policies and instruments to maintain wider sociopolitical and economic stability. Yet in this area there is always the risk that transferring significant decision-making power and resources to fractious localities may destabilize the regions, and possibly fuel demands for full independence. There is also evidence in, for example, the PRC, that fiscal devolution has served to enhance the powers of more affluent provinces, and thus may be exacerbating tensions in poor provinces with large minority populations.

With respect to overall trends in devolution in Asia, the case studies presented here show that fiscal devolution varies greatly depending on circumstances and institutions. Typically, several different forms of devolution co-exist within a country. No form is inherently better or worse than another; what matters is that the form selected is appropriate to the cultural and administrative context where it is applied, and that responsibilities are balanced by accountability, resources, and institutional capacity

Has economic growth and poverty reduction in the region been affected by devolution? Over the last 20 years, the East Asia and Pacific region recorded the highest growth rate and best performance on poverty reduction of any region in the world. Numerous studies have shown that this strong growth and poverty reduction performance in Asia-Pacific has resulted from many factors, including market-friendly policies, fiscal balance, macroeconomic stability, sharp increases in labor intensive exports, and large inflows of foreign capital. In no case examined in this study has economic growth been attributed or mainly to devolution.

Rapid development of physical, social, economic, political and fiscal infrastructure, and improvements in service delivery are highly evident as is the devolution trend—but even in the recent past many goods and services delivered to the public were provided exclusively or largely through central institutions. The PRC may be advanced as a primary example here, but this experience appears to be idiosyncratic to that country and not easily transferred. Still, it may be argued that a low level of past devolution in most countries helped to promote fiscal balance and macroeconomic stability by avoiding the soft budget constraint and moral hazard evident in some countries more advanced in their devolution. This has, in turn, may be viewed to have contributed to the market-friendly environment in Asia-Pacific countries, and in turn, to high rates of growth and poverty reduction.

The preliminary findings from the case studies in this chapter underscore how simple definitions of "devolution" cover an extraordinary range of relationships, different meanings and forms, often overlaid and occurring simultaneously. Devolution has become the acceptable face of governments of all political persuasions—consider the range from Thailand, to China to the Philippines—such that leaders advocating devolution may not quite know what devolution is, even less how it might work, but they do know that devolution is regarded worldwide as a progressive trend.

It is hoped that case study research such as that presented here (if performed properly—see Barzelay & Campbell, 2003), accompanied by a burgeoning comparative literature on devolution, will encourage an appreciation of the slippery and polysemous nature of a highly differentiated set of institutional arrangements and instrumentation. In turn, it is desired that the emergent body of evidence and thought in this area may be used by policymakers in the region and elsewhere to advantage, that is, to encourage continual experimentation rather than doctrinaire application of only uniform approaches adopted on the basis of OECD or even single country experience. There is in the Asia Pacific region no convergence toward one type of center-local, state-society relationship, although there is certainly universal interest in these matters as they are typically framed in the discourse on devolution and decentralization. Consequently, it is important to recognize that the level of generalization about net benefits (positive and negative) and risks often articulated in rhetoric at the theoretical level and in many political venues is replicated at the level of practical application. The intention is to raise and sustain critical attention to issues addressed in this chapter and to stimulate close scrutiny of hypotheses taken for granted in policy discourse on the virtues and dangers of fiscal and governance devolution across the region and around the globe.

CONCLUSIONS ON MANAGEMENT REFORM INITIATIVES IN ASIA

To conclude with respect to Asia, a number of methods have been launched in a variety of nations in the region by a variety of agents to strengthen performance in public sector management. Definition and measurement of resource inputs, workload, outputs, and outcomes within a results based framework is widely advocated by a number of sources including some of the best known scholars and most prestigious organizations in the world. Managing for results in various forms continues to be applied in a number of developed nations including the United Kingdom, the United States of America, Canada, Australia, New Zealand, Switzerland, and in other western European nations. The keys to this approach from our perspective are development of accurate databases and measurement methodologies, and application of performance measurement in decision making, for example, for strategic planning, budgeting, human resource management and investment, infrastructure development, acquisition and procurement, and in sectoral planning and resourcing, for example, health, education, social services, environmental protection, and others.

Critical to the success of these initiatives in our view is creation of knowledge cultures in public sector and nongovernmental organizations. Because improvement in performance is always linked to learning and human capacity development, the knowledge culture is an essential ingredient for success in strengthening performance in both developed and developing nations. A purely methodological approach of defining and measuring outputs and outcomes and relating results to costs is not sufficient in itself to forge lasting progress in enhancing public sector performance. In fact, where a purely methodological approach is taken, very quickly many, if not most, participants in the effort will become consumed by the details of measurement and verification to the detriment of actual improvement of management results and socioeconomic outcomes. Critical to the implementation of performance measurement methods is that measures and results must be useful for deciding about future courses of action when alternatives are present to policy and resource decision makers. In other words, to succeed performance measurement and results based analysis must be translated effectively into performance management (Argyris, 1993). All performance measurement approaches should be continually assessed against the criterion of cost versus value of information for decision. And, Ingraham et al. (2000) have pointed out, as noted earlier in this chapter, that performance management must include investment in human capital building at all levels of organizations, that is, leadership, staff, and line managers into the field. This is particularly the case for developing nations where capacity deficits present real barriers to implementation of performance and results based management initiatives. For this reason the value of working to create a knowledge culture that encourages self-assessment and learning, management innovation, and increased investment in human resources and information technology is probably higher in developing countries than in developed nations.

Finally, the relationships between strengthening performance in the public sector and ability and willingness of leaders, managers, and organizations to adapt to new economic circumstance with alternative organizational and governance arrangements must be stressed. The international economic order is undergoing a massive transformation. Its technology, its problems, and—to a considerable extent—its economics are radically different from those that traditional, highly-structured and rule-bound Weberian type bureaucratic organizations were created to cope with in seeking to advance production and problem solving. In today's world, many old problems bureaucracies were designed to deal with well have been wiped away. However, new problems are awaiting new technologies and the formulation of new governing instruments that are more adaptable and better able to network to solve the problems they confront, for example, poverty reduction, prevention of wars, economic planning and development, environmental protection, and species preservation, response to natural disasters and threats from the spread of new, highly virulent diseases. The painful lessons of failure of contemporary unilateral action by bureaucratic organizations to crises of all sorts are plentiful in today's world.

We are by no means the first to recognize the changes that are taking place in the world economy, markets and threat environment, and the potential lessons from experience about how to improve performance responsiveness in conduct of the public's business. Nor are we the first to suggest that performance management represents a wholesale change in the tactics and responsibilities of government. Schwartz (1994), for example, observed, "a profound shift toward a new kind of regime ... not simply a shift toward less state, but also a shift to a different kind of state" (pp. 527-555) He attributes this shift not to conservative politics but to international market pressures. He stresses that many of the governments that have embraced the performance and results oriented management are or were dominated by social democrats. We would emphasize that increased market pressure is largely a consequence of reduced transaction and transportation costs, both manifestations of the computer and the information revolution—the same forces that have driven change in the private sector since the 1970s.

NOTES ON REFORM IN NEW ZEALAND AND AUSTRALIA

Scholars have perhaps focused most on the New Zealand, and to a lesser extent, Australian reforms (Guthrie, Humphrey, & Olson, 1997; but see also Guthrie, et al., 1999, 2005; Jones & Schedler, 1997). New Zealand and Australia were at the vanguard of the new public management experiment. Their strategies and tactics heavily influenced the broader scholarly debate as well as the practice in many other nations. Any understanding of the NPM, therefore, will consider these reforms, especially in their prime in the late 1980s and 1990s.

For a comprehensive analysis of the New Zealand reforms see Boston, Martin, Pallot, and Walsh (1996; see also Newberry, 2006; Pallot, 1998). Much of the external attention given to New Zealand's public management reforms has focused on its efforts to improve the quality of external financial reporting practices: the adoption of accrual accounting and reporting on performance. New Zealand was the first country to publish a rational set of government accounts that includes a balance sheet of its assets and liabilities and an accrual-based operating statement of income and expenses. However, the changes made in the structure of the government of New Zealand designed to promote effective resource use and investment are even more significant than are the changes in its financial reporting practices (the following is based on Newberry, 2006; Pallot, 1998; Scott, Bushnell, & Sallee, 1990. First of all, New Zealand's Parliament privatized everything that was not part of the "core public sector." The residual "core public sector" includes a mix of policy, regulatory, and operational functions: military services, policing, and justice services, social services such as health, education, and the administration of benefit payments, research and development, property assessment, and other financial services.

Second, Parliament redefined the relationship between it and the heads of government agencies. Agency heads lost their permanent tenure and are now known generically as "chief executives." They are appointed for fixed-terms of up to 5 years, with the possibility of reappointment. Each works to a specific contract, the conditions of which are negotiated with the State Services Commission and approved by the prime minister. The State Services Commission also monitors and assesses executive performance. Remuneration levels are directly tied to performance assessment.

Third, Parliament changed the way it appropriates funds for use by the remaining government agencies. It has tried to link appropriation to performance, allowing Parliament to control the level of resource use and the purposes to which resources are put, but, at the same time, providing greater flexibility for agency heads. The basis of appropriation depends on the agency's ability to supply adequate information about its performance.

The decisions that had the most significant future consequences for the government of New Zealand's stakeholders were clearly those which had to do with the kind, quantity, and quality of service provided by the citizenry. Under this system of appropriations and financial reporting, those issues must be explicitly confronted when cabinet enters into long-term contracts with agencies, state-owned enterprises, and firms to deliver service outputs and its consequent liabilities must be stated in present value terms. However, according to Newberry and Pallot (2005, 2003) and others this last task was not done correctly, as supposedly intended by the government, and was in fact done incorrectly so as to mislead and draw attention away from the real purpose of the grand reforms—to shrink the size of New Zealand government (see also Ezzamel, Hyndman, Johnsen, Lapsley, & Pallot, 2004, p. 145; Newberry, 2001; Pallot, 2001).

Jonathan Boston (2001) explored some the hard questions of New Zealand's cutting-edge reforms. For example, he asked at what stage of reform in the public sector does it become possible to conduct a thorough appraisal of results and how does one know when this stage has been reached? How should such an assessment be undertaken? Boston argued that most assessments have focused upon specific changes in management practice, including the introduction of performance pay, the move to accrual accounting, the growth of contracting-out, the separation of policy and operations or the devolution of human resource management responsibilities. Some studies have dealt instead with management changes in particular policy domains—such as health care, education, community services or criminal justice—or within a particular organization (department, agency, or private provider). By contrast, there have been relatively few macroevaluations including comprehensive assessments of the impact of root-and-branch changes to the system. Boston provided broad reflections on the limitations to policy evaluation in the field of public management, and more particularly explained the obstacles confronted when assessing the consequences of systemic management reforms. Given his understanding of reform in New Zealand, his warning underlines the importance of the evaluation problem.

In his study of New Zealand, Laking (2001) agreed that serious debate about the New Zealand reform has been bedeviled by the limited evaluation. In fact, he concluded that the assessments of the successes and failures of reform in New Zealand seem not to be particularly concerned about the absence of comprehensive evaluation. Laking found that most evaluations tended to assert overall gains in efficiency as a result of reform, but they were far less specific or negative about the consequences for effectiveness, equity and service quality and quantity, issues that non-reformist New Zealand governments have wrestled with since the elections of 2000 at what may be argued was the end point of the nation's *grand reform* era.

On the other hand, according to Gill (2001), who was a player in the *grand reform* era, despite the lack of clear evidence about New Zealand reform impact, the elegant simplicity of the reforms had a seductive quality for analysts. Gill found that much of the "elegance" of the reform agenda evident in the early 1990s had been obscured in the intervening years, but that the yield from the reforms was significant. The trick in evaluating the New Zealand experience with public management reform, he argued, was to compare it with real world alternatives. In using the existing reforms to guide future questions, Gill attempted to unravel the disparate threads about "what remains to be done" by distinguishing four categories of problems: (a) Political problems that are inherent to the political arena, and are evident under a range of public management regimes; (b) Incompleteness problems that provide evidence the system is incomplete in some areas, but do not suggest inherent difficulties; (c) Implementation problems that stem from the way the system has been implemented; (d) Inherent problems that flow directly from the nature of the New Zealand regime, which might be different in other systems (Gill, 2001, p. 144).

Few observers write about the New Zealand reforms with more authority than Graham Scott (2001), one of the movement's chief architects for more than 20 years. In looking carefully at the New Zealand experience and comparing it with reforms around the world, Scott identified important lessons. Among other things, he concluded, the success of management reform depended on: (a) the clarity of roles, responsibilities and accountability in the implementation of management reform; (b) the importance of matching decision capacity to responsibility; (c) the significance of ministerial commitment and clarity of expectations; (d) the structural innovations within the New Zealand cabinet; (e) the need to analyse disasters carefully for what they teach; (f) approaches to embrace and foibles to avoid in implementing performance management; (g) problems caused by confusion over ownership and improper assessment of organizational capability; (h) the fact that actually doing strategic management in the public sector is hugely complicated; (i) that it is time to put an end to the notion that there is an "extreme model" of public management applied in New Zealand; and (j) that public management, government and governance innovations in New Zealand are no longer novel compared to those advanced in other nations. Scott concluded with an admonition to avoid too quickly drawing the conclusion from New Zealand's change in government that past reforms must be quickly and radically changed—or that the New Zealand model has failed, as he has argued elsewhere (Scott, 2001). For a critical analysis of Scott's views, see Newberry, 2003.

A senior public servant in the New Zealand treasury, Andrew Kibblewhite (2001), agreed with Boston, Laking, and Scott on the need for detailed analysis of results and a careful consolidation of the lessons. He suggested that much of the initial energy for reform has faded, that it was time to assess what had and had not been achieved, and that it was important to search for ways to move forward. He noted that the election of a new government in November, 2000 stirred a sense of anticipation, as well as some apprehension, across the New Zealand public sector. As New Zealand moved into a new phase of reform, one of the key challenges was to take advantage of what had already been achieved to make government even more effective. Kibblewhite argued further that central agencies could sharpen the specification of outputs by being clearer about the basic management framework, and by being more flexible about how that framework is applied. Outcome measures should be refined and used along with outputs where feasible, he advised. However, he suggested, some outcome measures should be abandoned where they do not provide useful information. And, in fact, after this time New Zealand abandoned for all intents and purposes its emphasis on outcomes and moved to more easily measurable outputs, as was done from the beginning in Australia.

The New Zealand reforms, however, have certainly drawn critics. Robert Gregory (2001) contented that a price had been paid for the overly narrow theoretical framework used to design state sector reforms. According to Gregory, the way ahead was to be best informed both by more eclectic theoretical input, as well as by closer dialogue between theory and practice. He argued that the state sector reforms in New Zealand, especially in their application to the public services, had been too "mechanistic" and too blind to the important "organic" dimensions of public organizations. They focused too much on physical restructuring and they tried too hard to reduce complex government practices to artificial dualities, such as "outputs" and "outcomes," "owner" and "purchaser," "founder" and "provider." They tended in his view to ignore the less quantifiable and more holistic elements that underpinned a strong culture of public service trusteeship in New Zealand prior to reform. Gregory argued that it was difficult to conclude that reform had all been for the good. There is too much evidence to the contrary, he asserted.

Tooley's (2001) analysis of the New Zealand school system helped to identify some of these tensions. Despite the rhetoric about decentralization and democratization through devolution of governance and decision making to the level of the individual school and principals as chief executives, there was a concomitant strengthening of central control over curriculum and tighter monitoring by the education review office. These changes reduced citizen choice in school education, turned principals into managers instead of skilled leaders and, ultimately, wrested control over education from educators and into the control of politicians. Tooley suggested that the educational "experiment" in New Zealand should be reversed because of its inability to deliver the outcomes promised from reform. And, in fact, more recent changes proposed by the government demonstrated its intent to rein back some of the more "market-oriented" elements of the educational reforms and, in particular, to soften some of the key features of the managerialist approach to education administration. Tooley concluded that the reforms failed almost completely, and that the coalition government elected in November, 2000 should reverse many of the changes made under previous governments, and it did.

Newberry's (2001) study of the operation during 1996 of a public hospital emergency department likewise revealed serious problems. Hostility between the hospital's clinical staff and management escalated to the point that the hospital's medical staff association released a report to the public titled, "Patients are Dying: A Record of System Failure and Unsafe Healthcare Practice at Christchurch Hospital." The report detailed the story of four patient deaths and alleged that deteriorating conditions within the hospital contributed to those deaths. The Medical Staff Association sought a public inquiry, but the health and disability commissioner announced a more-narrow consumers' rights inquiry. Newberry (2001) revisited that inquiry and recast its findings in the context of the NPM. She found that, although the hospital-based reforms were structurally sound and had real value, they did not address the broader issues of performance and accountability. She concluded that NPM as applied in New Zealand needed to create better structures, involve customers more directly in evaluation and decision making, and be more accountable to the public for results. Also, Putterill and Speer (2001) likewise found problems in information technology in New Zealand. New Zealand had benchmarked its IT innovation and development against its own policy aims and the achievements of a set of peer countries, chosen for similar size and technical sophistication. However, Putterill and Speer concluded that peers nations have significantly outperformed New Zealand. The New Zealand government had maintained a "hands off" stance in terms of helping the private sector to develop while most of the peer countries actively promoted IT involvement. Putterill and Speer questioned past policy direction, called for more active industry involvement by the New Zealand government, and argued for more industry-friendly policies to advance competitiveness in the region.

With respect to Australia, major reform began at the national level under Prime Minister Hawke in the early 1980s and continued well into the 1990s. Successive governments implemented substantial reforms in financial management and civil service laws and processes accompanied by budget reduction (some believe this was the driving motivation), multiyear budgets with carry-forward provisions (that were not used much because budgets were lean and there was no money left at year end to carry over to the next year), performance measurement (emphasizing outputs rather than outcomes as was the case in New Zealand) and also began a considerable wave of deregulation, sales of government assets, privatization, contracting out to the private sector, and public-private partnerships (O'Faircheallaigh, Wanna, & Weller, 1999).

At the state level, English and Guthrie (2001) analyzed NPM as implemented in Victoria, Australia's second largest state, between 1992 and 1999. These reforms were far-reaching and aimed at a major shift in the role and accountability of government. The Victorian model grew on a well-articulated theoretical framework from classical economic theory, and it was well supported by a series of specific government directives and manuals. The reforms attempted to be comprehensive, tackling all components of the public sector and its subsystems. The output-management models developed to determine and report on expenditure, planning, financial management, control, and evaluation were comprehensive in both scope and implementation. The reforms, however, promised more than they delivered. In particular, the speed and massive scale of contracting out and privatization proved difficult to implement. In fact, Hughes and O'Neill (2001) argue, the public management reforms introduced in Victoria by the Kennett government led to somewhat contradictory consequences. While the government implemented arguably successful reforms, particularly in sale of government assets and privatization of services and balancing the budget after serious deficits, cuts in social services also appeared to have contributed to Kennett's electoral defeat. The new public management may have some payoffs, but the political consequences can be significant and unanticipated.

Carlin and Guthrie (2001) examined efforts in Australian and New Zealand public sectors to implement accrual output-based budgeting. While agreeing on the need for public sector accounting reform, the authors use two detailed case studies—Queensland, Australia and the New Zealand national government—to show that the reforms have not accomplished all that their governments had hoped. For example, there is little real difference between the old cash-based and the new accrual budgets. That led the authors to wonder about the effectiveness of management reforms if decision making was unchanged. Carlin and Guthrie identify three conditions to be met if reforms in public sector accounting are to succeed. First, carefully defined and appropriately specified outputs that relate directly to the activities of the agency are needed. Second, appropriately specified and measurable outcomes must be identified to provide accountability as to the degree to which public resources are achieving public goals. Third, performance indicators and performance measures should provide a link between outputs and outcomes.

In summary, New Zealand and to some extent Australian reforms were for awhile the benchmarks by which reforms around the world were judged. A careful look at those reforms or, at least, at what analysts have written about them, reveals how much we have yet to learn about what truly has worked and why. Moreover, as the work of some researchers show, serious issues, both managerial and political, lurk just below the surface. Only more careful analysis and comparison can sort out the claims and counterclaims of success and failure, and of intentions (Newberry, 2006; Newberry & Pallot, 2005). What nation presently is regarded as the role model for what might still be termed NPM-like government? The United Kingdom is the example most often cited as the new model. But this goes beyond the scope of our inquiry.

THE EXPERIENCE OF THE UNITED STATES AND IMPLICATIONS FOR OTHER NATIONS

Although public management reform was embraced in the United States in the 1990s (Gore, 1993) and was influenced by many of the reforms undertaken during the Reagan and Bush presidencies from 1980 to 1992, and arguably the content of important laws passed by Congress in the 1990s including the Chief Financial Officers Act of 1990, the Government Performance and Results Act of 1993, the Government Management and Results Act of 1995 and the National Performance Review's call for mission-driven, results-oriented budgets as well (OECD, 1995, p. 230), it has had little or no practical effect in the U.S. until recently.

There are two explanations for this fact. The first is that many students of the expenditure process reject the notion that responsibility budgeting and accounting can be reconciled with the American legislative budgetary process. Some people even assert that it can be practiced only by responsible unitary governments on the Westminster model, although that claim seems to be belied by the Swiss example (Schedler, 1995). Of course, it would not be easy to reconcile responsibility budgeting and the American legislative process, but they are necessarily incompatible either (Thompson, 1994).

The second explanation for its failure to influence significantly government accounting and budget practices in the United States is that, unlike most other countries, America has large, well organized associations of government accountants, auditors, budgeters, and program analysts, supported by teachers of government accounting and budgeting, who have a vested interest in differentiating public from private practice, since it is that difference which gives value to their expertise. Anyone inclined to doubt the significance of this explanation should look carefully at the politics of the U.S. Federal Accounting Standards Board (FASB), Government Accounting Standards Board (GASB), and particularly the Federal Accounting Standards Advisory Board (FASAB).

The progress, or lack thereof, of reform in the United States must be viewed from a longer term perspective, as with all nations, to fully understand how it developed and what has stimulated reform, particularly reform oriented toward performance measurement and management (PM) and the integration of PM into budgeting. In this regard the following observations may be made about the U.S. case and lessons from the U. S. that may be applied to developing nations (LDCs) and elsewhere.

1. Performance measures are not well integrated with budget decision processes in the United States. and in LDCs. To integrate them is not an easy task and required highly sophisticated staff expertise

and development of a process and methodology to routinize the integration.

2. The problem is not that PMs do not exist in many cases, although we all acknowledge the difficulty of developing and applying good measures. Rather, the problem is the absence of any regular methods or processes that systematically cause PMs to be considered in budgeting.

3. In the U.S. PMs were first theorized in the early 1900s by researchers in the New York City Bureau of Municipal Research. However, in practice in the federal government they were not applied until the 1950s when under the Eisenhower administration they were developed by the president's Bureau of the Budget (BoB) and used in formulating agency budgets. Many of these measures were crude one line workload proxies that were applied to simplify estimation and calculation of budgets, for example, X number of acres of reforestation planting for the Forest Service will cost on average Y$ per acre. Many of the measures developed in the 190s are still in use in U.S. federal budgeting today.

4. During the 1980s two presidential commissions (the Grace Commission and the Packard Commission) reported the need for increased efficiency in the federal government, and included reference to PM in their recommendations, either directly or indirectly. The recommendations from these Commissions significantly influenced the development of PM elements in the National Performance Review (NPR) under the Clinton administration in the 1990s and passage by Congress of the Government Performance and Results Act of 1993 (GPRA) and the Government Management and Results Act of 1995 (GMRA). Thus, in the 1990s both Congress and the executive branch called for increased performance measurement and management. However, although progress was made under the leadership of the president's Office of Management and Budget (OMB) in implementing these initiatives (agencies developed long range strategic plans that were articulated into comprehensive annual plans and to some extent budgets), it was not until 2001 that PMs began to be developed and used in review of agency budgets by OMB.

5. Beginning in 2001, under direction from President Bush, OMB developed what is known as the Performance Assessment Rating Tool (for more information on PART see the OMB Web site http://www.whitehouse.gov/omb/part/index.html). PART required agencies to submit performance data on a number of dimensions of management (e.g., use of human resources, use of IT resources,

extent of contracting, extent of integration of PMs into budgets, etc.) that were initially evaluated by OMB using a "stoplight" indicator evaluation method (green for good progress, yellow for needs improvement, red for failure to comply). Since its first use PART has been refined to evaluate and report using a multivariable scorecard and a 1 to 5 scale. PART has been lauded as a success by a wide range of entities in Washington D.C. Congressional review has judged it a success in implementing the spirit of GPRA and GMRA, the Government Accountability Office (GAO), the audit arm of Congress, has testified to Congress that PART has shown progress in improving the integration of PM in executive budgeting.

6. Critical to the success of PART is the improvement in quality of feedback from OMB budget examiners and analysts to agencies on areas where they needed to improve management practices. A number of agencies have reported that both their strategic planning and budgeting processes have been improved as a result of PART analysis and feedback. However, use of PART as a feedback mechanism is one thing; using it to cut budgets is another. Beginning in 2005 and continued more assertively in 2006 PART has used to assist decisions about reductions in domestic program budgets and in some cases program termination as the Bush administration has gotten serious about cutting the annual federal budget deficit. Cutting spending in the U.S. is particularly difficult because approximately 70% of spending is driven on "auto-pilot" through mandatory spending (permanent appropriations determined by formula) for entitlement programs including Social Security, Medicare and Medicaid. Thus, discretionary spending excluding that for national defense (which has been increasing due to the war on terrorism, and conflicts in the Middle East) constitutes only approximately 17% of total annual government spending. It is against this 17% that cuts must be applied. The Bush administration proposed and Congress accepted approximately $5 billion in cuts in 2005 and deeper reductions have been proposed in 2006. Whether PART continues to be popular and as highly regarded when it is used to cut budgets remains to be seen but already some critic have argued that the method has been diverted to serve the Bush administration's political and ideological preferences. Such criticism is typical at any time when budgets are reduced, and especially in a congressional election year such as 2006.

What are some of the lessons from U.S. experience with integrating PM into budgets? The following may be observed:

- Even under the best of circumstances where political support is present it takes a long time to develop and integrate PM into budget decision making. In the United States it has taken approximately 50 years—in a highly developed budgetary process where staff expertise in PM emerged by the 1990s. This, expecting result in PM and its use in budgeting to emerge quickly is inappropriate and unrealistic.
- If staffs are not trained in the techniques of PM then no progress will occur. Development of HR capacity is critical to development of PM and its use in budgeting.
- Less is better than more in the sense that attempting to develop too many measures of performance muddies the water and ends up in the reporting of meaningless data. Thus it is best to concentrate on a few core measures (e.g., no more than six) rather than many.
- While PMs can be developed and measured by agencies, finding and tying high quality cost data to PMs is difficult. Often cash based accounting does not render data in ways that are amenable to cost analysis.
- Political support over a long period of time is necessary to integrate PM into budgeting, and continuity of political support from both left and right of party leadership is needed for success.
- Related to continuity is the need for the successive reform agendas of succeeding governments to include emphasis on PM and budget integration. Typically, each new government brings in its own reform agenda when it takes office. This agenda may or may not be consistent with what has been done under previous reform initiatives. In the United States there was a considerable degree of consistency of support for PM when viewed from a broad perspective from the administrations of Bush 1989-1992, Clinton (1993-2000) and G. W. Bush (2001-2008). This is a period of 20 years if as expected PART continues to be used until 2008.
- Constant waves of different reforms frustrate progress in developing PM and integrating PM into budgeting. When this occurs staffs cannot determine which reform has priority and whether new initiatives cancel out earlier initiatives, or what data they should be developing and reporting using which methods or systems.
- For agencies, typically it is easier to develop PMs based on resource inputs or workload measures. However, while workload measures are easily integrated into budgeting, such measures usually reveal

little or nothing about what amount of work is needed to achieve desired results.
- Due to the confusion in trying to define PMs that differentiate workload from output and outcomes, it is often better to concentrate on definable results and the management and resource requirements needed to achieve highest priority results.
- U.S. experience teaches that to be successful in integrating PM into budgeting a specific unit of government such as the president's Office of Management and Budget needs to take responsibility for leadership and ownership of the results assessment and review process. When this agency also is responsible for preparing the executive budget, as is the case with OMB, then integration is more likely to occur. However, in the United States the willingness of Congress to lend support to the executive branch PM/budgeting integration initiative has been critical. In nations that have parliamentary government support from the legislature and particularly within cabinet is similarly critical.

LESSONS FROM DECADES OF PUBLIC MANAGEMENT REFORM

What lessons spin from the past few decades of public sector reform and transformation, including those initiatives attempted under the rubric of new public management? A review of the experiences of a variety of nations around the globe suggests the following series of propositions:

1. Public management reform never stops and is never over.

Analysts and practitioners alike have sometimes been tempted to view the reforms with cynicism. For some, the lack of clear or full success led to the conclusion that the reforms had failed. For others, the evolution of new strategies led to the conclusion that earlier efforts had been abandoned. In fact, history shows that public management reforms recur, with each new piece woven—sometimes seamlessly—into the next. There are several reasons for this. First, no reform can ever fully solve the problems that led to its creation. Lingering issues tend to breed the next generation of reforms. Second, public management is not so much a problem-solving activity as a problem-balancing enterprise. Any reform strategy requires making choices at the margin that focus on some problems more than others and that emphasize some values more than others. Because no solution can ever be complete, each reform necessarily leaves problems unaddressed and under-addressed and every reform therefore breeds the next. Third, because management problems tend to recur and the bag of management tricks is relatively limited, reforms tend to cycle between accepted strategies—periods of centralization followed by episodes of decentralization, deregulation replacing bureaucratisation. Careful observers of administrative reform can detect the recurring patterns.

2. The "new public management" provided a fundamentally different approach to reform.

Some critics have therefore dismissed the new public management as worthless nostrums or old ideas dressed up in new clothes. The experience over the last two decades, however, shows that there truly has been something new in the "new" public management. To the dismay of some detractors and to the hopes of some reformers, the new public management introduced a heavy dose of economic models and tactics into public management. From privatization to performance contracts, the new public management sought to replace bureaucratic authority with economic incentives. Contracting out and other market-based strategies, of course, have been around for decades, if not centuries. But the new public management pursued them with a single-mindedness unseen previously. Moreover, the new public management reforms spread around the world with an energy and simultaneity never seen before with any kind of management reform. The rise of the Internet and relatively inexpensive international air travel helped drive this movement. So too did the near-universal rise of citizen discontent over the cost and performance of government. Never before have so many governments tried such similar things in such a relatively short period of time.

3. Political reality drives management reform more than management concerns.

Scholars have examined numerous public management reforms around the globe, including America's ill-fated reinventing government, for theoretical insights. Enduring analytical conclusions have proven elusive because the reforms have been so different. Different nations have gone down different paths because their high-level officials have been trying to solve different problems and cope with different political realities. Even relatively similar nations, such as the United Kingdom, Canada, Australia, and New Zealand, have produced markedly different strategies. Finding common ground with other nations' experiments has often proven difficult. In large part, this is because top officials launched the management reforms for fundamentally political reasons: to cope with budget crises, to sustain public services without increasing taxes, and to signal concern about citizens' disaffection with government. Top officials sustained the reforms as long as they had political value; they transformed them or backed away when political pressures demanded. When asked to comment on the New Zealand reforms, one careful observer immediately began discussing the proportional representation plan for the parliament—not the 15 years of management reforms that preceded it. A New Zealand official tells audiences of his mother's constant question about the management reforms: "Why does it still take so long to get a gall bladder operation?" Politics lies at the core of management reform, not vice versa. Management reforms have their genesis and sustenance in the degree to which they help solve political problems.

4. The political clout of the public management reform has been negligible.

Over a period from 1980 to 2006, it has become clear that the effort provided little political clout in any nation, with the possible exception of Switzerland, where new public management persists because it has been written into law (See Buschor, 1994; Knechtenhofer & Schedler, 2003; Rieder & Lehmann, 2002; Ritz, 2005; Schedler, 2001; 2003; Schedler & Proeller, 2000; Steiner, 2000). Even in Swiss cantons there are mixed results. Some of them are successful (Lucerne, Zurich, Solothurn, Berne), some others have decided not to implement NPM (Basel, St. Gallen, Geneva).

In the U.S., President Bill Clinton significantly downsized the bureaucracy and proudly proclaimed the smallest bureaucracy in 30 years, only to have Republicans win control of both houses of Congress for the first time in 40 years. Vice President Al Gore barely mentioned his reinventing government effort on the presidential campaign trail in 2000 and got no political credit for having led it. Prime Minister Tony Blair made little of his own management reforms in the 2001 elections or subsequently. And while the administration of George W. Bush has put many of the principles of NPM into practice as noted in this chapter, there is little evidence that management reforms have translated into electoral victories or, even, into modest political gains.

5. Despite the lack of traction from management reform as a political issue, it is a puzzle with which elected officials nevertheless feel obliged to wrestle.

Even if public management builds little political capital, management problems do have the potential to cause enormous headaches. Prime Minister Blair found himself struggling with the management of the foot-and-mouth outbreak as he geared up election campaign, and these struggles in fact shifted the timing of the elections. In the language of political consultants, management reform has little upside potential but can pose a tremendous downside threat. In other words, it might not help, but it certainly can hurt. Management problems have a recurring tendency to develop, and elected officials must deal with them effectively or risk serious political damage. Thus, management reform springs eternal.

6. 6. Public management, reforms have moved increasingly from restructuring to process reengineering.

In most countries, public management for generations had built on the traditions of hierarchy and authority. The Prussian influence was especially strong in European nations and in other countries, like the United States, that borrowed heavily on these ideas. As these nations developed their empire, the traditions spread as well. When these approaches encountered problems—as inevitably they did—the instinct was to reorganize the structure and reorient the authority. The launch of the public management reform movement was a frank recognition that hierarchy and authority, in all their variations and reforms, had reached their limits. Most public management reforms have emphasized market incentives and contract-based approaches. These reforms, in short, sought either to supplement or replace traditional structure-based approaches with process-based reforms.

7. Despite wide variation in reform strategies, there is a convergence of reforms around general themes.

The enormous variation in reforms has long frustrated analysts, who have struggled to define more precisely the agenda of public management reform. Assessing whether public management reform initiatives actually constitute an identifiable set of ideas, let alone whether nations are increasingly pursuing more-similar ideas, is a daunting problem. No less an authority than Graham Scott (2001), however, has observed, "For most of the world, the late twentieth century has been about reducing the scope of government. But this process must inevitably slow down" (p. 140). In time, he suggested, the pace of downsizing will inevitably slow and governments will face the task of managing the programs that remain. That, in turn, will likely turn more governments to the American reform strategy of making government "work better and cost less." As Scott concluded,

Over time, the rest of us will look more and more like the United States, as the problems of what the government is going to do become less urgent and we deal with them by marginal adjustments rather than sudden and radical change, and focus more on the steady processes of improvement around the organizations that will persist. (p. 140.)

This has not happened yet, but given what is noted above with respect to PART use by OMB, it may occur. The United Kingdom also provides a contemporary model that deserves additional analysis.

8. Developing nations have different management reform problems than developed nations.

For at least some observers, the convergence argument suggests that nations that are serious about performance pursue management reform and that most reforms are moving in at least loose synchronization (Pollitt & Bouckhaert, 2000, 2004). However, Allen Schick (1998) bluntly warned that "most developing countries should not try New Zealand reforms" or other "new public management" strategies (p. 24). Indeed, facing a huge need to grow their economies and shrink their governments, many developing countries have found the reforms irresistible. Schick contended that the new public management-style reforms require a foundation of governmental rules, vigorous markets, and broadly accepted dispute-resolution processes that many developing countries lack. Seeking short cuts, Schick concluded, risks sending developing nations into dead ends. Different nations in different positions with different traditions, structures, and capacities need different strategies, even if they attempt to follow a new public management course.

9. Pursuit of public management reform strategy has revealed a mismatch among practice, theory, and instruction.

Unlike some previous reforms around the world, where scholars charted at least some of the course, public management reform has evolved with only modest theoretical foundation. Formal theory has suggested concepts like moral hazard and adverse selection, but most of the hard work has come from pragmatic officials cobbling together approaches to very hard problems. As noted above, theorists have struggled to determine what the public management reform consists of, how it differs from country to country, whether it has succeeded, how it might transform itself, and whether it will prove a lasting phenomenon. Public officials, pressed with high public demands and limited resources, have rarely stopped to ask such questions. Meanwhile, in public policy programs around the world, academic leaders have struggled to assess whether they need to transform their curricula to prepare students to supply the tools to drive public management reform. For the most part, these leaders have understandably taken a cautious approach. However, this has left public officials with an even greater problem of finding young managers with the skills to operate effectively in the new program strategies. Of all the options, the one sure bet probably lies in forecasting rapid change. The tensions at the core of the practice, theory, and instruction dilemma thus will only increase.

10. What roles should national versus local governments play in implementing reform?

Osborne and Gaebler (1992) inspired some officials and enraged others by suggesting that the government of the future ought to steer, not row. Central governments around the world have found themselves in the midst of a fundamental transformation, with simultaneously more globalization and devolution of power (Kettl, 2000b). What role can and should central governments play in a world where their traditional roles have become more marginal yet their importance has only increased? Managers of central government agencies have sought greater leverage in the management of networks and the creation of information systems, among other tools. How to weave these new tools together into a freshly defined role, however, has proven anything but clear.

CONCLUSIONS

Learning from the experience of public management reform strategy within and across national boundaries is daunting. The tendency is to say that context dominates all lessons. However, the lessons reviewed here and elsewhere suggest some interdependence. In many regions of the world, cross-national organizations, like OECD, the Asian Development Bank, the World Bank, the International Monetary Fund, have encouraged management reform and have stimulated reform networks across national borders. There are elements of isomorphic transference in the reform experiences of some countries: in Hong Kong, in Taiwan, and from New Zealand to almost everywhere.

One nation's copying the reforms of others can help improve the effectiveness of public services and attract greater investment. Information technology has spurred the spread of reform ideas. The Internet reveals, at least to the computer literate, the success or failure of policy adventures in different countries and analyses of reforms by academics and others.

The media play an important role in identifying policy problems and comparing solutions among nations. Consultants have spread many ideas among their clients. As a result, nations engage in far more rapid policy reproduction and perhaps even learning than has been evident in the past. However, the conception that "one size fits all" in reform should be resisted because this isn't the case. Reforms have to be constructed and implemented within the context of the national and organizational cultures in which they are implemented. To lose sight of this fact is to misunderstand one of the major lessons of international public sector reform.

Public management reform invites evaluation of convergence: how much, of what kind, and in what directions. Boston's assessment of New Zealand invites questions about the degree of unison in reform. He finds clear benefits, but the dearth of "before and after" studies, or even thoughtful quasi-experimental designs, prevent genuine evaluation of the effectiveness of public management reforms. Boston terms the broad nature of evaluations about reform as "counter-factual," because gauging the impact is difficult without greater specificity. Similarly, Wescott's analysis reinforces this picture of diversity with his analysis of methodological problems in defining and introducing reforms. In Gregory's account, the "mechanistic" adoption of reform in New Zealand created long-term implementation problems, which proved especially notable compared with the enthusiasm that first greeted the reform process.

Convergence versus divergence is a long-standing debate in public administration and management. Principles of economic efficiency and effectiveness, or choice and market forces would suggest that rhetorically one would expect to see a more consistent picture of reform in the past decade or so. There is ample evidence of a convergence in rhetoric. Reformers speak eagerly of "reinvention," "entrepreneurial management," and "results-based approaches." Indeed, the work reviewed here suggests that there indeed in some convergence. However, there clearly are instances of divergence as well, because of the special circumstances of nations, regions, and the developed-developing nations contrast. On balance, there appears to be a convergence in the reform agendas and implementation efforts in the United Kingdom, in most British Commonwealth nations, in selected OECD nations, and the United States. The convergence emerges among developed nations. The experience of developing nations is more diverse.

Even assessing the convergence/divergence question, however, requires far greater precision in defining the problem and developing a useful language for exploring it. Roberts' analysis of the inability to define "problems" accurately shows the underlying problems affecting both the formulation and implementation of management reform. That, she suggests, is why cooperative strategies can prove useful. Similarly, both

Wescott and Shand suggest that while diversity exists, cooperative tools can assist in the reform process and are applicable across borders.

Nevertheless, application of the same or similar approaches in different nations may succeed or fail in different ways. Reform is about building capacity to do the old things in different ways and to discover new things that need doing. Reforming public organizations may provide institutional remedies, but traditional restructuring cannot eliminate the changes of retrograde tendencies or prevent problems from recurring. This comparison, moreover, suggests the need for more careful analysis about what constitutes "good reform." Is it merely locating the definition of a "problem" in the standard NPM line-up and finding the relevant "solution?" Is there greater need for refinement of interpretive and epistemological skills before nations embark to mimic what is done elsewhere? A significant lesson, thus, is this clear definition of the problems to be solved is the first step toward successful change.

From there nations need to move toward experimenting with various methods, and carefully gauging results, until the combination that best solves their problems emerges. This experimentation takes time, energy, patience and a commitment to careful, unbiased, and unvarnished evaluation. It requires the will to ask questions when the answers could prove inconvenient or embarrassing. Then there is the question of building the political will to move in the direction the evaluation points. Politics plays the crucial role throughout this cycle in determining how the problem is to be defined, what methods may be tried, whether evaluation is to be done and by whom, and whether the results are to be heeded and followed.

Other lessons apply to the role of the state. English and Guthrie (2001), and Hughes and O'Neill (2001) emphasize the importance of strengthening the institutions of governance. Accountability is a paramount virtue in governance. Reform per se is not sufficient to ensure greater accountability; it is necessary to strengthen the institutions of governance *and* management. Shand and Wescott concur in this observation. Neale and Anderson outline the challenges for the New Zealand performance reporting process with respect to parliamentary utility. Jones and Mussari suggest (2001) that the U.S. Congress and the Italian Parliament may not benefit from the accountability mechanisms they have enacted. Conversely, Schedler (2001) demonstrates the value of performance budgeting in Switzerland to result from a unique balance between freedom and regulation, between the rigidities of the law and the needs of politicians.

Institution building is not likely to be achieved by enlarging the role of the state, but by *rediscovering* the tasks and roles that governments are best suited—and most needed—to perform. Those tasks can include building critical capacity for planning and evaluation. Reform might well produce more effective service delivery institutions as well as governments that work more effectively with the private sector. It might also produce new forms of regulation that more productively shape market behavior.

The manifestations of public management reform are many and varied. Debate about its variations can be awkward because of widespread differences in governance problems, political cultures, and reform language. This reinforces the need for a conceptual framework and language for public management reform, allowing for contribution from different disciplines. Barzelay (2001) argues that without a common frame of reference and language, meaningful dialogue on public management reform cannot occur.

The public management reform movement has also framed new questions. What role should the nation-state play as but one player in a new architecture of governance where networks of organizations comprise more effective problem solving entities than single governments? How can public bureaucracy effectively solve complex governance problems without sacrificing the public interest? New organizational forms such as hyperarchies, flatter and more decentralized entities with greater delegation of authority and responsibility and faster learning-adaptation-action cycles (Jones & Thompson, 1999, pp. 3-4,174-176; see also Evans & Wurster, 1997, p. 75), appear likely to be more effective than traditional bureaucratic organizations to manage networked programs.

For us at this point we conclude that NPM did not and does not represent a new managerial "paradigm," in the Kuhnian sense. Indeed, it is not clear whether the question about its impact has meaning, and it certainly is clear that not enough information is available to try to answer it. Management reform, in fact, has proven a far more subtle enterprise that extends over the medium and long-term in order for any political or managerial regime to succeed relative to the ambitious agendas proposed and the need for assessment and feedback using an appropriately broad set of evaluative measures. The survival of governments, politicians, and managers advocating reform and attempting to implement comprehensive change appears to depend upon relatively slow and careful implementation. Moreover, any theory of public management by necessity is highly contingent. As we have emphasized in this book, new public management is no longer new. Many of the reforms labelled as NPM have been under implementation for 10, 20 or more years. Although academics can claim to have defined the techniques and terminology of the new public management with a reasonable degree of precision (see Barzelay, 2001; Borins, 1997; Hood & Peters, 2004; Jones & Schedler, 1997), much of the dialogue about NPM, pro and con, is confusing, disconnected and, in effect, a distraction that inhibits sincere attempts to determine the outcomes of management reform.

Out of the decades-long experience in observing the emergence of public management as an academic discipline have emerged a number of criticisms of it by academics from a variety of social science disciplines. Indeed, critics of various public management reform initiatives, including NPM and so called managerialism or neo-managerialism appear to outnumber advocates in academe, if not in the practitioner environment. Some of this may be related to the fact that academics face professional and career incentives to find fault rather than to extol success. Additionally, some criticism of public management reform may derive from the fact that it is perceived to draw conceptually too strongly from a business-driven perspective. This approach threatens the traditions of public administration and public policy programs, which build on the primacy of government aggressively pursuing the public interest. The reform debate will—and should—continue, and as it does it should move toward a better structured and more informed dialogue about reform more generally. Several works on NPM and public management reform published in the past five years or so have attempted to clarify this dialogue (see, for example, Barzelay, 2001; Hood & Peters; 2004; Kettl, 2000a; Jones & Thompson, 1999).

We conclude that there can be no single theory or set of managerial prescriptions to guide the strengthening of performance in the public sector, whether positive or normative, that is sufficient for all times or circumstances. Any institutional arrangement has the potential to improve upon another. Conclusions about the utility of new organizational and institutional governance arrangements depend essentially upon a comparison of information costs under each of the alternatives. The information revolution has dramatically transformed information costs and, thereby, the relative efficacy of various institutional arrangements to deal with crises, threats and changes in markets. Many of the consequences of these changes can be lumped together under the rubric of performance and results based management. Inevitably, these changes will refashion the institutions of government and public management and, perhaps, even the nature of the state itself.

At the core of the reforms lurks the issue of equity, which neither academics nor practitioners have considered carefully enough. In particular, public officials have not sufficiently addressed equity goals while pursuing managerial efficiency. It is surely the case that those who support increased public sector efficiency will (or wish to) ignore the risk of greater income disparity, impaired earning capability for many citizens, increased poverty, and worsening of health, social, and educational services. Much reform appears to be directed with a high degree of insularity of purpose to change governments internally without much attention to distributional consequences. Any careful review of the implications of management reform must address those linkages. As our late colleague Frieder Naschold would caution, unless better government and improved services result from reform, why should change be undertaken?

NOTES

1. SARD development management nations include Afghanistan, Pakistan, India, Nepal, Bhutan, Bangladesh, Sri Lanka, and Maldives. These initiatives are reported in Asian Development Bank (2005b, October, 17), *Draft Technical Assistance project paper "Mainstreaming MfDR in Support of Poverty Reduction.*
2. See for example, OECD, Managing for Development Results, 2005a, www.mfdr.org.Sourcebook.html; World Bank, Managing for Development Results, 2005, http://Inweb18.worldbank.org
3. This section draws on Wescott, C. with Jones, L. R. (2005). *Fiscal Devolution in East Asia*. Manila: Asian Development Bank
4. The term deconstruction is used here as defined and applied by Charles Perrow in his various works (see, for example, 1986a, 1986b).

CHAPTER 4

PHASES OF ORGANIZATIONAL TRANSFORMATION AND RESTRUCTURING

Organizational transformation through reform typically begins with what is referred to as restructuring. This chapter defines restructuring and its application and explains why restructuring is the first step in the process of public management reform. To restructure an organization initially entails defining all of the skill areas and work processes where an organization has special or unique skills and knowledge, that is, its core competence relative to the capability of other organizations. Second, restructuring requires an assessment of those core competence areas that fit within its overall mission and objectives. Third, under restructuring the organization contracts out noncore competence work that needs to be done to fulfill its mission to other organizations, including those in the private sector, that have core competence comparative advantage. The comparative advantage of contractors may lie in the superior quality of their products or services, or may be the result of ability to produce products or services at lower cost with no loss of quality. Finally, restructuring meets its goals only where the organization then eliminates everything else that does not contribute value to the services and products delivered to the citizens and stakeholders served by the organization, that is, non-core competence work processes and that work not contracted out.

At the beginning, restructuring requires a careful assessment (typically a reassessment) of the mission and objectives of the organization, an evaluation of the organization's strategy relative to its target markets for products or services, definition of criteria for determining core competence, and value engineering to define what work materially contributes to mission and goal achievement, and the extent of the contribution. Restructuring demands a comparison between the costs and performance of work performed by the organization and that of potential alternative service suppliers. This step is essential to decide where to contract out, or where a service or product should not be supplied by the organization at all. And, because restructuring requires cost and performance comparison, activity based-cost analysis, or what is termed or responsibility accounting in the public sector must be employed to permit such comparisons to be made. Responsibility accounting, budgeting, and management control are techniques or methods that enable the organization to define its core competence and costs of product and service production.

According to the principles of mission or responsibility accounting, budgeting, and management control, the components of the organization should be classified according to their primary mission or responsibility, for example, mission centers, revenue centers, expense or cost centers, internal service centers, investment centers. Each is evaluated in terms of its contribution to the delivery of services that meet citizen demand. Restructuring may result in significant "delayering" or flattening of organizational structure, considerable delegation of authority, responsibility and decision making on day to day operations to levels of the organization closer to its constituency. Restructuring usually means shedding jobs. Indeed, large-scale productivity improvement in government depends upon the elimination of hundreds of thousands of jobs. However, restructuring should also include increased employee education and training, especially in the use of new technology and work processes.

WHY RESTRUCTURE?

Why should public organizations restructure? Part of the answer lies in the significance and relative performance of the U.S. services sector. Services now constitute 75% of GDP (gross domestic product). This means that the United States must increase service productivity to grow wealthier and in recent decades increases have been glacial. Government productivity poses an especially severe problem. The 20% of the American workforce employed by government generates less than 15% of GDP. Value-added per worker is only 5% lower in private services than in manufacturing, but government productivity lags manufacturing productivity by a third. In contrast, in 1958 value-added per government worker was 40% higher than in the goods sector.

A second part of the answer goes to the organization of service delivery. Arguably, bureaucracies were once relatively effective. Bureaucratic organizational arrangements successfully provided security, jobs and economic stability, ensured fairness and equity, and delivered the "one size fits all" services needed during the era of government infrastructure development that lasted from the turn of the last century to the mid-1960s (Osborne & Gaebler, 1992, p. 14). During crises such as the Great Depression and two world wars, bureaucracy saved us. In the meantime, however, the hierarchical, centralized, rule-driven organizational arrangements invented during the industrial era have become increasingly anachronistic.

Global economic competition, international capital mobility, and breathtaking improvements in telecommunications and information storage, processing, and retrieval are producing a knowledge-based economy —one where workers demand autonomy and citizens/customers demand high quality products, superior service, and extensive choice. Old-fashioned business bureaucracies cannot meet these demands; neither can old-fashioned government bureaucracies. Meeting these demands requires flexible, adaptable, innovative, and customer-focused organizations that offer an array of high quality goods, tailored to individual wants and needs. However, few public officials or managers have had much experience restructuring. Consequently, better methods for management are needed. Additionally, better evaluative frameworks against which reduction options and actions may be assessed also are required.

PATTERNS OF RESTRUCTURING AND CUTTING BACK ORGANIZATIONS

How has the public sector tended to approach restructuring in the past? A reasonably similar pattern or sequence of events appears to characterize the restructuring initiatives of many public organizations. The first response to restructuring typically involves denial. This is usually followed by short-term measures to reduce spending, accompanied by efforts to assign blame. Organizations at this point must chose between reducing services and cutting positions. Many public officials balk at this choice, arguing that budget cuts should be made gradually, that organizations are better off relying on employee attrition, withdrawal of vacant positions, cuts in support budgets, and even deferral of maintenance than on across-the-board personnel reductions or cuts targeted at specific programs or services. When push comes to shove, they cut "soft" services first. Then they cut things that are invisible to the public, for example, in support operations and maintenance, employee training, and capital asset replacement. These cuts eat up an organization's accumulated capital and often demoralize its employees who understand that ignoring maintenance and investment will lead to higher costs later. Nevertheless, massive layoffs are also costly. When severance pay, replacement costs, loss of morale and valuable skills, not to mention the dislocation experienced by the employees who lose their jobs, are considered, staff reductions through attrition may actually be more cost-effective than termination—especially poorly targeted terminations.

The next phase of restructuring usually involves deeper, across-the-board budget cuts, often accompanied by hiring and salary freezes, increased use of part-time and nonpermanent employees, and other initiatives to reduce total salary costs. However, the across-the-board strategy tends to weaken organizations throughout. It is especially damaging in that high-demand programs and high quality personnel are cut the same amount as programs with lower demand and quality (Jones, 1984; Jones & Bixler, 1992; Jones & McCaffery, 1989). Unfortunately, many public organizations and their employees appear to prefer the across-the-board and attrition approach, with nonessential services cut first and the last-hired employees the first to lose their jobs. Application of length of service rather than merit criteria often eliminates less experienced and younger staff. Unfortunately, these employees may be more adaptable to change than those with longer records of service. Employees cut in this phase may include a higher proportion of new entrant women and minorities than is represented in the total organizational workforce. There also may be an accompanying loss of highly skilled employees who find better employment opportunities elsewhere in a less stressful working environment.

HOW SHOULD RESTRUCTURING BE MANAGED?

A number of variables in addition to those mentioned at the beginning of this chapter must be addressed in restructuring management. Once the organization has reviewed and assessed its strategic and market plans, determined its core competence areas, performed value chain analyses, decided on what work processes will be retained, contracted out or eliminated, then it must begin to address a number of issues related to managing reduction. Typically, the first issue is how to deal with personnel reduction. As noted previously, personnel may be reduced by attrition or by layoff and termination. It is essential for the organization to develop a deliberate strategy on personnel reduction and then stick to it. Public organizations often attempt to reduce through attrition, a slow yet effective method given that the costs of this approach can be afforded. Attrition takes longer and is more costly in the long-term; termination appears to be more cost-effective in the long-term but costs more up-front because of the necessity for paying employees for accrued benefits, and in some instances bonuses. Legal constraints, union contracts and other strictures make termination more difficult in the public versus the private sector. Numerous political and other constraints seem to force public organizations toward the attrition approach. However, it should be kept in mind that termination is used more often in the private sector because of its apparent long-term cost advantage and for other reasons, including sustaining employee morale for those not terminated and the advantages gained from shifting the organization rapidly toward the achievement of new goals and market opportunities. With respect to strategy, we advocate use of both attrition and termination, in short depending on the circumstance and degree of political and market pressure to change.

To manage employee reduction, the criteria for cuts and rules on how cuts will be made must be developed and communicated clearly to employees. Some public organizations have developed, procedures to mix length of service and merit criteria in determining layoff or employment termination schedules. Employee performance evaluation systems may be designed so that employees generate service credits for high performance ratings. These credits are then added to other credits earned through length of service and total service credits are then used to define employee layoff order and rights to move into the positions held by less senior employees in the same or similar job classification elsewhere in the organization.

The service credit system also may be used to set priorities for employee reassignment to new positions within the organization, either at the point where personnel cuts are made or after a period of layoff. While reduction-in-force rules often include the provision of replacement or "bumping" rights across organizational units, unlimited bumping is stressful, disruptive and may cause serious losses in employee morale and productivity. A "single bump within class" system that restricts movement rights to a single choice and compares the qualifications of those seeking to replace other employees with requirements for the contested positions appears to be a preferable option. Union contracts may constrain the close application of qualification and requirement definitions, as may civil service rules.

One of the most important dimensions of personnel management under restructuring is the extent to which the organization invests in education, training and placement of employees whose jobs have been cut. Education and retraining may be necessary to enable reassignment of employees to new positions within the organization. Investment in education, training and placement services, and job search assistance is costly but desirable in most instances. Responsible management of job loss can build rather than reduce morale, and may help sustain or even promote the productivity of employees whose jobs are not cut, particularly for those continue to face the threat of elimination.

We have stressed that strategic planning and the establishment of both program and personnel priorities should guide restructuring. Maintenance of service quality and the retention of valuable employees must continue to be of paramount importance to the restructuring organization. Under conditions of program reduction and termination, enforcing priorities requires strong political support, effective strategic planning, a sophisticated information base for decision making, and considerable attention to negotiation with employees, citizens receiving services and stakeholders. All of this can be assisted through definition of critical mass program and core resource operation levels, i.e., resource levels below which programs cannot operate and still achieve their mission and objectives satisfactorily (Jones, 1985).

Evaluation of value-added to the services delivered to citizens and employee and stakeholder participants is critical to effective restructuring. The capable manager will recognize that cuts ought not to be based on organizational prestige, program longevity and employee seniority, budget size, or other convenient but nonvalue added criteria. Regrettably, the program information needed to do otherwise is often lacking. At this point, the implementation of a strategic planning process that generates accurate and reliable information about market and citizen demand patterns and shifts in demand and to enable comparisons between programs, service production costs and productivity is critical. The planning process and strategic plans also ought to fit with longer-term financial, debt management, and capital planning. In attempting to plan and execute restructuring effectively, managers are likely to be frustrated as they recognize the extent to which they have under invested in or simply squandered valuable accounting, planning, program and policy evaluation, information technology, and other analytical resources in the past.

The issue of participation in restructuring decision making is sensitive and may be dominated by management-labor contracts to a considerable extent. Arguments for broader participation of employees are often made on the grounds of fairness, contribution to employee morale, and adherence to democratic management values. A much stronger argument for participation is that employees and program constituents have information that needs to be assessed by program managers in deciding whether and how to restructure. Many of the best suggestions on how to save money and increase efficiency are likely to come from program managers, their staffs, and citizen consumers if they are asked.

Centralization of planning and the reassessment of priorities are typical in public sector restructuring. Prolonged dependence on one or a few individuals to make restructuring decisions can result in reintroduction of many of the bureaucratic weaknesses that contributed to the need to restructure in the first place. A "Chinese mandarin" system of management by personal influence is inimical to effective restructuring because of its effect on workplace moral and on the openness of the organization to restructuring, reengineering, reinvention, redesign, and rethinking. However, the degree of centralization of authority in restructuring may be less important than other variables in explaining successful restructuring. Smoothing the impact of cuts, continuity of leadership, the extent to which restructuring is politicized, ability to define and communicate organizational mission and goals, the extent to which service priorities are established and budgeted, form of government, and degree of cooperation between executive and legislative arms all appear to be more important variables than centralization per se.

The dilemma of centralization of decision authority versus broader participation in restructuring comes down to a fundamental trade-off — either centralize and limit representation for purposes of decision and execution efficiency, or allow decision participation to be more open and, consequently, open to greater fragmentation and delay. Open access and participation in restructuring more fully utilizes the knowledge extant in the minds of employees, those served by the organization and stakeholders. However, broad participation often limits the ability of public organizations to establish new priorities quickly and to target cuts. Broad participation may make significant restructuring impossible as all parties have the opportunity to articulate reasons why the organization should remain as it is rather than adapting to new market, social, and political conditions. Either way, something of value is sacrificed, which reinforces our view that the best approach may be a combination of the two wherein politicians and managers cooperate but employ a procedural mechanism to limit choice and constrain the time in which choices can be made and appealed. In the closure of military facilities in the United States, the Congress, and executive branches of government used such a constraining procedural mechanism to close hundreds of military bases, the specifics of which had been debated in some cases for decades (Thompson & Jones, 1994).

RESTRUCTURING UNDER FISCAL STRESS CONDITIONS

Where the organization faces fiscal stress or financial crisis, prolonged, acute mismatches between jurisdictional means and policy commitments may severely inhibit the ability to continue in the status quo. Budget deficits may accrue and interest payments increase as a percentage of total revenues and spending. Credit ratings may suffer, and the ability of public organizations to finance capital construction and to borrow to meet short-term cash shortages may be impaired. In many instances, the need for restructuring may not be recognized until the government as a whole or specific public organizations face a financial crisis and cannot continue to earn revenues either through the political/budget process or from the market, then the need for restructuring becomes readily apparent. Where public organizations, including those in state and municipal governments, rely in part on deficit financing and borrowing, the ability to get credit from external lenders may become impaired or lost.

Where the confidence of elected officials is lost in ways that affect budget decisions and willingness to fund programs, and where loss of external market user revenues and credit-worthiness has occurred, longer-term financial planning and action is needed to evaluate the effects of program and service demand shifts and, from a financial perspective, to improve cash flow, cash management, and investment practices. Under conditions of fiscal crisis, special attention must be given to insure entitlement and pension fund solvency, to limit debt load to fit tax base and debt service capacities, to assess property and equipment leasing or liquidation options, to develop accurate capital asset depreciation and replacement costs and schedules, to improve inventory management and, in some cases, to establish sufficient fund reserves to support the budget in the event of future revenue short-falls.

Long-range program and financial planning may require the counsel of financial management consultants and may involve the participation of other public entities, bankers, municipal bond market advisors and others to rebuild confidence in the accountability and credit-worthiness of the enterprise. Public organizations often discover, as have many private organizations, that long-term productivity improvement requires risk capital for investment in new equipment, employee training, additional program analysis and market research. Because restructuring requires analysis of service value, additional costs for accounting system modification, data collection, analysis, and decision making is inevitable. Of course, some organizations are penny wise and dollar foolish—they avoid these costs by cutting deeply across-the-board without regard to the capacity to deliver quality services in the future. This approach is not a model for successful restructuring despite the obvious advantages of expedience and ease of compromise it gives to elected and appointed officials. Indeed, it is possible only where governments practice cash rather than accrual accounting, which means that organizations can convey a false impression of fiscal health by play games (often in violation of the law) with the timing of income and expenditures, for example, in New York City in the fiscal crisis of the mid-1970s. Fiscal smoke and mirrors sometimes will suffice to persuade the news media and the public that a crisis has been averted, apparently without serious long-term loss. Unfortunately, the costs of mismanaging the financial component of restructuring are high and are borne for a long time, for example, as in Orange County, California.

OPPORTUNITIES FROM RESTRUCTURING

The most important contribution restructuring can make to increased productivity may come from the replacement of out-of-date technology. In many public organizations shortsighted, across-the-board budget cuts made over a multiyear period create substantial technology and employee education and training gaps. This issue is addressed more fully in the chapter to follow on reengineering.

Under restructuring, some of the ideas proposed to resolve organizational and citizen problems may initially appear to be too radical but may later prove to be workable. For example, under the pressure of fiscal necessity, the city of Oakland, California sold the public building that housed its museum to private investors. However, the city continued to provide museum services under lease agreement with the new owners. Similar sale and lease-back agreements have been successful for other cities. These arrangements enable local governments to reduce their maintenance and operation costs while private investment incentives help to insure proper maintenance and care for facilities. Users of facilities may be required to bear a larger proportion of costs through user fees. Better cost accounting can help in setting prices and appropriate fee levels relative to measures of ability to pay.

Justifications for provision of services by government must be thoroughly reevaluated by public officials in making decisions about user fees, program reductions, or whether to continue provide the service at all. The trend toward privatization has been driven by recognition that many of the services provided traditionally by government can and ought to be provided by the private or not-for-profit sectors of the economy. Restructuring, contracting out, and privatization are compatible in many instances as a means of reducing the scale and scope of government.

In general, restructuring has to be managed taking into account the rigidities and constraints built into hierarchical public bureaucracies. Typical manifestations of such constraints include overspecialization of function, devotion of inordinate amounts of time to self-defense rather than to problem solving, problem avoidance through obfuscation, resistance to the implications of new information, and a fear of adaptation to new social and economic conditions. Inability to adapt reduces the probability of survival. Recognition that these rigidities and constraints exist should cause us to devote more resources to the study of restructuring and to the education and training of public decision makers, managers, and service providers in methods for diagnosing the need for and managing public organizational change.

THE CHALLENGING CONTEXT FOR RESTRUCTURING THE PUBLIC SECTOR

Beginning in the United States in the mid-1970s and continuing through the 2000s, considerable public discussion of the need to reduce the size, scope and role of government in the economy was undertaken. To a considerable extent the debate in the United States paralleled that occurring elsewhere in the world. Examples of this may be found in the debate in this era that took place in the United Kingdom, Sweden, and selected other European nations, Canada, Australia, New Zealand, and elsewhere. The stimulus for dialogue about the size, scope, and role of government and the need for government restructuring during this period appears to be essentially economic in origin as we have noted. However, politics always plays an important role in influencing and reflecting both economic crises and public opinion. Views on the pervasiveness and relative disadvantage resulting from the broad social and economic role played by government in general, and perceptions of inadequacy of public service performance specifically are subject to interpretation based on different political and ideological perspectives. Further, the condition of the economy may be, in some cases, somewhat independent of views on the need for restructuring government. In the United States, political demand for restructuring continued during a period of unprecedented economic growth that produced a balance federal government budget in the 1990s and into a period of federal budget deficits in the 2000s.

Where public dissatisfaction increases, typically some politicians are able to orchestrate public frustration resulting from reduced economic opportunity, or uncertainty in the case of the U.S. economy in the 1990s and 2000s, into a voter support for greater government programmatic and fiscal control and restructuring. Over the period in question in the

United States and a globally, public sector revenues and expenditures were constrained or redirected for number of reasons including (a) economic competition and recession that reduced economic growth, employment and tax revenues; (b) major political change (e.g., the end of the Cold War and corresponding economic and social reformulation in Germany, Central Europe, and the nations of the former Soviet Union), (c) tax limitation measures approved through popular vote, for example, Proposition 13 in California; (d) reductions in federal government transfer payments to subordinate governments; (e) changes in government funding priorities for domestic services, social assistance, health care, defense, and other programs. Expenditure cuts and shifts in policy priorities made by governments in this period resulted in part from reductions in tax and nontax revenues as well as from the application of different social philosophies regarding the costs and value of many services provided by government. Political motivation to curb or redistribute government expenditures, or to actually reduce spending levels nominally or in constant dollars, may be viewed to emanate from a variety of factors independent of public dissatisfaction with government and the public sector performance.

The dilemma in facing the need for restructuring the public sector results in large part from the fact that for more than 50 years Western societies and economies have become accustomed to and to some extent dependent upon continued growth of government. Growth has fitted well with both the motives of political decision-makers seeking electoral and financial support on the basis of providing jobs, public works projects and welfare assistance, and of citizens desiring the benefits of political representation for their causes, needs, and preferences. Labor union power, although diminished in some nations including the United States, typically resist restructuring, although the inevitability of budget and salary and staff reductions in government eventually have to be faced and negotiated carefully by union leadership.

Restructuring is not particularly attractive to politicians who, because of it, are no longer able to reward constituents. Neither is it attractive to public managers desiring to preserve their programs and jobs, or to citizens benefiting from the provision of transfer payments and services by government. It is little wonder that, collectively, we tend to want to avoid thinking about public sector restructuring given that its outcomes are likely to displease great numbers of citizens and politicians.

Among the issues that must be addressed when public sector officials and managers face restructuring in response to economic challenges and changes in patterns of political and social demand that threaten or actually reduce or shift revenues are the following: Should the scope of public policies, programs and organizations be reduced? Why do government policies become immune to review, modification, and termination? How can we tell which policies and programs should survive and which should be modified, reduced, or terminated? How should decision-makers attempt to reduce or terminate public programs or organizations where this appears desirable? Elected officials, public managers, policy analysts, and the public have had to respond to the necessity for changing policies, cutting or shifting spending and restructuring organizations since the 1970s. However, before this era, few public officials or managers had much experience in restructuring. And we may wonder to what extent the lessons from success and failure produced as a result of having to cope with the challenge of restructuring during this period have been learned and internalized so that we may do better in the future.

CONCLUSIONS

This chapter has provided information that elected officials, public managers and others need to understand to better assess alternative methods for improving the management of economic and fiscal stress through restructuring. Evaluation of restructuring may be segmented into the determination of: (a) the causes of economic and fiscal stress, (b) methods for improved management of restructuring, (c) the issues and dilemmas faced by public officials and managers attempting to manage restructuring, and (d) methods for either achieving or avoiding restructuring. The range of nonmutually exclusive approaches to management of restructuring includes:

- Doing nothing, likely to work only for a short time if economic and fiscal stress persists,
- Increasing revenues and/or reducing expenditures,
- Increasing employee and organizational productivity and employing a set of more innovative responses that are productivity-related of the type presented in this chapter.

The third category of productivity-related responses includes a number of approaches not discussed to any extent in this chapter but important in restructuring the role of government as a whole. These include increased cooperation between and networking with other organizations, programs and their constituents, strategic co-optation of other organizations, increasing citizen volunteerism in provision of services to the public, mission and program reorganization and merger, joint service and purchase agreements within and between governments, contracting out and privatization.

Before developing plans to manage restructuring, prudent elected officials and public managers will attempt to define the components of demand for restructuring. In doing so, they may wish to consider responding to this demand in a holistic manner rather than in the piecemeal fashion that has characterized attempts to restructure the public sector and public sector organizations in the past. Finally, restructuring must be tailored to the contextual demands of each national, regional, local, and organizational circumstance in which it is applied around the world.

CHAPTER 5

CHANGING PROCESSES

What Works, What Does Not, and Why?

Business process reengineering is an inevitable and attractive initiative to be undertaken by public management reformers because reducing costs, cutting service production cycle time, and improving quality and productivity so often depends on moving beyond the constraints imposed by traditional and highly bureaucratic ways of performing work. Business process reengineering endeavors to establish efficient work processes and reengineering concentrates on "starting over" rather than on trying to "fix" existing process problems with marginal or incremental "band-aid" solutions. Business process reengineering require thinking about processes and not functions and positions in organizational hierarchies. The goals of reengineering are increased customer satisfaction and improvement in service quality combined with greater efficiency as measured primarily by reduced cycle time and cost. Reengineering takes advantage to the greatest extent of computer and other information technologies. It requires repeated pilot testing of alternatives proposed to replace existing work processes prior to implementation of new systems and processes.

From Bureaucracy to Hyperarchy in Netcentric and Quick Learning Organizations: Exploring Future Public Managment Practice, 111–128
Copyright © 2007 by Information Age Publishing
All rights of reproduction in any form reserved.

Only a brief attempt is made here to define reengineering as much has been written about it, most notably by Hammer (1996), Hammer and Champy (1993), and Hammer and Stanton (1995). Reengineering is a top-down process wherein the organization, typically driven by resource constraints and competitive market pressures, attempts to serve its customers better by reducing work process cycle time which, in turn, can reduce costs either in the short or long-term. Reengineering does not attempt to modify existing processes. Rather, it replaces existing processes with more efficient ways of doing business. Critical to accomplishing the goals of reengineering is increased use of computer and other information technologies to allow fewer employees to do the work formerly performed by more people. Reengineering alters work flow and sequential or reciprocal task dependent relationships, short-cutting older processes in part through substituting computer assisted data gathering, analysis, decision, and management for manual human reform unitor. However, the key is not so much replacing people with technology as much as it is working smarter, eliminating unnecessary, duplicative, paper-heavy work methods. Not surprisingly, reengineering can result in organizational flattening or "delayering" as fewer lower and midmanagement employees are needed to do the same or better work after processes have been reengineered. This enables redeployment of some personnel to direct customer service, depending on demand, ability, aptitude, and training. Essential to reengineering is investment in education and training of staff to operate new processes effectively. Reengineering success examples are numerous (Hammer, pp. 174-190; Hammer & Champy, pp. 150-199; Hammer & Stanton, pp. 204-227, 254-273) and often show reduction of work process steps of 70 to 90%, cuts in cycle time of 60 to 80% and reduction of costs from 20 to 80%. In other words, reengineering is intended to make quantum rather than marginal performance improvements.

The process of reengineering involves a commitment by executives to fully support the initiative, the selection, and prioritization of processes to be reengineered, assignment of project responsibility to work teams, selection of work team members representing older processes and many or all of the stakeholders in the process outcomes, assignment of team leadership and reporting / liaison responsibilities, analysis of existing processes, development of alternatives to the status quo, pilot testing and evaluation of alternatives tested, integration of trial and error lessons in redevelopment of alternatives, refinement of the best alternative and, finally, implementation of the new process and discontinuance of that which it replaces.

Some simultaneous operation of old and new processes may be necessary temporarily. Selection and tasking of work teams is critical to achieving desired results. Continuity of executive support for testing and insulation for failure is essential. Some or many errors should be expected in attempting to define new processes. Full commitment of resources to see the reengineering initiative through also is essential. Staff time, technological support, and funding must be provided as needed by process action teams. Furthermore, support for the effort must be virtually open-ended in terms of time schedule, that is, teams must be free to work on alternatives until they have succeeded. Setting artificial end dates by which process must be reengineered is not productive. Instead, teams should be asked to work until they "get it right."

The bottom line for evaluating the success of reengineering is improved customer satisfaction (i.e., results). Cycle time and cost reduction are not ends in themselves. Rather, they are the results of better work processes. Metrics are critical to determining whether reengineering is successful and, consequently, methods for evaluating results and comparing them to those achieved under previously used processes have to be built into the reengineering effort. Without a means for measuring quantitatively and qualitatively the improvement in service reengineering is virtually pointless. There are simpler ways to cut costs if this is the only objective. This means that results indices must be identified, data bases and collection procedures designed and constructed, data must be gathered, analyzed, and compared. Accounting data must be related to results measures to permit cost analysis s well as consumer response to process alternatives whose costs differ. Typically, different parts of the customer base will prefer different mixes of service quality and cost. Reengineering must attempt to accommodate such preferences, which is also the objective of change.

Proponents of reengineering recognize that many organizational work flows, job designs, control mechanisms, and structures are either superfluous or obsolete. Reengineering processes, accompanied by restructuring and downsizing, intends to improve administrative performance and, by slimming the organizational bureaucracy, save money. As Michael Hammer (1990) explains,

> It is time to stop paving the cow paths. Instead of embedding outdated processes in silicon and software, we should obliterate them and start over. We should reengineer our [organizations]; use the power of modern information processing technology to radically redesign our ... processes in order achieve dramatic improvements in their performance.... We cannot achieve breakthroughs in performance merely by cutting fat or automating existing processes. Rather we must challenge the old assumptions and shed old rules. (pp. 104, 107)

Hammer illustrates reengineering with the revolution that took place in the Ford Motor Company system of accounts payable. In the early

1980s, Ford auditors carefully studied accounts payable activities and concluded that, by consolidating, by rationalizing processes, and by installing new computer systems, payroll staff could be cut 20%—from 500 employees to 400. Ford was pleased with its plan to slim the accounts payable payroll—until it looked at Mazda, whose entire accounts payable organization consisted of five clerks. Consequently, Ford did not "settle for the modest changes it first envisioned. It opted for radical change—and achieved dramatic improvement." Through reengineering, Ford cut the required number of manual accounting transactions and reconciliations associated with processing and paying for the goods it used from nine to three, thereby producing, "a 75 percent reduction in head count, not the twenty percent it would have gotten with a conventional program." Hammer also notes that the changes Ford made in its accounts payable operation resulted in improved materials management and more accurate financial information

PRINCIPLES OF REENGINEERING

The principles of reengineering are fairly simple. First, whenever possible, design jobs around an objective or outcome instead of a single function—functional specialization and sequential execution are inherently inimical to expeditious processing. Second, whenever possible, have those who use the output of activity perform the activity and have the people who produce information process it, since they have the greatest need for information and the greatest interest in its accuracy. The use of modern data bases, expert systems, and telecommunications networks provides many, if not all, of the benefits that once made administrative centralization and specialization of administrative functions such as reporting, accounting, purchasing, or quality assurance (economies of scale, high levels of coordination, and standardization) attractive, without sacrificing any of the benefits of decentralization. Third, capture information once and at the source. Fourth, coordinate parallel activities during their performance, not after they are completed. And last, give the people who do the work responsibility for making decisions and build control into job design (Hammer, 1990, pp. 108-112).

The contrast between how Ford handles its accounts payable and standard operating procedures in governmental organizations could not be more striking. In the U.S. Navy, for example, research showed that in the early 1990s it took 26 manual accounting transactions and 9 reconciliations—35 steps in all—for a user to obtain authorized supplies from a qualified vendor (Hemingway, 1993, pp. 8-12). This system was not only cumbersome, it often led to bad service and excessive investment in inventories. This system caused frequent delays in obtaining repair parts. And these delays keep a large proportion of the Navy's cars and trucks out of commission, which forces the Navy to buy 10% more vehicles than it really needed.

Research demonstrated that computerization could eliminate over half of the steps in the Navy's accounts payable process (Hemingway, 1993, p. 25). But the process reengineering question is why are 14 steps, let alone 35 accounting records needed by the Navy where Ford gets by with three? One answer is that Navy fails to capture information once and at the source. Moreover, the people who produce information do not process it. Processing is handled by financial management specialists at every level from the cost center to the Financial Information Processing Center of the system-wide centralized U.S. Department of Defense Finance and Accounting Service (DFAS).

However, the most important reason that explains process bloat is that the Navy, like many public organizations, has not build financial controls into job designs. Navy commanding officers, for example, have had insufficient discretion as to the mix or quantity of resources used by their commands. Even in peacetime their effectiveness in managing resources has little bearing on the evaluation of their performance. Their budgets are determined at a higher level. The system of ordering and processing supplies is primarily intended to insure that neither they nor higher level authorities exceed their obligational authority divided into multiple separate accounts, numerous management codes, and several thousand of accounting lines.

The principles of process reengineering imply that Navy operational commanding officers should instead be held responsible for their purchases and supported by a standardized information system. Under this approach the Defense Finance and Accounting Service would be responsible only for maintaining a standardized information system and monitoring purchases made by commanding officers. The Defense Logistics Agency created a database on vendors that it uses to negotiate contracts with vendors on behalf the organization as a whole and which it plans to share with commanding officers. Instead of rules preventing them from incurring excess obligations, commanding officers could be evaluated during peacetime at least in part on the basis of their success in managing costs. Adoption of this approach would permit the number of individual accounting entries needed to make a purchase to be reduced.

At Hewlett-Packard, adoption of this approach resulted in substantial cost savings and a better than 100% improvement in service (Hammer, 1990, p. 110). Could this and other more recent examples of reengineering successes of the types noted above be achieved in most public organizations? The answer appears to be affirmative where public officials understand and effectively support reengineering efforts for a sufficient period of time so that alternatives may be thoroughly tested, training needs are met, and where results are carefully evaluated and integrated so that the organization learns from both its successes and failures.

UNIVERSAL SUCCESS FACTORS FOR SUCCESSFUL BUSINESS PROCESS REENGINEERING

According to the public management reform practice literature and research conducted by the authors in the course of writing this book in U.S. federal government agencies including the Department Of Defense, managerial innovation depends on several factors that may be controlled or influenced by practitioners themselves. Where these factors are absent or attenuated, change usually fails. This is so regardless of innovation content or organizational identity. These are:

(a) Commitment at the top of the organization.
(b) A meaningful, clear vision, a set of goals, and a plan of action.
(c) Organization-wide understanding of the vision, goals, and plan of action.
(d) A sense of urgency.
(e) An understanding of obstacles to change and persistence in overcoming them.
(f) Performance measures and a willingness to learn from one's mistakes.
(g) Recognition of successes and extraordinary efforts.
(h) Institutionalization of continuous improvement.

To understand the relative significance of these factors we interviewed representatives from more than 70 of the initiatives, in most cases, several representatives, and the change reform unit coordinators from each of the military departments and defense agencies. In some cases, follow-up interviews were conducted. Our findings relative to the criteria are summarized below.

Committed Leadership

Most of the reform practitioners interviewed for this book believe that solid support from senior managers is the sine qua non of change. Representatives of successful innovations consistently praised the support of top management; failures more often than not were blamed on their bosses.

Unequivocal top-management support appears to be an element common to all efforts.

In some of these cases, senior leaders adopted change as a personal goal. In a few, the senior leaders actually initiated the change. This is not surprising as many senior leaders are the chief executive officers of their organizations. Contrary to the general public perception about the inefficiency and backwardness of government managerial knowledge and capability, many leaders interviewed kept themselves abreast of contemporary management change and better business practice theory and research. Further, they were keen to apply techniques of better business practice. Consequently, many senior leaders willingly invested the resources at their disposal to improve the performance of their organizations.

Unfortunately, reengineering and change are not free. Change in work processes costs time and money and takes key people away from their day-to-day jobs. Lacking a good reason for so doing, few bosses are likely to divert the resources needed to implement innovative, long-term projects. In many cases, however, grass roots managers exploit exigencies to win the support of top leaders.

Change agents evidently do need continued support from top management to overcome resistance to change. At a minimum, this means that reengineering teams must keep bosses involved by keeping them informed. The most successful initiatives went beyond this minimal level of involvement. In some cases, they persuaded top leaders to take ownership of the change campaign and its accomplishments. In contrast, loss of top management support usually left committed managers vulnerable and, in many cases, rendered their best efforts ineffectual.

We may note that change initiatives in government departments and agencies with a reputation for supporting managerial innovation seemed to be more likely to have made significant changes in the way they did business than those in departments and agencies with a reputation for managerial conservatism.

A Clear Vision and a Plan of Action

The second characteristic of successful reengineering teams appeared to be an ability to envision a payoff and to figure out how to make it happen. Waiving bureaucratic rules seems to be a key factor here in stimulating reengineering and reform. In contrast, despite the importance of the reform process to the change effort, some working level representatives, especially those from the less successful initiatives, often complained that they did not even know how to request a waiver of rules or who to contact to find out. Most of reform unit representatives expressed the opinion that there was no coherent corporate plan that they could follow to ensure that their waiver requests were given a fair and expeditious hearing. Instead, requests seemed to disappear into "a black hole" somewhere in upper level management, never to reappear again.

Frustration caused by ambiguities surrounding rule waiver processes may inspire some pretty radical suggestions. For example, one reform unit representative called for a central agency, to be given, "blanket authority to waive any government regulation that didn't impact public health or safety." Another went even further, insisting that, "change agents need to be free to reinvent." The unit representative said that the organization should, "unleash innovation, unleash creativity, by granting change initiatives blanket waiver authority." "Don't hold us accountable," she said, "for compliance with regulations, but for reporting the waivers we've taken and for the consequences of our actions."

Organization-Wide Understanding

New ideas have to be explained and sold throughout an organization. Selling means persuading and, because it is axiomatic that people are not persuaded by others but must persuade themselves, selling means listening to what people have to say about change. One must listen to persuade, both because only the persuadees can say what it will take for them to be persuaded and because an appearance of open-mindedness and fairness on the part of the persuader encourages confidence in the persuadee. Organizational change usually involves persuading the members of an organization that change is necessary and obtaining their commitment to the specifics of the change—what, how, when, where, who, and why. This means more than just briefing people about the plan of action or how it affects them. Moreover, it is not sufficient for senior leaders to repeat this message many times over, although this latter may be necessary if the members of the organization are to be convinced that change is a serious priority.

The more successful change unit representatives consistently stressed the importance of communication—up, down, and all around. One reform unit leader, for example, stressed the importance of communicating the organization's vision of itself as being important to high-level officials, to its potential customers, and to every member of the organization. Moreover, he claimed that the unit's vision and its plan of action had been successful in large part because they were not imposed from top down, but were crafted with the participation of many members of the organization and reflected their contributions of intelligence and energy.

Based upon discussions with reform unit representatives, far too many of the change initiatives were completely out of the information dissemination loop. Many were unaware that they had any obligation to communicate their goals or accomplishments either up or down in the organization. For example, a midlevel manager observed that his office had been designated a change reform unit by the CEO of the organization. However, he said he had never heard from the CEO and, to the best of his knowledge, there had never been any change activities announced there. He also noted that according to the guidance from the CEO, change initiatives were supposed to submit quarterly reports on their activities, including processes improved or savings accomplished, to his office. He had not received what he deemed to be a satisfactory report in over a year. This indicates that while reengineering and other changes were taking place in the parts of the organization, many sponsors and implementers of these initiatives were unaware of standing reporting requirements.

Not surprisingly, initiatives that were not communicating or communicated also were among the least successful. One of the clear messages heard from the reform unit representatives was that a communication network was needed that would let people find out what the initiatives were achieving or not accomplishing.

A Sense of Urgency

Revolutions are not made in a leisurely fashion although, as noted, reengineering takes time to do effectively. What is critical is for large-scale organizational change to occur, it must be pushed forward by a sense of urgency—by a need to act and act now. Otherwise, it is likely that little will be done. As articulated by one line manager, to accomplish results his team tried to create an, "atmosphere of crisis in order to prod people to seek solutions to problems that otherwise might not seem very important to them." However, after much promising effort, little beyond internal reorganization was achieved. The sense of urgency that propelled the reform unit to change was smothered by organizational rigidity and risk aversion toward experimenting with new ways of delivering services.

Understanding the Obstacles to Change and Persistence in Overcoming Them

There is no substitute for persistence. Initiatives that demonstrated persistence and creativity usually succeeded in improving business processes. Many reform unit managers admitted that more than a few of their ideas were unrealistic at the outset or "half-baked." In contrast, those who identified the obstacles they faced, adopted realistic plans, and were persistent in their efforts to overcome roadblocks were also much more likely to be among those reporting some or significant progress and claiming measurable performance improvements, or at least initial positive results from their efforts.

Persistence was especially critical to obtaining reform results. While an organization's stated philosophy is that the burden of proof rests with regulators who must show why a waiver should not be granted, rather than on the change reform unit to show why a waiver was needed, that is evidently not how many of the regulators saw it. The typical experience of reform unit representatives was that they had to convince regulators beyond a shadow of a doubt that a waiver was a good idea—in some cases, not just for them, but for the entire organization, which missed the whole point of the reform unit exercise as an experiment with innovation.

Performance Measurement and Willingness to Experiment

Change reform units that unambiguously achieved significant operational improvements or financial savings are were committed to measuring their accomplishments. Every one of the initiatives reporting significant changes in the way they did business also reports that they had established one or more metrics by which their performance could be measured. The reform units benchmarked performance against best commercial practices, measuring their costs, cycle time, and customer service against "world class" standards. The measures they used focus on cycle time and service quality -- including rework, work hours, space utilization, overproduction, transportation and conveyance, inventory, unnecessary motion, unnecessary processing, and waiting time. Moreover, as one manager explained, the workout team consciously treated their efforts as experiments: "We don't know ahead of time that we will be successful and we won't know if we are unless we have a good baseline to weigh our results against." He also noted that success depended on tolerance for failures. He concluded that, "Leaders must be willing to accept failure if processes are to improve"

It is important to note that activity cost measures were critical to many of the initiatives that could show unambiguous performance gains. For example, activity costing enabled one unit to analyze alternatives before they acted and document savings after their actions were carried out. One manager observed that this exercise also made them aware of wasteful operating practices—such as using $30.00 per hour government employees to sort wood, when a local private contractor would do the job for $7.50 per hour.

It is noteworthy that almost all of the initiatives studied had invested in performance measurement. The problem with implementation was that their metrics were usually based on local operating measures, collected on a statistical basis. Measures could rarely, if ever, be verified by reference to basic transaction records tied in to the standard system of accounts. Consequently, owing to fundamental flaws in federal government bookkeeping and accounting systems, far too few of reform unit success stories can be substantiated by hard data. Without these data, it is difficult to know precisely what to make of the change enterprise—although we applaud the extraordinary efforts of the successful initiatives. Measurement of value added and costs is an area that needs improvement as is the case throughout the U.S. federal government.

Recognition of Successes and Extraordinary Efforts

Change reform units were supposed to empower staff "down in the organization" to use their knowledge of the system's workings to make things better, and then to publicly reward them for their efforts—for the risks they took and the contributions they made.

Organizational recognition probably was a more effective motivator than anything else staff or executives could do for the members of change initiative units. Some reform unit representatives expressed frustration with the attention and recognition they received for their efforts. In the words of one, their senior leadership, "wants to appear to be involved with the least possible effort." Many claimed that actual reform unit efforts were entirely ignored or even, in a few cases, punished.

Continuous Improvement and Learning

Managers need and like to leave a legacy. They need to do this because after promotion to senior ranks, their careers depend on it. They must be perceived and evaluated to be effective leaders. Moreover, as they receive responsibility for managing large organizations, their interest in private-sector management practices seems to intensify. Astute change managers will accommodate these considerations in getting their projects off the ground. However, episodic performance improvement does not constitute reengineering or change. As explained, by one observer, "Successful initiatives will not declare victory and quit after reinventing one process, but will continue on the path of change—moving from success to success."

The goal of change managers was to institutionalize continuous improvement by integrating it into their vision, mission, goals, plans, data measurement, and corrective action. Of course, governments always are characterized by islands of administrative excellence. The problem is that these islands rarely are linked up to form continents. All too often they have been overwhelmed by the rising tide of indifference to change. Only the level of budgeted resources seems to make a difference across-the-board in forcing organizational change. One reform unit representatives put it this way:

> Midlevel managers in are used to seeing new initiatives emerge on the scene almost every year; they're like new tunes on the Hit Parade—they reach great popularity, shine brightly for a time, then quickly fade, unnoticed by those too jaded to remember the lyrics or the melody.

For some, only the budget crisis of the day remained, to be dealt with in whatever ad hoc manner deemed appropriate for each phase of retrenchment and cutback. After change he first wave of reengineering reform came "best business practices," an initiative that continues. This has been the history of government reform since the later 1980s, exacerbated by constant appropriation reduction throughout most of the past decade.

Some of the more inventive change reform units tried to figure out how to institutionalize what had done. More than a few attempted to institutionalize continuous improvement as a part of better business practices. Managers of most change initiatives, outsourcing under OMB Circular A-76 for example, found it difficult to see beyond the crisis of the moment—a crisis defined by reductions in programming that cut billions dollars across the government through the millenium. This is unfortunate, but not surprising. As a former government comptroller, the late Charles Hitch, used to observe: "It's hard to remember that you are there to drain the swamp when you are up to your ass in alligators."

The National Performance Review (NPR) of the 1990s in the federal government was an attempt to prevent management reform from fading from the charts like a fallen top 40 tune. The same may be said for the more recent best business practice and outsourcing initiatives. Still, a lot more work will be required to convince decision makers and managers, let alone the rank and file, that these initiatives are more than merely the latest management fads to sweep through the organization (Pollitt & Bouckhart, 2004). Many advocates of reform want deeply to believe that this is indeed the case, but even they are dubious. The most typical hope is that the budget circumstance will improve. While appropriations may increase, the demands for funding government operations and war fighting, for capital investment, for investment in people to make government careers more attractive, and the costs of maintaining a satisfactory infrastructure will continue to exert pressure for achieving management savings through whatever initiative are available. The reason for paying close attention to the NPR and subsequent government reform experiments including implementation of the Government Performance Reform Act and Government Management Reform Act is that they reveal lessons for all management reform initiatives in the federal government, and in other public organizations.

CONTINGENT SUCCESS AND FAILURE FACTORS

In light of our conclusion above, we need to articulate some of the barriers to managerial innovation identified in evaluating change initiatives that seem to be especially severe in the U.S. federal government in particular, and some of the steps that might be taken to remove them. These are problems that nearly all of the reform unit representatives we interviewed identified, whether or not they were successful

First, most change reform unit representatives were genuinely enthusiastic about the opportunity to do a better job, but even they were often apprehensive about the consequences of improving business processes. But experience has taught them to duck responsibility. Most seem to believe that management change threatens powerful interests—particularly but not exclusively in functional communities. Many conclude they are more likely to get into trouble rather than being rewarded if they instigate change. It is quite remarkable that many, nevertheless, still commit themselves to change. But then, what is the alternative? The alternative often is to exit the organization.

Numerous studies show that dedicated "fanatics" are needed to overcome the ambiguities, time delays, and resistance inherent in the process of large-scale organizational change. It is unlikely that enough champions of innovation will step forward to make a noticeable difference throughout organizations if there is no payoff for doing so. Nor will the change agents have very many followers if support at the top of departments is not conspicuous, unequivocal, and emphatic. If organizations are serious about management reform, they must recognize and reward success.

In well-run organizations, managers who find ways to increase productivity or performance are generally given greater responsibility and authority. Teams that increase their performance are rewarded and given new jobs to do. Managers who fail to increase productivity and performance are shunted aside or terminated. In an environment of resource constraint, and where the members of less productive teams are shed—their jobs may be reallocated to more productive employees. A surprising number of reform unit representatives seemed to believe that they were much more likely to lose promotions or even their jobs if they increased productivity than if they did nothing. Virtually everyone asked said that they actually believed their employees were at greater risk if they increased productivity than if they did nothing. Several talked about how their agencies punished success. A few noted that change initiatives were the first units of their organizations to be terminated.

It is hard to show performance improvement if performance is not measured objectively. It is nearly impossible to demonstrate increased productivity where unit costs are not accurately captured, even if the organization is fortunate to have a numerous units performing similar activities, or where appropriate financial targets have not been established. In the short run, it might be acceptable for the organization to take the change advocates at their word, especially where they have developed satisfactory benchmarks, and to reward them accordingly. Perhaps, as several reform unit representatives suggested, by allowing "initiatives that cause direct dollar savings ... to retain savings as an incentive to keep innovating." In the long run, however, the conceptual and practical shortcomings of organizational accounting and control systems may doom almost any serious attempt at wholesale management reform to failure.

Why has this been the case? The problem was clearly outlined by a Department Of Defense acquisition specialist interviewed, who noted, "Acquisition reform within DoD has made great strides in creating a new culture for program managers to execute the duties of their jobs." He then went on to say, "What is lacking is any visible significant financial reform—program managers are stripped of any accountability or sense of program success through the culture and reality of the spending process, reprogramming thresholds are too low; and the system is geared for short term results, not long term success." "Why," he asked, "has budget and financial reform not kept pace with acquisition reform?" He concluded, "If you are going to preach empowerment, why not apply that concept to the spending process as well and develop new measures of success for program managers?" (Jones & McCaffery, 2005).

One of the factors that works against consistent support for management effectiveness efforts in government is management turnover. Several of the reform unit representatives complained that their bosses changed every 2-3 years. This inhibits initiative. As one reform unit representative asked: "Why start something new when chances are it will be terminated by the next change of command?" Another representative then chimed in, saying, "We just had a change of leadership 12 months into the change process; the new CEO does not support the new environment—self-directed work teams—and plans to reorganize back to old traditional hierarchical structure." Management tenure also leads to short planning horizons. According to another reform unit representative, the bosses he has known, "are reluctant to buy-in to any change that will extend pass their tenure—they tend to look for a quick fix." Investments explicitly biased toward short-term wins and against projects with far higher net present values are more attractive.

Moreover, as a general rule, management teams do not move from assignment to assignment together. Rather, management teams are frequently little more than collections of strangers. The organization appears to treat individual managers like interchangeable parts, to be moved around willy-nilly from one slot to the next, without consideration for organizational performance or team cohesion. There may be good and sufficient reason for this style of personnel management where units have to respond quickly to crises, but for the two thirds of organization that provide support services, it makes little or no sense. Management turnover is especially costly to reform, not only because inexperienced managers tend to cling to what they know best—rules, regulations, standard operating procedures, but also because inexperienced managers are far less likely delegate authority and responsibility. If they do not know their subordinates, they will not trust their judgment. Moreover, if they know that they will not have to rely on their current subordinates in the future, they are unlikely to invest in subordinate employee development now.

Some of the reform unit representatives also complained about having to go to the agency that imposed a rule for relief. As one reform unit representative explained, "The process to secure waivers has built in gate keepers who continue to prevent each request getting a fair hearing." Another put it more pungently, "We have to go to the proud parent and tell them their baby is stupid and ugly ... it's no surprise that they don't want to hear that." This complaint has two versions: the first is that many of these agencies suffer from a "one size fits all" mentality and, as a consequence, are simply not as forthcoming as they might be; the second is that some of these agencies are threatened by change or are philosophically opposed to its basic thrust and are doing everything in their power to subvert it. It is in fact fairly common for CEO staff offices to forget that they are service centers, not mission centers, and to see the organization as means to their ends rather than the other way around. It is a nevertheless pathological response and should be avoided.

The "one size fits all" mentality is not really a bad thing where a unit undergoing management experimentation is collocated with another entity or at a higher level of the organization. In such instances, waivers create duplicate processes for the organizations that support both entities. The solution here lies in a no-fault policy that would automatically extend approved waivers to all the entities being serviced by the supporting organization, following an appropriate notice and comment period.

Many of the reform unit representatives complained about their inability to get relief from mandatory "in house" sources of supply. They noted that commercial suppliers could provide better quality service at a lower price for each of these services. One individual asserted that, "substituting commercial suppliers for in-house service providers would reduce total operating costs by 3%."

Such rules need closer attention. Clearly, rule waiver approval processes ought not to go through in-house suppliers where mandatory in-house supply rules are concerned. However, allowing units to purchase services elsewhere could, in a number of instances, unnecessarily raise costs due to captive purchasers. In this instance the problem seems to be a consequence of the prices charged by in-house suppliers. The standard internal transfer pricing rule where suppliers are not permitted to refuse service and customers are not permitted to go elsewhere, is: whichever is less, market price or cost—not whichever is more (Anthony & Govindarajan, 1998, chapter 6). If there is a difference, it should be charged to the policy that necessitated the mandatory rule in the first place or to general overhead—in which case the rule would likely get the scrutiny it deserves.

In addition, we would note one more barrier to significant management reform within public organizations. We were repeatedly struck by the squeamishness of even committed change advocates to shedding employees. They seemed to be genuinely averse to people losing jobs as a result of their efforts, even if those jobs were somewhere else in the organization. It would appear that large-scale productivity improvement depends to a considerable extent on the elimination of thousands of government jobs. The source of squeamishness is not clear. Perhaps some naively believe that supporting low productivity jobs will somehow lead to higher total employment levels in the United States, but this view cannot possibly be widespread. It seems more likely that it reflects a legitimate concern with the dislocation experienced by employees who lose their jobs. If this sentiment reflects a sincere desire to minimize the transition costs to the affected employees, it should be understood that the best way to minimize those costs would be to reduce while employment opportunities in the private sector are relatively more abundant. Regardless of the source of this sentiment, if management reform, including better business practices, is going to have more than symbolic value, it will have to be changed. It would be much better for everyone concerned if the positions that are lost are those which are less productive. However, management initiatives taken toward the end of the decade of the 1990s in the federal government lead us to question whether productivity was a genuine concern of leadership.

In assessing management effectiveness it is difficult to reconcile financial management priorities with organizational needs. The highest priorities of any system of accounting and control should be mission support. Top managers should demand the installation of governance arrangements and accounting systems that align individual and organization self-interest with the public interest (Jones & Bixler, 1992; Thompson & Jones, 1994). The lack of such a system affects outcomes and achievements in every area of defense policy, often profoundly. Instead, the focus of government efforts continues to be on compliance with legislative intent and fiduciary control. These are the by-products of a well-designed accounting and management control structure, but they do not replace it (Jones & McCaffery, 2005).

Government initiatives seem to focus first and foremost on ferreting out fraud and misuse of funds through increased emphasis and spending on audits of both small and large programs and amounts of expenditure. This approach is characteristic of a fundamental misunderstanding of how to create a more productive and cost-effective organization. First, with reference to increased audit effort, to paraphrase Allen Schick, "Some butterflies are caught, most elephants escape." Audits of low cost transactions inevitably cost more than they save. Second, this initiative reinforces an organization's worst management proclivity, to "manage to audit." Managing to audit means to manage reactively, while constantly looking backwards, rather than proactively, looking forward. This is the opposite of the types of management initiatives that have been successful in the private sector, that is, those that enhance productivity through use of strategic planning and marketing.

Spending federal government energy in amassing and reviewing vast amounts of largely paper transactions is perhaps one of the most wasteful of enterprises launched in government in the post-World war II era. It represents a control philosophy that cannot be cost-effective in an organization of the size and complexity of the U.S. government. Perhaps such a management approach would seem attractive to a student of divinity trying to keep thieves from stealing from the church "poor box." However, it is highly wasteful, even foolish, in sophisticated and complex organization.

This style of management demonstrates the essential managerial expertise bankruptcy in the leadership of the federal government. It may be characterized as an approach that says, in effect, if you cannot succeed at doing something well, do something bad. Therefore, if an organization cannot manage to perform its financial responsibilities effectively, put it to work auditing so that it can be shown to do something defensible, that is, use a "smoke-screen" tactic to hide incompetence. As one staff member put it, "Dilbert is alive and well in government! Nothing says 'I don't trust my employees' better than continuous audits."

Advocates of management to audit in government might point out in defense that it is always good to focus on fraud prevention. While this may be true from a political perspective, given how closely the executive is watched by congressional oversight committees, the general accountability office, inspectors general, and the media, these efforts may be characterized as "window dressing" (i.e., to look good while doing little of substance) in absence of support for more significant and effective management change. The U.S. federal government can be managed more effectively in the future.

CONCLUSIONS

This chapter has reviewed why organizations need to reengineer, how reengineering is supposed to be accomplished, and what reengineering is intended to accomplish. In reviewing the experience of the U.S. federal government we understand factors that both stimulate and retard reengineering initiatives. Many of these same factors affect other types of change in the same way. However, as explained in the next chapter, there is a dramatic distinction between change that is guided by strategic planning versus reengineering. The latter is applied within organizations primarily to increase efficiency. In contrast, strategic planning is something that takes place as organizations attempt to adapt more effectively to change in their environment, as we explore in the next chapter.

CHAPTER 6

IMPLEMENTING THE CONTINUOUS LEARNING CYCLE TO IMPROVE STRATEGIC PLANNING AND ORGANIZATIONAL PRODUCTIVITY

Reform to implement the cycle of continuous learning within an organization is perhaps the most ambitious initiative to be undertaken by officials and managers as a part of public management reform. The learning cycle requires strategic thinking and planning develop markets, services and products, and service delivery methods beyond what the organization has done in the past. Consequently, it presents the greatest challenge to the status quo of bureaucratic organizations. As we have explained, organizations can become more efficient through restructuring and work process engineering. However, mere efficiency is not what the public expects generally, or even wants most typically, from public sector organizations. The objectives of government and, therefore, of public sector organizations, should focus more on the provision of equity and service quality, however we may define these attributes, rather than efficiency per se. This is what public officials and service providers should emphasize most in attempting to respond to perceptions of public wants and needs.

In this chapter we accept that equity, effectiveness, and responsiveness are the legitimate and primary goals of government and governance. Our purpose is not to challenge the rationale for government participation in the economy or the incentives that cause elected officials to direct and guide public managers as they do in participative democracies. Rather, we put our effort on defining how public organizations may become more effective. We argue that to become more effective, public sector organizations must learn to adapt better and more quickly to citizen demands and preferences, and to other changes in their environments. In this regard, public organization need to develop better approaches to adaptation, and these approaches should be designed or should evolve to fit into overall organization strategy and long-range planning.

In essence, to accomplish the ends we seek in the public sector we argue that it is necessary to adopt a quick learning cycle approach that assesses and enables comprehensive changes in an organization's customer service orientation and what we term its service market strategy, particularly relative to competition or the threat of competition. This implies a transition for public bureaucracies that is essential for them to continue to fulfill their assigned missions, and in some cases, to survive in an ever changing, more competitive world. As part of operating in a long-range strategic planning orientation under conditions of competition, and perhaps of fiscal austerity, public organizations need to give greater attention to program outcomes, alternative service development, production and distribution methods, that is, to how they market their services to constituents. Improved public sector marketing as well as better accounting, as we detail in the next chapter, as components of better long-range strategic planning, are among the key ingredients to implementing the learning cycle through improved strategic planning.

Inevitably, implementing the learning cycle and strategic planning requires new approaches to thinking about the manner in which public organizations should be made to operate. Initially, an acceptance of strategic planning as something worth doing is needed—this chapter attempts to explain why it is essential. Second, elected officials and managers need to understand the definition of marketing in the public sector as something more than mere advertising and selling, that is, as simply adopting private sector techniques designed to develop and merchandise products. Part of the change in emphasis to a service market strategy in the public sector requires recognition of the importance of market research to define citizen/consumer preferences, demand attributes, attitudes, and behaviors. This information is vital for strategic thinking and planning. Attention to the various components of what in the private sector is termed the marketing mix (product, price, sales, and distribution) will result in better understanding of citizen demand for public services. Relationships between market research, program development, pricing, distribution, advertising, promotion, sales, and evaluation of public services and consumer behavior all is part of the strategic planning process and organizational adaptation to new markets as we define these initiatives. For example, the importance of research on citizen ability to pay should be part of any effort to establish or reevaluate tax and service pricing policies. Better information on citizen demand attributes (what it is exactly that citizens want from service providers in terms of what, when, where, how, etc.) should be seen as essential in policy formulation and setting of organizational objectives. The importance of learning more about market segmentation (according to citizen socioeconomic status and other variables) also has to be recognized so that services may be provided to the correct citizens at least cost for meeting their preference profiles, for example, quality/price expectation trade-offs where fees are charged directly to the public. Accompanying the acceptance of a service market strategy orientation must be an awareness of essential differences between private and public sector marketing in terms of its product versus service orientation, and the obvious consequences of the fact that often in the public sector there is no direct consumer payment for services rendered.

A service market strategy orientation in public organizations recognizes that because large portions of financial support come from governments instead of directly from consumers, greater attention is needed to what may be termed internal political marketing in contrast to the external consumer marketing focus of private sector organizations. Political marketing is an essential but often misunderstood component of the public budgetary process. Most public organizations engage in a considerable degree of marketing activity, although it is often poorly organized, not well-coordinated with other units of government, and badly executed.

The desire on the part of decision makers, whether elected officials or managers, for better information on constituent preferences should stimulate governments to develop new procedures to determine citizen attitudes toward specific types of public services—and how these services should be provided. Definition of public service market segmentation through survey research is a first step in improving responsiveness to service quality, price, distribution, and other citizen/constituent preferences. To acquire better information on citizen preferences, public sector officials must become more willing to invest in innovative information gathering and communication procedures, for example, from voting by mail to computer-assisted, interactive television, and telephone voting and opinion sampling systems.

Effort to improve market preference assessment creates new challenges to be overcome, including dealing with information overload and financing experimentation with new information, and communication technologies. Managing increased citizen participation in government decision making becomes more difficult in this context as well. Having more and better information about citizen preferences may make it more difficult to justify policy, programmatic, and budget decisions based upon equity considerations. Citizen preference, where they do not support equity objectives over obtaining private benefits, may tend to erode support for many services currently provided by governments on equity grounds. Debate over reform of social security in the United States reveals that many citizens want to manage their tax contributions to the system on their own in proprietary accounts. This preference challenges part of the redistributive rationale for establishing the system in the first place. Another example is found in recent U.S. experience with welfare reform. Public objection to the idea that it is the obligation of government to provide welfare services for an indefinite period of time, and fundamental disregard for public goods justifications for provision of some government services, appears to be implicit in citizen demand to limit government welfare expenditures. Such preferences, refracted in the dynamics of the political process, led the U.S. Congress and President Clinton to enact sweeping welfare reform in 1997. Changes in federal policy have caused major alteration of the welfare policies of state governments. In summary, the emphasis on results-oriented government and increased public sector responsiveness to citizen preferences brings new challenges and places greater pressure for political and managerial adaptation.

Over the next decade and beyond, it seems likely that governments the world over will continue to alter their patterns of services provision, modifying and expanding them in some cases, reducing the range of services they offer in others. In some cases, governments will surrender the provision of services they now provide to citizen groups, to nonprofit organizations and to the private sector. Some services simply may lapse, for better or worse. Under the learning cycle, we should expect continued evolution of alternative service development and delivery methods, ranging from means testing for all transfer payments to individuals to improve equity on one hand, to increased application of user fees and charges to generate revenue to pay for delivery of services with higher private benefit composition on the other. Concomitant with such changes should be a reorientation of the manner in which public financial resources are allocated. Approaches such as the voucher system to provide consumer-citizens with money or credit to spend for services delivered directly may improve the manner in which public demand, government marketing strategy (including pricing and other service distribution policies and procedures) are defined. Increases in the already prevalent use of private sector contracting, intergovernmental service provision arrangements, shared service contracting, innovative financing techniques for public works, new types of joint lease, and purchase agreements, and so forth, all are consistent with the adaptation to environmental change and increased competition characteristic of the context for the learning cycle.

In this chapter we argue for the implementation of a strategic service marketing orientation in the public sector. We advocate the application of what we term "the learning cycle" to enable more rapid adaptation to conditions of increased competition for public services. To explain what we mean by the learning cycle we first reach back into history to draw upon the example of a private firm, the Hudson's Bay Company (Milgrom & Roberts, 1992, pp. 6-9). In 1670, the king of England granted a royal charter to a firm called the Governor & Company of Adventurers of England Trading into Hudson's Bay, giving it the exclusive right to trade in most of what is today Canada. Now known as the Hudson's Bay Company, this firm is the world's oldest commercial entity. It almost did not survive due to failure to adapt to competition in the marketplace. Let us investigate why this almost happened and how failure was turned into success. An excursion into the nineteenth century will permit us to extract the lessons from this example applicable to adaptation in the public sector of the twenty-first century.

In the early 1800s, the Hudson's Bay Company was completely beaten by its rival, the North West Company. The North West Company was successful despite an overwhelming disadvantage—it was in violation of the law. Concealing its trespasses against the royal franchise forced it to operate through Montreal rather than by the shorter route to London through Hudson's Bay. This increased both North West Company's transportation costs and its working capital requirements—the Hudson's Bay Company could sell its furs within 6 months of buying the goods it traded for them; the North West Company faced a lag of 18 to 24 months. As a result, its logistical costs were nearly double those of the Hudson's Bay Company.

Organization was the primary ingredient of the North West Company success. Not only did it locate its trading posts closer to its customers, it also adopted a structure that motivated its members to serve the interests of the firm. The North West Company was a partnership with two classes of partners who shared in the profits of the organization. The senior, Montreal-based partners were responsible for financing, acquiring trade goods, and selling furs at the London auction. The wintering partners ran the trade in the field. The two groups met annually to exchange information and set policy, but operating decisions were left to the individual wintering partners on site, who were motivated by their partnership shares to respond to circumstances with effort and imagination. Other employees were chosen for their ability to adapt to the entrepreneurial organizational culture of the North West Company. They too were given real responsibility and were paid for performance. Outstanding performance led to full partnership and a share of the firm's profits. In contrast, the Hudson Bay Company was run as a rigid bureaucracy.

> Rules and controls from distant London circumscribed every action and decision of its employees in the field, leaving little responsibility for flexibly responding to emerging conditions. Innovation was discouraged or even punished, and performance was rewarded only by the possibility of someday gaining a promotion to the next rung of the bureaucratic ladder. Employees were chosen for their ability to withstand the excruciating boredom of their service on the frozen bay and for their willingness to work cheaply and follow orders. They were disciplined by floggings for breaking the company's myriad regulations. (Milgrom & Roberts, 1992, p. 8)

In 1809, a new set of owners acquired the Hudson's Bay Company. They responded to North West Company's challenge by mimicking their rival. They moved the Hudson's Bay Company's trading posts inland to compete directly with the North Westers, decentralized authority within the organization, instituted a performance-based profit sharing plan, and recruited a new class of employees who would fit with the aggressive, entrepreneurial organization they were trying to build. Ten years later the North West Company was beaten. In 1820 the two companies merged under terms that gave control to the Hudson's Bay Company.

This story illustrates a number of points: the importance of staffing, of measuring and rewarding performance, the significance of getting close to the market, and the value of aligning organizational structure with one's product/market strategy. Most importantly, it shows the critical importance of time in organizational competition (Dixit & Nalebuff, 1991, pp. ix, 3). Because organizational competition takes place in real time, success often depends upon the ability to perform a series of steps (the learning cycle) faster than the competition. The North West Company's wintering partners could promptly respond to new conditions and situations. Before 1809, the Hudson's Bay Company made its operating decisions in London and communication between Hudson's Bay and London was extremely slow. The lag between the reporting of information about the situation in the field and receipt of a response from the management in London was frequently as long as 15 months. Not surprisingly the Hudson's Bay Company's actions were frequently inept and it was consistently bested by its rival.

That organizational competition is time based is an extremely important point and one that is increasingly recognized in the management literature (Blackburn, 1991; Meyer, 1993; Nonaka, 1990; Stalk & Hout, 1990; Thomas, 1990; Vesey, 1991). Senge (1990), for example, argues that the ability to learn faster than one's rivals is the key to competitive success (p. 4). Christopher Meyer (1993) observes that the product-development cycle is essentially a learning cycle or learning loop and concludes that faster teams and organizations outperform their competitors because they have more complete opportunities to learn (p. 31). However, those who write about time-based competition often focus on internal process improvements—on reducing product development time (Stalk & Hout, 1990), on reducing manufacturing time (Meyer, 1993), on reducing red tape (Hammer, 1990), or on improving internal communications. In so doing, they imply that organizational competition is primarily a game against nature. This means that material factors predominate.

However, the story of the Hudson's Bay Company reminds us that organizational competition is not merely a game against nature. Market competition is a struggle between rivals for dominance and survival. And it is also a game in which defeat is often "deeply rooted in the loser's strategy" (Bower, 1990, p. 49). In real-time strategic games, the learning cycle is of critical importance. Under our definition it consists of four steps. The first of these steps is observation. Organizations start by observing their positions, the environment, and their competition. Next, on the basis of observation, each orients itself to the situation and then decides on a course of action. Finally, each puts the decision into effect; that is, it acts. Then an organization checks to see if its action has changed the market situation. Our description of what we term the learning cycle of observation-orientation-decision-action and its origins is based on the work of Boyd, as we will note, and that of Fallows (1981, pp. 26-34) and Smith (1985).

The significance of the learning cycle as we define it, consisting of observation-orientation-decision-action, was first noted during the mid-1970s by John Boyd, a captain in the United States Air Force assigned to study air-to-air combat during the Korean conflict. American aviators were especially successful in Korea, achieving a 10-to-1 success ratio against their opponents. Why had this occurred Boyd wondered? The first possibility was that Americans simply had better airplanes. However, as it turned out, by most measures of aircraft quality, the American F-86 was inferior to its Korean War opponent, the MiG-15. The MiG-15 could climb and accelerate faster and turn quicker than the F-86. Nevertheless, the F-86 had two advantages over the MiG-15. First, its pilot could see out better. Second, it had quick, high-powered hydraulic *controls*, and the MiG did not. This meant that, although the MiG could perform many individual maneuver activities—turning, climbing, accelerating—better than the F-86, the F-86 could switch from one activity to another much more quickly than the MiG.

Using these two advantages, American pilots developed tactics that forced the MiG into a series of maneuvers. Because the pilot of the F-86 could see how the situation had changed and could switch faster to another activity, at each maneuver the F-86 gained a beat on its opponent. With each switch, therefore, the MiG's responses were less appropriate to the situation, until they were so inappropriate that the MiG was exposed to destruction. Often it appeared that the MiG pilot realized what was happening to him and panicked, which made the American pilot's job all the easier.

Boyd then turned to ground combat to see if circumstances paralleled those of the air war over Korea. He found a similar pattern. One side presented the other with a sudden, unexpected challenge or series of challenges to which the other side could not adjust in a timely manner. As a result, the side with the slower response was defeated, and it was often defeated at a small cost to the victor. Moreover, the losing side was frequently materially stronger than the winner and, in many cases, the same sort of panic and paralysis the MiG pilots had shown in Korea seemed to occur.

What do the winners in these cases have in common? Boyd's answer was that they consistently went through the learning cycle faster than their competitors and, thereby, gained tremendous advantage. By the time opponents acted, they were doing something different. With each cycle, the slower side's actions were less apt and it fell farther behind. This is also what happened in many of history's most decisive battles. Hannibal went through the learning cycle faster than the Romans at Cannae and won one of history's greatest tactical victories. The Germans beat the French in 1940 and the Japanese beat the British in Malaya in 1942 because they went through the learning cycle faster than their opponents. In some of these cases, a single, sudden action was enough. In others, a series of cycles was required. In every case, the critical competition was in learning time, and the faster side won.

If one of the rivals in a market can consistently go through this learning cycle faster than the other, it gains a tremendous advantage. By the time the slower side acts, the faster is doing something different from what it had observed or anticipated, and, while it may benefit from a lucky or inspired guess, more often its actions will be inappropriate to the situation. With each The learning cycle, the slower side's actions will tend to become less apt. Even though the slower side strives to do something that will work, each of its actions is less efficacious than its predecessor and the slower side falls farther and farther behind. Frequently, it panics. Ultimately—and often suddenly—it breaks down.

That is precisely what happened in story of the Hudson's Bay Company. Initially, the North West Company's organizational design gave it a huge advantage in learning cycle time. Not surprisingly its responses were often far more appropriate to the situation than were those of its rival. In the end, the owners of Hudson's Bay Company panicked and unloaded it at a price of twenty cents on the dollar. Once the aggressive new owner-managers and their allies purged the Hudson's Bay Company of its organizational handicap, it quickly overtook its rival. Its inherent logistical edge meant that it could go through the learning cycle faster than the North West Company. The 10 years that followed witnessed fierce and even bloody competition between the two rivals, but the advantage lay with the Hudson's Bay Company, and the ultimate outcome of the struggle was never really in doubt.

The importance of observation and orientation to the development of a sound organizational strategy is highlighted in a survey in *The Economist* ("A Guide to Better Buying," 1993). It stated:

> change is not unique to the computer industry. But its pace, and the fact that it is happening in so many areas at once, may be. So to succeed, or even to survive, computer firms now have to put an inordinate amount of effort into ... watching other firms ... [and] monitoring technology. Firms must keep a close eye on the actions of others, even those with whom they have no formal alliance or do not compete. Most firms depend upon those in other layers of the industry to succeed. If a firm stumbles in one layer it can deal a mortal blow to firms *in other layers.* (pp. 14-15)

The ability to perform the learning cycle faster and more appropriately than the competitors is the crux of success in organizational competition. We must inquire why the ability to perform the learning cycle strategically in a competitive market "game" faster and more appropriately than competitors is of paramount importance to survival and organizational vitality.

Entrenched services or products have several competitive advantages. First, they are familiar to customers. Later entrants must overcome consumer awareness and reputation if they are to capture market share. Lacking a superior service or product or a significant cost advantage, this is hard to do. Early entrants also have production experience. Organizationally they are, therefore, likely to have moved farther down the learning curve and to have lower costs than later entrants. In some cases, the initial entrant grows large before potential competitors can act. Because it has already spread its fixed costs over many units of output, its per-unit cost is lower than that which any follower could hope to soon achieve. Moreover, getting to the market first often means that the early entrant can make mutually advantageous arrangements with suppliers, giving it preferential access to parts and raw materials. Similar arrangements are possible with service providers who interact directly with the public. These arrangements can be substantial barriers to entry on the part of potential competitors (Carlton & Perloff, 1990, p. 181).

Knowledge of the early entrant's competitive advantages is often enough to deter potential competitors. As Porter (1980) explained:

> Good defense is creating a situation in which competitors, after [considering the factors] described *above or actually attempting a* move, will conclude that a move is unwise. As with offensive moves, defense can be achieved by forcing competitors to back down after a battle. However, the most effective defense is to prevent the battle altogether. (p. 98)

The very fact that the initial entrant has made the first move gives it a major advantage. It has already taken a position, made investments, and acquired product or service-specific assets (that is, sunk costs) that make it unlikely that it will exit the industry without a fight. Moreover, this commitment gives the entrenched entity an incentive to spend more money to defend its position than potential competitors are willing to spend to take it away from them.

This is not to say that attacking an entrenched service or product is impossible. Organizational competition in which fast-moving, fast-thinking entities isolate and dominate a stationary opponent demonstrates this fact. For example, where competition is dominated by technological advances, by anticipating future developments a fast-moving, fast-thinking organization can surround the dominant service or product with an impenetrable barrier and leave it to wither and die. Obviously, however, the secret of success in such an attack lies in moving much faster than the opposition, which requires either an exceptionally complacent opponent, deception that prevents the defender from observing or understanding the attacker's moves, or a significant advantage in the part of the attacker (Porter, 1980, pp. 95-98; see, however, Fudenburg & Tirole, 1986). It is also a fact that organizations make fundamental errors in observation.

The point is that an entrenched organization can counterattack employing a variety of maneuvers involving price, product or service, promotion, location and other attributes of the marketing mix. Owing to adjustment costs, other things being equal, the more quickly followers try to enter a market, the higher their costs (Alchian, 1959). With respect to pricing, where this option is available in the public sector, this means that the entrenched organization has the option of following a passive pricing policy, treating its hard-won monopoly as a cash cow and milking it, in which case, it will start by charging a high price for its service or product. Ultimately, subsequent entrants will erode the entrenched entity's market share and gradually force it to lower its price to the competitive level. The speed of this process will depend upon its head start, the height of the barriers facing potential entrants, and the initial price. Because it has an interest in deterring entrants, the entrenched organization may set a lower price than it would if it simply ignored the future. But, because revenues today are worth more than future revenues, its managers might instead choose to "take the money" in the short-term. Alternatively, through the creation of advantages that are not easily copied, an early leader can try to preempt potential competitors.

The organizational strategy literature is full of advice about what to observe how to orient one's organization and its services or products with respect both to the market and the competition so as to exploit fully one's strengths and mask one's weaknesses (Porter, 1980, pp. 88-125, 191-298), and how to choose a course of action (Porter, pp. 299-357). Much of the rest of management literature is concerned with the effective implementation of these actions. This is certainly the basic thrust of managerial control. Unfortunately, this literature has almost nothing to say about the importance of learning cycle time, at least not explicitly, let alone about how to speed it up. Fortunately, however, there is nothing arcane about the means by which an organization reduces the learning cycle time. The secret of moving faster than one's opponent lies in reducing friction through simple, reliable administrative structures and the use of flexible tools that can be adapted rapidly in response to changing tactics.

Many managerial innovations are justified in terms of the contribution they make to organizational reliability and adaptability, including decentralization, employee empowerment, principle-centered leadership, flexible manufacturing, cycle-time burdening, and transaction cost accounting. Most students of management believe, for example, that the effectiveness of large, complex organizations improves when authority is delegated down into the organization along with responsibility. Decisions are then made by those with the most pertinent knowledge of the situation and with the highest stake in their outcome. What is novel is justifying the adoption of innovations such as decentralization in terms of their contribution to reducing the learning cycle and, therefore, their direct contribution to organizational strategy.

We have argued using the Hudson's Bay example how centralization is inimical to fast learning cycling and that decentralization is one key to successful adaptation. Under centralization, subordinates must do what they are told to do. If they observe that the situation has somehow changed, they must report the changed situation up through the chain of command and wait for new instructions. Often, by the time they arrive, the situation has again changed, and the instructions are useless. Decentralization and employee empowerment permits those who are best situated to observe a new situation to act upon it. Besides, centralized organizations often treat people as if they were machines. However, as we have noted, machines are rarely a source of competitive advantage, since the material inputs used by organizations, the equipment and technology, the functional skills and organizational designs that are available to one tend to be equally available to all. People are a source of competitive advantage only where they contribute their intelligence and initiative to the organization, that is, where they are treated like people.

There is also evidence to suggest that decentralizing along service or project or program rather than functional lines can increase organizational speed and flexibility, especially in the process of developing new products. According to Takeuchi and Nonaka (1989):

> emphasis on speed and flexibility calls for a different approach for managing new product development. Under the old approach, a product development process moved like a relay race, with one group of functional specialists passing the baton to the next group. The project went sequentially from phase to phase: concept development, feasibility testing, product design, process development, pilot production, and final production.... Under the new approach, the development process emerges from the constant interaction of a hand-picked multidisciplinary team whose members work together from start to finish. Rather than moving in highly structured stages, the process is born out of the team members' interplay. The shift from a linear to an integrated approach encourages trial and error and challenges the status quo, and it stimulates new kinds of learning and thinking within the organization at different levels and functions. (pp. 85-86)

Many fast-cycle time theorists argue that all jobs should be designed around objectives or outcomes instead of single functions—that functional specialization and sequential execution are inherently inimical to fast cycle time. Hammer (1990), for example, claims that modern data bases, expert systems, and telecommunications networks provides many, if not all, of the benefits that once made administrative centralization and specialization of administrative functions such as reporting, accounting, purchasing, or quality assurance (economies of scale, high levels of coordination, and standardization) attractive, without sacrificing any of the benefits of decentralization. Meyer (1993, p. 49; see also Stalk & Hout, 1990) goes even further. He argues that not only organizations should be made up of interdisciplinary task forces or project teams, but that team members must be located in direct physical proximity to each other. This approach is consistent with what Jack Welch put into practice at General Electric later.

We agree that sequential execution is often inimical to fast cycle time, especially where task performance involves multiple, interdependent activities that have to be carried out simultaneously. However, there is more than one way to coordinate parallel activities. The military's Joint Tactical Information Distribution System, for example, ties specialized military units and maneuver elements into a single real-time, spatially structured information system that permits activities to be coordinated as they are carried out (Coakley, 1992).

A number of private sector firms have experimented with a similar approach to the coordination of parallel activities. Like the military, they use powerful computer programs to chart all workflows within an organization, to keep track of progress being made at each stage of each internal transaction, and to prod tardy participants into action, thereby encouraging employees to take the initiative and to coordinate their activities amongst themselves. For want of a better term, this approach might be described as "virtual proximity." According to *The Economist* (1993, p. 80), virtual proximity "has helped IBM trim its workforce at the Austin plant from 1,100 to 423; increase its range of products from 19 to 85; cut the time taken to develop new products from more than two years to eight months; and shrink the average manufacturing cycle from 7.5 to 1.5 days."

Organizational culture and values including building a shared vision of the future (Senge, 1990; Sergiovanni, 1992) also increases organizational speed and flexibility. By getting employees at every level to adopt the organization's external goals and purposes as their personal goals and values, a shared vision helps employees to orient themselves to new situations and to decide on a course of action that will serve the interests of the organization.

How does this process work? Our best examples in the literature are those from the private sector. For example, in many Japanese firms, goals and purposes are inculcated by everything the organization does— from starting the workday by singing the company song, through wearing uniforms, sharing onerous tasks between workers and management alike, and dispensing rewards and incentives. On a day-to-day basis Japanese firms try to get their employees to evaluate everything they do to in terms of the overall goals and purposes of the firm. Their employees still have individual jobs, but they are expected to use their intelligence and initiative to work within and beyond those jobs to serve the organization's interests.

Peters and Waterman (1982, pp. 38-39) use the following example to demonstrate the benefits of shared vision. In their fable, an American bank is acquired by a Japanese bank. The Japanese bank sent over a new management team that explained the parent company's values and goals to its new employees. At first, the Americans were mystified. They expected detailed, specific instructions, not pep talks. Morale dropped and their productivity plummeted. But the Japanese were patient. They kept on explaining company goals and values and continued trying to get the employees to understand that they, not management, were supposed to figure out how to accomplish those goals. Finally, some of the bolder employees took the initiative to act on behalf the company's interests. Their tentative initiatives were recognized and applauded, even when they weren't always successful. Ultimately, everyone caught on and the bank's performance soared. What this example omits is that the bank's employees were highly skilled professionals. In most cases, it is necessary to do more than merely explain the organization's values and goals to employees. A high degree of education and training also are needed to teach employees what to do and how to do it.

It is also worth mentioning that personnel stability helps organizations react to and anticipate change. Education and training will not pay off for the organization if the employees that are trained leave or, even worse, if management moves them willy-nilly around the organization. Moreover, strangers do not work well together; sometimes they do not work at all. If people do not know each other, they won't trust each other. They will not count on each other for support, and they may not even care what others think about them, in which case they are unlikely to contribute their intelligence and their initiative to the organization. Additional views on this topic are provided in chapter 7 where we analyze motivation and productivity more closely.

Another attribute distinguishing organizations that adapt quickly to new or changing market conditions is flexibility. Flexible service or product development or redevelopment is usually justified in terms of enhanced productivity and product quality, but it too can help to speed up the learning cycle. The greatest advantage of flexible development is that it reduces both the time it takes to move a service or product from concept to market and the cost penalty associated with hastening the date of first delivery. It thereby increases the likelihood that an attack or a counterattack will succeed. Flexible development and delivery also tends to reduce if not eliminate the competitive advantage that accrues to organizational scale, one of the main advantages possessed by entrenched organizations.

For example, during the 1950s and 1960s, General Motors (GM) was the dominant firm in the American automobile industry. Lower per-unit costs were the principal source of GM's market power. GM's production volume allowed it to use less labor per-unit of output than either of its domestic rivals, Ford and Chrysler. Furthermore, GM could profitably accommodate union demands for higher wages, because, under the CIO's system of pattern bargaining, wage increases granted by one of the big three auto makers had to be met by the rest of the industry, and, since higher wages increased GM's unit costs less than those of its rivals, they actually served to reinforce its cost advantage—the main source of its market power. U.S. Steel was evidently similarly situated during that period. In both industries, tacit collusion between the dominant firm and the union evidently led to far higher wage and benefit levels than in other American manufacturing industries.

According to the logic of international comparative advantage, this is one reason why the automobile and steel industries were especially vulnerable to foreign competition (Niskanen, 1982, Crandall, 1981 & 1986). It wasn't until Ford and Chrysler found ways to lower their break-even levels, in part by following the precepts of flexible production, pricing, distribution and delivery (in other words, throughout their marketing), that they were able to get out from under the dominance of GM, and in the case of Ford, surpass it. Approximately the same thing happened in the steel industry—highly flexible minimills thrived where giants collapsed. Size and scale advantages may be overtaken through greater flexibility and adaptability.

Activity accounting, explained in the chapter that follows, also turns out to be essential for fast learning cycle implementation. Building state-of-the-art, flexible facilities, in which economies of scope replace economies of scale, reduces labor's direct role in the service or product development process. This means that controlling overhead costs, including procurement costs, product development cost, and setup and rework, is now more important than ever before to organizational survival and success. Consequently, many organizations have modified their managerial cost accounting systems to focus the attention of responsibility center managers, marketing and service development teams, and especially service or product designers and engineers on controlling overheads.

Two concepts have been critical to this effort. These are cycle-time burdening and the recognition of transaction costs. Adoption to these concepts also speeds up the ability to perform the learning cycle by increasing flexibility and reducing service or product complexity and in some cases directly by reducing processing time designed into the service or product. Consequently, systems intended to affect the internal strategy of an organization can also play a critical role in its external market strategy. Activity-based cost systems were designed to motivate improvements in the speed and flexibility in the service or product development process. The goal of the system is to reduce the number of unique components in services or products.

Cooper and Turney (1990) described how activity-based cost systems were designed to motivate improvements in the speed and flexibility in the manufacturing processes of three business firms: the Portable Instruments Division at Techtronix, Hewlett-Packard's Network Division, and

Zytec. The goal of the system at Techtronix was to reduce the number of unique components in their products, thereby reducing parts inventories and ordering costs as well as simplifying the manufacturing process. Hewlett-Packard took a similar approach with respect to procurement costs. It split these overheads into two pools: one related to the number of assemblies and the other to the number of parts. The costs of production planning, product logistics, product specification, and service scheduling were allocated to individual products based upon the number of assemblies they required; purchasing, storage (including space, heating, and insurance), parts specification, and material planning costs were allocated using the number of parts they required. This information was provided to product designers to influence them to minimize the number of assemblies and parts needed to make the products they designed. At Zytec overheads were pooled and allocated to products based upon the time elapsed from project initiation to shipment of the finished product, providing a direct and unambiguous incentive to reduce the factors that cause cycle time to be long. Time-based performance measures are needed to get people within an organization to take cycle-time seriously and to manage it efficiently.

Information gathering and processing also are critical to fast cycle learning. Teece (1993) reminds us that there is considerable empirical support for the notion that organization routines for gathering and processing information, linking customer wants and design choices, and coordinating activities are main determinants of competitive advantage, not plant or capital investment (Clark & Fujimoto, 1991; Garvin, 1988). At the same time he acknowledges that firms generally lack the organizational capacity to develop these tacit, firm-specific assets quickly. Longer-range asset planning and acquisition is needed to provide the organization with the capability to effectively employ information management to strategic advantage.

The point of the preceding discussion is that the steps of the learning cycle—observing, orienting, deciding, acting—are themselves processes contained within an overall strategic market and organizational approach to competition. They are amenable to the standard rules of process reengineering improvement as detailed in the previous chapter: design jobs around outcomes instead of individual tasks; have information producers process it and have the people within the organization who need the output of a process carry it out; capture information only once and at its source; coordinate parallel activities during their performance, not after they are completed; and, build control into the job design. Then, once an appropriate structure is in place, the key is practice.

Does this mean that all the organizations are equally capable of minimizing learning cycle time? If so it might be concluded that, aside from windfalls owing to good luck and barring self-imposed handicaps on the part of one's competitors, learning cycle time cannot be a consistent source of competitive advantage or organizational success. There is some truth to this inference, but its truth is somewhat paradoxical. Process improvement usually implies routinization—standardization of one's responses and behavioral repertoire. Routinization is ultimately inimical to successful service-market tactics because routine behavior is predictable behavior. Rigid formulas and recipes can be identified, anticipated, and defeated. If one cannot surprise one's opponents, one cannot present them with difficult situations faster than they can deal with them. Pascale (1984) reminds us, for example, of the success the Japanese have had in defeating routine strategies:

> While they do not reject ideas such as the experience curve or portfolio strategy outright they regard them as a stimulus to perception. They have often ferreted out the "formula" of their concept-driven American competitors and exploited their inflexibility.... Yamaha plowed ahead and destroyed Baldwin's dominance [in pianos]. YKK's success against Talon (a Textron subsidiary) and Honda's outflanking of Harley-Davidson (a former AMF subsidiary) in the motorcycle field provide parallel illustrations. All three cases involved American conglomerates wedded to a portfolio concept that had classified pianos, zippers, and motorcycles as mature businesses to be harvested rather than nourished and defended. (p. 48)

Carl von Clausewitz, the greatest philosopher of war and one of the greatest writers on strategy and tactics who ever lived, reserved his special scorn for thinkers who reduce the reciprocal action of conflicting wills to the clarity and precision of a geometric exercise and for the misguided leaders who have followed their advice into bloody disaster. According to von Clausewitz, there is no action—no strategy or tactic—that cannot be undone by prompt counteraction. The problem lies in seeing through "the fog of war" and in overcoming its frictions. Furthermore, given the uncertainty inherent to the clash of human wills, a bold decision made in time for aggressive execution is often better than one that is more elegant but too late.

CONCLUSIONS

The key to implementing the cycle of constant learning in an organization is integration of this approach into the strategic planning process. Unless this integration occurs, improved organizational learning likely will lead to improved efficiency but not necessarily improved competitiveness in the government or the economy. However, organizational leaders should be suspicious of those who reduce service market strategies and tactics to a set of formulas and who "preach" rules that guarantee success. That is not our purpose here. Speeding up the learning cycle will not guarantee success. In the best of circumstances, observation may be inaccurate, orientation faulty, decisions wrong, and resultant actions clumsy or ill-timed. Furthermore, increasing the efficiency of the processes of observing, orienting, deciding, and acting will not defeat an inspired hunch that grasps at a stroke the essential truth of the situation. It is nevertheless pretty good advice that managers ignore at their peril. Adopting the learning organization approach through strategic planning before it becomes widespread can bring success for a time, which is all most managers can expect. We argue that reducing learning and response time to translate new information about markets and consumer demand and preferences leading to faster service and product redevelopment is critical to the learning cycle and successful strategic planning that embraces this approach in both the private and public sectors.

CHAPTER 7

MATCHING INSTITUTIONAL STRUCTURE TO STRATEGIC PLANNING AND POSITIONING

Matching institutional structure to strategic planning and positioning consists of changing organizational structure to match the service market strategy developed under strategic planning. In essence it is implementation of the strategic plan and market strategy adopted by the organization. The concept is straightforward: match the organization structure to the new strategy to obtain desired goals and to motivate management and employees. Matching institutional structure to strategic positioning requires diagnosis of the strategy-structure mismatch where it exists in the organization and adaptation to create different structures and alternatives that may be applied under different conditions. Matching institutional structure to strategic positioning should result in a contingent organizational structure consistent with emerging market opportunities and the strategy developed under the learning cycle. Matching institutional structure to strategic positioning has serious implications for accounting and budgeting of the organization, for example, different types of accounting and budgets should be employed for different purposes. Matching institutional structure to strategic positioning seeks to create a "fast cycle time" organization to respond quickly to changes in the market and constituent/stakeholder environment. In this sense it is a direct extension of the learning cycle. Matching institutional structure to strategic positioning, in essence, is the implementation of the learning cycle strategy. However where the learning cycle is concerned with changes in how the organization operates in the external market, matching institutional structure to strategic positioning focuses on change within the organization.

The initial step in matching institutional structure to strategic positioning is establishing a responsibility structure within the organization, a topic we explore in depth later in this chapter. Establishing the responsibility structure requires clarifying and delineating the role of budgeting, cost analysis and costing systems, and the use of cost information in the organization. Understanding cost analysis and costing systems, in turn, permits us to specify how responsibility budgeting is used to guide matching institutional structure to strategic positioning initiatives. Implementation of responsibility budgeting causes us to rethink the precepts of organizational structure. Thus, initially we need to understand the nature and use of budgeting and control systems in contemporary public organizations. In developing this understanding we point out some of the problems with budget and control practices in the U.S. federal government, and the directions for correcting these pathologies.

THE KEY ROLE OF IMPROVED SYSTEMS FOR ACCOUNTING, BUDGETING AND MANAGEMENT CONTROL

Many public organizations do not employ capital, operating, and cash budgeting and accrual accounting in a way that conforms to the organization's responsibility structure. However, under matching institutional structure to strategic positioning, accounting, and budgeting must serve this structure to make the responsibility system fully congruent with and accountable to the responsibility structure. Establishing this linkage enables analysis of the relationships between the organization's goals, and its inputs, outcomes and results. Linking budgeting and accounting to the responsibility structure establishes the means by which the organization controls itself, that is, the management control system.

The attributes of capital budgeting and management control systems used by well-run organizations in the private sector are similar in some ways to those used in the public sector but the differences are great and in several respects decisive. In the first place, most well-managed businesses employ multiple budgets: capital budgets, operating budgets, and cash budgets. In this context, capital budgeting is concerned with all policy decisions—that is, all decisions that have long-term consequences for the organization, including those governing operations and not just those involving the acquisition of plant and equipment. The time horizon of a capital budget is the life of the decision; its focus is the discounted present-value of the alternative in question. Operating budgeting is concerned with the behavior of responsibility center managers. It seeks to insure that they carry out the organization's policies as efficiently and effectively as possible. Consequently, it comprehends both outlay and responsibility budgeting and accounting, a topic we delve into in detail subsequently in this chapter. Its time horizon is the operating cycle of the responsibility center in question, perhaps a month or even a week in the case of cost and revenue centers, usually longer where investment and profit centers are concerned. Its focus is on the performance of the responsibility center, outputs produced and resources consumed—where possible these are measured in current dollars. The cash budget is concerned with providing liquidity when needed at a minimum cost. Its time horizon is the cash-flow cycle, the temporal pattern of receipts and outlays experienced by the entity.

In contrast, many governments have a single "budget." In the U.S. government, the only problem the federal budget and financial control system is well-designed to solve is the liquidity problem, since the U.S. government's cash flow cycle has a period of 1 year and its accounts are maintained on cash as well as an obligation and a purchases basis. Paradoxically, however, liquidity is not a serious problem for the U.S. government.

Furthermore, private-sector capital budgeting is selective, usually concerned only with new initiatives, and then only with changes in policy that are expected to yield benefits for longer than a year. In the language of public administration, one might even say that private sector capital budgeting is radically incremental (Wildavsky, 1966, pp. 96-98). In contrast, the U.S. government's requests for budget authority are absolutely comprehensive. They reflect all planned asset acquisitions, including current assets—assets that are acquired and consumed during the fiscal year in support of continuing policies—as well as all long-term assets that will be consumed over an extended period, including those which replace existing assets that have been lost or worn out (Wildavsky 1964; Wildavsky, 1966; Wildavsky 1988; Wildavsky & Hammond, 1965).

In the second place, private-sector capital budgeting tends to be a continuous process. Most well-managed firms always have an array of policy proposals under development. The decision to go ahead with a proposal is usually made only once, when the proposal is ripe, and is usually reconsidered only if the investment turns sour. In most cases, the proposal's champion within the organization is given the authority and the responsibility for implementing it (Bower, 1970). In contrast, budgeting in the U.S. government tends to be repetitive; all programs are reconsidered annually on the basis of a rigid schedule. New initiatives must be supported by elaborate analytical justifications and reviewed and approved by hundreds of people all along the line from the lowest to the highest echelon. The purpose of this repetitious review is evidently that, if one keeps hammering away at them, bad decisions will be defeated by attrition. The reality is that this process leads either to paralysis by analysis or to endless logrolling among the interested parties at every level. Moreover, the new initiative's principal advocate is seldom assigned responsibility for its implementation, although according to Vincent Davis (1973), this is precisely how most effective innovations are carried out. Instead, responsibility is usually given to someone else, often in an entirely different administrative unit than the one championing adoption of the proposal.

Another difference is that the objective of capital budgeting in the private sector is the identification of all policy options with positive net-present values, since in the absence of real limits on the availability of cash or managerial attention, the welfare of a firm's shareholders will be maximized by the implementation of all projects offering positive net-present values. Strategic planning in the U.S. federal government, as it is being implemented under the requirements of the Government Performance and Results Act (GPRA) mimics private-sector capital budgeting in that it shows the future implications of current decisions, albeit in a somewhat truncated manner. Moreover, many of these decisions are informed by cost-benefit and cost-effectiveness analysis. But nothing in the government's requests for budget authority depicts the future implications of current decisions in present-value terms. Otherwise Congress would not routinely stretch out weapons systems acquisition programs, often thereby increasing program cost by as much as 60%, to reduce the deficit and to avoid borrowing at interest rates of 10% or less. In content, the budget requests transmitted by the president to Congress are more like pro forma cash budgets than anything else found in the private sector. The biggest difference, however, between the budget authority given to federal departments and agencies and the capital budgets approved by top management in the private sector lies in its relationship to departmental management control structures.

Management control is supposed to be a process for motivating and inspiring people, especially subordinate managers, to serve the policies and purposes of the organizations to which they belong. It is only secondarily a process for detecting and correcting unintentional performance errors and intentional irregularities, such as theft or misuse of resources.

In most well-managed businesses the primary instrument of management control is operational budgeting, which embraces both the formulation of operating budgets and their execution. In operating-budget formulation, an organization's policies, the results of all past capital budgeting decisions, are converted into terms that correspond to the domains of administrative units and their managers (Anthony & Young, 1988, p. 19). In budget execution, operations are monitored and subordinate managers evaluated and rewarded.

The government's budgeting system does this, of course. But there are critical differences between program decision making and budgeting in departments and standard practices in well-run firms. The federal appropriations process produces a detailed spending or resource-acquisition plan that must be scrupulously executed just as it was approved. In contrast, operating budgets in the private sector are remarkably sparing of detail, often consisting of no more than a handful of quantitative performance standards. This difference reflects the efforts made by firms to decentralize authority and responsibility down into their organizations. Decentralization means giving departmental managers the maximum feasible authority—or, in the alternative, subjecting them to a minimum of constraints. Hence, decentralization requires operating budgets to be stripped to the minimum needed to motivate and inspire subordinates to maximize their contribution to the organization as a whole. Most large decentralized firms produce fairly comprehensive operating reports describing many relevant aspects of the performance of their component departments and managers, but only a few of these are used to evaluate operations and to motivate subordinates. Ideally, the operating budget of a decentralized organization would contain a single number, goal, or performance target (e.g., a sales quota, a unit cost standard, or a profit or return-on-investment target) for each administrative unit.

In summary, effective decentralization is possible in the private sector in part because capital budgeting and operational budgeting are treated as related but distinct processes. An organization's responsibility budget should reflect its commitments. Thus, a decision to invest resources in a new initiative should be reflected in the operating budgets of all the responsibility centers affected. The controller should revise operating budgets to reflect the increases in organizational performance that justified the decision to go ahead with the initiative. Controllers should specify the increases in performance expected of each administrative unit or responsibility center, revise evaluative standards to take account of anticipated improvements, and assign responsibility for realizing them. But the purpose and the content of capital and operating budgets—deciding and doing—are supposed to be kept distinct. Finally, for the responsibility structure and budget and accounting systems to serve the needs of the overall organization, they must be embedded within the management control system.

It is essential that the organization selects the appropriate control system relative to its internal requirements, the demands placed upon it by its sponsors (the Congress in the example of the U.S. federal government), and the nature of the market in which it seeks to compete (for a detailed discussion of alternative control structures and the criteria that should be used in deciding between them, see Thompson & Jones, 1994, chapter 6). In any case, it is inarguable that the U.S. federal government and numerous other public organizations overuse before-the-fact controls —rules and regulations—when other governance mechanisms would be more appropriate.

COST ANALYSIS AND COSTING SYSTEMS

One of the biggest needs of governments worldwide is to be able to perform cost analysis and to use modern activity-based costing systems. Obviously, better cost information is necessary to carry out make-or-buy decisions, but that is not the most important use for such a system. Rather, adequate costing and cost accounts are needed to implement a sound responsibility budgeting system. The lack of a sound responsibility budgeting system is by far the greatest mismatch between control system design and circumstances that we have observed in the U.S. federal government. We also think it likely that such a system would show that many of the activities performed by the government, especially overhead staff, support, and administrative control activities, are essentially unproductive and could be contracted out or eliminated.

In attempting to understand cost and cost behavior it is important to recognize that economists and accountants mean two different but related things when using the term cost. Economists define cost in terms of opportunities that are sacrificed when a choice is made. Hence, to an economist costs are simply benefits lost (and, in some cases, benefits are merely costs avoided). Costs are subjective—seen from the perspective of a decision maker not a detached observer (Buchanan, 1969, pp. 38-39)— and prospective. Moreover, cost is a stock concept—costs are incurred when decisions are made.

Accountants define cost in terms of resources consumed. Hence, from an accountant's standpoint, costs are objective—seen from the perspective of a detached observer—and retrospective. Accountants usually define costs as flows. Costs reflect changes in stocks (reductions in good things, increases in bad things) over a fixed temporal interval. To distinguish between these two cost concepts, we refer to what economists do as cost estimation and what accountants do as cost measurement. Our treatment of the topic will emphasize cost measurement.

Both concepts have much in common. Both accountants and economists would agree that, for want of a better yardstick, costs should be measured in dollars (money). Both would agree that cost necessarily means cost to do something—it is meaningless to talk about cost without identifying a cost object (or cost objective as the Cost Accounting Standards Board (CASB) calls it). The corollary to this concurrence is that there are as many different costs as there are cost objects. Finally, both would agree that standing matters. Cost necessarily means cost <u>to</u> somebody—preferably real people, because ultimately all costs (and benefits) are borne by individuals, although for some purposes a legal entity (organization) will suffice.

Cost measurement is the special domain of managerial accountants. Managerial accounting is a design science that uses a set of languages and behavioral controls to solve specific organizational problems. The vast majority of accountants, however, are financial accountants. They prepare and interpret general purpose financial statements: balance sheets, income statements, sources and uses of funds statements, and so forth. In the public sector, many financial accountants focus on fiscal accountability —insuring that government spending is lawful and consistent with legislative intent—which implies a preoccupation with the timing and purpose of cash outlays rather than cost (resource consumption).

Generally speaking, financial accountants deal with things that all entities have in common: assets and liabilities, capital, revenues and expenses, sources and uses of funds, cash flows, using standardized definitions, categories, and arrays. In contrast, managerial accountants deal with things that are unique to an organization: its costs and cost objectives, its products, activities, policies and procedures, its customers, and its strengths and weaknesses, opportunities and threats.

Why Measure Costs? Approaches to Cost Measurement

Why measure costs? There are two generic answers to this question: to facilitate decisions and to influence decisions (Demski & Feltham, 1976). Because time only runs one way, both uses of cost information are problematic. In the first instance, a cost description (estimate or measurement) is provided to decision makers before a decision is made. Unfortunately, costs can only be measured after the fact. This means that cost analysts must estimate the costs of the alternatives under consideration. In some cases, measured cost is a reliable predictor of future costs; in other cases it is not. Regardless of its reliability, however, it is all we have in most instance or, perhaps, can have. In the second instance, cost is measured after decisions have been made and implemented. Only the measurement method and its consequences are conveyed prior to the decision. In this second case, measured costs are used to evaluate managerial performance, with the purpose of influencing management choices. Consequently, managers must be informed as to how their performance will be measured and how measured performance will affect outcomes they care about—promotion, pay, esteem, and so forth. It is useful next to outline the basic approaches to cost measurement and then show how cost measures can be used to facilitate and to influence decisions.

Cost measurement is fundamentally a simple process. In most cases, cost analysts begin by measuring resources consumed (cost items). Next, they match (assign) cost items to cost objects. Finally, they account for the prices paid (historical cost) to acquire cost items and adjust those prices to reflect economic reality.

Nearly, anything of interest to a decision maker can be a cost object. Insofar as organizations exist to benefit customers or clients by means of their products or services, however, organizational decision makers should be (and usually are) especially interested in product costs. Sometimes, a final product consists of several intermediate services, each of which is produced in one or more organizational units, which implies several layers of cost objects.

Matching Cost Items to Cost Objects

There are four ways a cost item can be matched (assigned) to a cost object: (1) direct matching, (2) averaging (apportioning), (3) allocating, and (4) allocating and then apportioning. Cost items that benefit a single cost object—a department, an activity, a process, a service, or an individual's efforts—may be directly matched to the cost object in question. Cost items that are exhausted to produce a single cost object are always direct costs. Cost items that benefit one cost object at a time, but are not used up producing a single cost object, must be averaged or apportioned, in this instance over time. Cost items that are exhausted to benefit two or more cost objects must be allocated to each on some basis, so that each bears its fair share of the cost of the item. Cost items that benefit two or more cost objects at a time, but are not used up as a result, must be both allocated and apportioned.

These distinctions can be illustrated by the production of mutton and wool. To produce mutton and wool, one must acquire sheep, grazing land, and grain, and hire shepherds. Each leaf of grass or gram of oats will be consumed by one and only one sheep. In theory, then, we could treat each sheep as a cost object and directly match it to the items it consumed (although, if this were not a 4H project, the measurement costs of doing so would be prohibitively high, since it would be necessary to fence in the sheep and monitor its consumption). There is a difference, however, between grass and grain. Grain is purchased by the kilo, grass by the hectare. The cost of grain can be matched directly to the cost object; the cost of the land used must be averaged or apportioned by calculating the rent per hectare for the period in question and then, if the cost object in question were kept in pen 1/10 of a hectare in size, by dividing the rent by ten. If the cost objects were kept in a herd, the cost analyst could average the land rent in much the same way, simply by dividing the rent by the number of sheep or the total weight gain of the herd, in which case the rent could then be allocated back to each animal, if the analyst had a reason for doing so (this approach is called *process costing*). The cost of the shepherd could be handled in much the same way. Alternatively, the time the shepherd devoted to an individual sheep—getting it off a rock or out of a tree, say—could be assigned the sheep in question (*job order costing*) and the rest of his time could be apportioned over the whole herd. Note that the main differences between process costing and job order costing are that in process costing, costs are first assigned to cost pools and then to cost objects, whereas in job order costing, costs are directly assigned to cost objects.

The analysis becomes trickier if the cost analyst wants to know the cost of mutton. This is because the cost items used in sheep production jointly benefit the production of both mutton and wool. The analyst must allocate the cost of bringing the herd to market to its constituent products, perhaps on the basis of the total revenue obtained for each. In which case a cost per kilo of mutton produced could be measured by apportioning the allocated cost by the total kilos of mutton sold.

The distinction between exhaustible items and nonexhaustible items is roughly equivalent to the financial accountant's distinction between current (short term) and fixed (long term) assets. Indeed, from the standpoint of preparing general purpose financial statements they are essentially identical. The difference is that cost analysts are concerned with many things that are not included in general purpose financial statements. Financial statements focus on things that all entities (of a given class) have in common. Cost analysts are primarily concerned with things that are specific to a particular entity. Besides, if the time horizon of the cost object (or objects) in question is long enough, all cost items save only capital and land are exhaustible. And, as a practical matter, under a positive discount rate, even land and capital are treated as if they were exhaustible.

These categories are somewhat heterodox, to be sure. Most accountants merely distinguish between direct and indirect costs: direct costs can be traced to a single cost object; indirect costs arise where resource consumption benefits several cost objects. The CASB, for example, says that costs are assigned to accounting periods. They are then allocated to cost objects within the accounting period. They may be either directly or indirectly allocated. However, this classification leaves the distinction between apportionment and allocation hopelessly confused—as explained below, this distinction is a lot more important now than it has been in the past.

Adjusting the Prices Paid to Acquire Cost Items to Reflect Economic Reality

Where a cost item is supplied by an efficient market and immediately exhausted (kilowatts of electricity, for example), the price paid to acquire the item satisfactorily measures cost. Some cost items are not instantaneously exhausted, however. Materials and supplies, work in progress or in transit, and finished goods awaiting delivery are held in inventory; plant and equipment are consumed very slowly. Land and capital are used rather than consumed.

Nonexhaustible items play a significant role in the delivery of services by government. For example, the federal government's investment in property, plant, and equipment exceeds $1 trillion. Consequently, the Federal Accounting Standards Advisory Board (FASAB) Statement No. 6, "Accounting for Property, Plant, and Equipment," directs that:

> General PP&E shall be reported in the basic financial statements: the balance sheet, and the statement of net cost. The acquisition cost of general PP&E shall be recognized as an asset. Subsequently, except for land which is a non-depreciable asset, that acquisition cost shall be charged to expense through depreciation. The depreciation expense shall be accumulated in a contra asset account—accumulated depreciation.

FASAB further directs that depreciation expense should reflect the estimated useful life of the asset in question, less its estimated salvage/residual value, taking into account factors such as physical wear and tear and technological change (e.g., obsolescence), and that any changes in estimated useful life or salvage/residual value shall be treated in the period of the change and future periods. In other words, FASAB Statement No. 6 moves the U.S. federal government toward and, in some respects, beyond commercial accounting practices, which probably represents a considerable advance over the status quo.

Service and Product Costing

Where the problem of measuring the consumption of non-exhaustible cost items has been satisfactorily dealt with, service and product costing in organizations that produce a single product or perform a single service or activity is straightforward. Full costs are the sum of all exhaustible and nonexhaustible cost items used for a cost object. Full unit costs are merely average total costs—the sum of direct costs and rents (sometimes called period costs) apportioned over the total number of units of products produced or services or activities performed. This situation also gives rise to a predictable set of cost functions.

Where there are several layers of cost objects (i.e., a final product/service consists of several intermediate services, each of which is produced in one or more organizational units) and processing is sequential or seriatim, product costing is equally straightforward. The cost object of one organizational unit is a merely a cost item for the next unit in line. This means that, where a single product, service, or activity is concerned, measured cost provides a reliable basis for estimating the cost of replicating the cost object (decision facilitating) and an unambiguous basis for evaluating managerial performance against a target, benchmark, or standard (decision influencing). That is to say, measured product/service cost is a highly useful guide to decisions about product provision (retain/divest) and pricing, alternate mixes of cost items, the rate, volume, and timing of production, and even alternative processing sequences, although in these instances counterfactual estimates must be derived from other measures. Where there are two or more layers of cost objects, measured product cost is also a useful guide to decisions about whether to make or buy cost objects (see Horngren & Foster, 1991; Kaplan, 1992). Indeed, whenever these issues can be decided on the basis of direct costs, measured cost will satisfactorily perform the decision facilitating function as well as the decision influencing function.

The utility of product cost measurement becomes problematical only where cost items are shared by two or more cost objects—these can be either final products or layers of cost objects. Where the service delivery process is dominated by joint cost items, cost measures that serve the decision influencing function will rarely, if ever, also satisfactorily serve the decision facilitation function. This means that different costs are required for different purposes (see Kaplan, 1992).

Financial accountants usually denied this fact. Perhaps, because it implied that their transactional accounting records were insufficient bases for managerial decision making, and they often tried to enforce the fiction that allocated costs were satisfactory proxies for both opportunity costs and responsibility costs. For a long time they got away with it. This was possible for three reasons: (1) most production processes could be traced to a single cost item (direct labor or machine hours, materials, etc.); (2) managers were held responsible only for <u>controllable</u> cost items (i.e., those that could be significantly influenced by the actions of the manager); and (3) given joint cost items, the only alternative to cost allocation was statistical cost estimation. Since statistical costs often cannot be tied directly to an entity's system of dual-entry transactional accounting records, accountants, especially financial accountants, were inclined to distrust their validity.

Cost Allocation

Traditional cost allocation is a two step process: (1) direct cost matching, and (2) indirect cost allocation. As a practical matter, many accountants do not distinguish between nonexhaustible cost items traceable to a single cost object, exhaustible cost items benefiting two or more cost objects, and nonexhaustible cost items benefiting two or more cost objects. They are all lumped together as indirect costs or overheads (i.e., any cost item not directly associated with a final cost object), pooled in cost centers, and distributed to cost objects. This step involves the selection of a basis of allocation (i.e., a measure of activity associated with the pool of common costs being distributed) and a method of allocation.

Cost accountants rely on three methods to allocate cost pools to cost objects. The simplest is known as single step allocation. Under this method, analysts allocate each cost pool to all the cost objects that use its services, but not to any others. For example, building maintenance and housekeeping services performed by a state department of administrative services could be allocated to various other departments and agencies based on the number of square meters of office space they occupy. Where there are several layers of cost objects, cost accountants usually rely on the two stage or step down method. Under this method, the cost pools are trickled down to other pools and cost objects using a variety of allocation bases. Usually analysts begin with the cost pool that serves the greatest number of other pools or final cost objects and spreads its costs over the others. They continue in this fashion with all other pools until all costs have been allocated to final cost objects.

For example, the allocation process could begin with depreciation of buildings and fixtures. These costs would be distributed across all remaining cost pools. The amount to be distributed from the next pool (building maintenance and housekeeping services) now includes not only its own costs but also the amount allocated to it from the previous step. This total would them be allocated to all the remaining pools, and so forth.

Two important aspects of the step down method are (1) no reverse allocation takes place; that is, once a pool's costs have been allocated, that pool receives no additional allocations from other pools; and (2) pool costs are allocated both to other pools and to final cost objects (or the administrative units directly responsible for their delivery), but final cost objects (or the administrative units directly responsible for their delivery) are not allocated to other final cost objects (or the administrative units directly responsible for their delivery). Because no reverse allocation takes place, the sequence of the steps in the step down is an important cost measurement decision. Although the effect of different step down sequences is rarely great, in a few circumstances the choice may have a huge influence on the measured costs of final products.

This problem can be mitigated by using the reciprocal method. Under this method, cost pools are not stepped down. Rather, the accountant develops a set of simultaneous equations that measure and allocate each pool's costs based on its use by all other cost pools, not just those below it in a step down sequence. Sometimes this process can become quite complex. For example, the cost model developed by the National Center for Higher Education Management Systems provides a structure for 338 equations and 13 relationships (over 6 billion) for allocating costs to student types and funded research activities.

Relevance Lost?

As discussed under the topic heading "using measured costs to influence behavior," overhead cost allocation systems retain utility insofar as decision influencing is concerned. Increasingly, however, they have been rendered obsolete for purposes of facilitating decisions by changes in organization and technology. Most overheads are transaction costs. They reflect the organization's policies, its operating and administrative procedures, and its customer relationships. They involve activities like purchasing, materials handling, marketing, accounting, and asset utilization. Once upon a time overheads could be allocated to final cost objects on the basis of direct costs without significantly biasing key operating decisions (provision, pricing, input/output mix, rate, volume, or timing) simply because overheads were relatively insignificant. In 1950, service industries played a minor role in the American economy and overheads accounted for a less than 15% of total manufacturing cost (direct labor and machine hours more than 50%). Nowadays, even in manufacturing, overhead activities often have a greater effect on expenses than production volume. In the average U.S. manufacturing plant, for example, direct manufacturing labor accounts for only ten to 15% of costs; materials and purchased components typically account for thirty to 40% more. This leaves roughly 15% for overheads. And that's the typical manufacturing plan; direct labor costs are practically irrelevant in the increasing number of high tech firms that rely on flexible computer aided design and manufacturing. In those organizations, 80% of life cycle costs are typically incurred before a product gets to market.

The U.S. Office of Technology Assessment (1984) defines flexible manufacturing as a system:

> capable of producing a range of discrete products with a minimum of manual intervention. It consists of production equipment workstations (machine tools or other equipment for fabrication, assembly or treatment) linked by a materials handling system to move parts from one work station to another, and it operates as an integrated system under full programmable control. (pp. 60-62)

Flexible, computer-aided design and manufacturing have had the effect of making manufacturing firms much more like service organizations. Most manufacturing costs were once engineered costs. The amount of labor and the quantity of material required to make products depended entirely on the volume of output. By contrast, most service costs have always been discretionary (i.e., they depend on policy decisions).

Paradoxically, however, although flexible production has reduced the significance of exhaustible cost items, where systems are linked by modern relational or object-oriented data bases, flexible production permits non-exhaustible cost items to be assigned to individual cost objects (job order costing) far more precisely than was ever before possible. In such an environment, cost analysts must still apportion expenses, but they rarely need to allocate them.

ACTIVITY BASED COSTING SYSTEMS

When it became increasingly evident that traditional cost measurement systems no longer provided the information managers needed, many tried something new. Of particular interest here is activity accounting. Activity accounting is oriented to overheads. Indeed, so far as direct costs are concerned, there is little or no difference between Activity Based Costing (ABC—also called transaction cost analysis) and job-order costing. What is new about ABC is that it reflects the premise that *all* organizational activities, including overheads, are undertaken to produce goods and services for customers and that they are the proximate cause of all costs. This means that all costs, including overheads, are ultimately product and service costs (Harr & Godfrey, 1991, p. 24). The problem is figuring out how.

Like traditional cost measurement, ABC starts by apportioning an organization's expenses to a set of cost pools. Unlike traditional practice, which ignores activities that do not vary with output volume, mix, or production rate, ABC compiles cost information on all the activities performed in the organization. Analysts use a variety of statistical methods to figure out which transactions cause these pools to vary in size. These are called activity drivers, resource drivers, or cost drivers.

Cost analysts typically use one of five methods to establish a relationship between cost drivers and cost pools: (1) High-Low Method, (2) Scatter Diagram Method, (3) Regression Method, (4) Incremental Method, and (4) Element Analysis. The last method is used when there are no historical data points available. The cost analyst must, therefore, estimate each cost category separately (e.g., salaries and wages) and decompose it into its various cost elements: fixed, step function, variable, semivariable. Once this is done, simplifying assumptions can be made concerning step function and semivariable costs, and the totals for each cost element can be summed to produce a total cost equation. These methods are described in greater detail by Anthony and Young (1994). Moreover, economists and management scientists have developed an array of analytic models that can be used in cost finding. One of the most popular is data envelopment analysis (DEA), a linear programming-based technique for measuring organizational performance in the presence of multiple inputs, outputs, and constraints. A quick computer search identified 106 articles published since 1990 explaining, using, or criticizing DEA. There is even a recent book on the subject focusing on public sector applications (see Ganley & Cubbin, 1992).

Examples of cost drivers in manufacturing (e.g., the Air Force's depot maintenance operations) include the number of inspections, work receipts, the number of components in inventory, machine setups, or change orders. Examples of cost drivers in a service environment (e.g., the Air Force's supply operations) include orders processed, number of unique items held in inventory, type of items issued, physical volume and weight processed, distance shipped, and supporting facilities and equipment acquired, operated, and maintained. More general examples include time, space, transaction, service, or commodity type, distance, and weight, as well as the old standbys, output volume, mix, and rate.

In many organizations, ABC is a by-product of quality management—the basic elements of which are process value analysis (PVA), statistical process control, customer feedback, participative management, and supplier cooperation (Hyde, 1997). Process value analysis involves five steps (Harr & Godfrey, 1991, pp. 25-26):

- Chart the entire flow of activities needed to design, create, and deliver a service;
- For each activity and step within the activity determine its associated cost and the cause of that cost, or cost driver;
- Determine whether or not the step adds value for the customer and, if it is nonvalue adding, identify ways to eliminate it and its associated cost;
- Determine the cycle time of each activity and calculate its cycle efficiency (value-added time/total time); and
- Seek ways to improve cycle efficiency and reduce associated costs due to delays, excesses, and unevenness in activities.

This approach has proved itself in a variety of settings, identifying activities and outcomes that do not add value and that arise out of defects in the service delivery process. A PVA of the Treasury's check-writing operation, for example, showed that it spent about 8 cents out of every dollar writing checks, 21 cents on administration, and 70 cents correcting errors (Keohoe, Dodson, Reeve, & Plato, 1995).

Moreover, insofar as quality management pushes significant operating decisions down to the lowest levels of the organization, cost measures and cost estimates are also needed at the lowest levels, as are measures of rework, activity cycle time, customer satisfaction, and so forth. Operators especially need cost/performance standards for each value-adding activity they perform. Such standards can be based on the best the organization has achieved over time (baselining), the best practice currently being achieved somewhere (benchmarking), or an engineering standard — in target costing, for example, price targets are set by the market (price less planned markup equals allowable cost) and evaluated for feasibility by computer simulation (drifting cost) (Tani, 1995).

A study conducted by Software Productivity Research of Burlington, Massachusetts in *The Economist*, shows how ABC works ("Software Engineering," 1993). It used a method called function point analysis to estimate the productivity and cost effectiveness of three kinds of software projects: small management information systems, large scale systems, and military systems. Based on a sample of thousands of software projects selected from around the world, Software Productivity Research found that American military software productivity lags behind France, Israel, Korea, the United Kingdom, Germany, Sweden, and even Italy. The same study showed that the United States is in first place in the production of management information systems and runs a strong second to Japan in large-scale systems software projects.

Differences in cost per function point are due primarily to the amount of paperwork required per point. Preparation of this paperwork takes a lot of engineering time, but contributes no value (function points) to the finished product. American military projects require five times as much paper and cost twelve times as much per point as management information systems projects. They are six times as costly per function point as big systems software projects, which are arguably comparable to military software projects. This comparison is particularly telling, because it suggests is that, for activities like software engineering, federal procurement regulations may account for more than half their cost.

Studies such as this one also confirm the weakness of traditional cost measurement systems. Focusing on direct labor costs and assigning overheads accordingly may have made sense 30 years ago when direct labor was the key to productivity, but it is unrealistic today and has probably always had the effect of diverting attention from transaction costs that arise out of the administrative process.

Field studies also show that ABC provides more accurate information for product costing than traditional cost measurement systems, which tend to understate costs for low-volume specialty-type services and overstate costs for high-volume standard services. It should probably be noted here that ABC's recent popularity is due in no small measure to the improvements in computing power and systems architecture.

Modern information technology has dramatically lowered the cost of establishing, maintaining, and using cost systems, but increasing the number of cost drivers and their associated cost pools still increases information costs. This is especially true where activity data must be manually collected and where it is often more cost effective to rely on sampling procedures than universal measurement. Consequently, users should carefully weigh the costs of greater measurement precision against its benefits. The organizations that are most likely to benefit from ABC are those with high overhead costs and widely diverse operating activities and service lines—which probably comprehends most government agencies.

Using Measured Costs to Influence Behavior

One area in which traditional cost measurement continues to play a significant role is management control (i.e., decision influencing). Management control is the process by which people, especially subordinate managers, are motivated to serve the policies and purposes of the organizations to which they belong. It is also secondarily a process for detecting and correcting unintentional performance errors and intentional irregularities, such as theft or misuse of resources. In many organizations the primary instrument of management control is responsibility budgeting, which embraces both the formulation of budgets and their execution.

RESPONSIBILITY BUDGETING AND ACCOUNTING

Information/transaction costs make it necessary to decentralize some decision rights in organizations and in the economy. Decentralization in turn requires organizations to solve the control problem that results when self-interested persons do not behave as perfect agents. Capitalist economies solve these control problems through the institution of alienable decision rights. But because organizations suppress the alienability of decision rights, they must devise substitute mechanisms that perform its functions. Three functions are critical: (1) allocating decision rights among agents in the organization, (2) measuring and evaluating performance, and (3) rewarding and punishing individuals for their performance. Responsibility budgeting and accountings systems are the most widespread mechanisms for performing these functions in business today.

In this following section we explain the nature of responsibility budgeting, its intellectual justification, its antecedents, and its present and future use in the public sector. This is not a straightforward task. We cannot simply explain how responsibility budgeting is used and how it works. Responsibility budgeting makes sense only as a part of a framework of structural, procedural, and monitoring/reporting relationships. We must, therefore, also explain the framework that gives it utility and power. At the same time, responsibilities budgeting and accounting, or their functional equivalents, make an essential contribution to the efficacy of this broader framework of relationships. One cannot arbitrarily mix and match administrative relationships and expect that the outcome will be productive. The efficacy of administrative relationships depends upon their congruity with each other as well as with the purposes and products of the entity in question and the productive and information processing technologies available to it.

Governance Arrangements, Administrative Processes and Contractual Relationships

All governance arrangements and administrative processes are primarily mechanisms for motivating and inspiring people, especially subordinate managers, to serve the policies and purposes of the organizations to which they belong. This means that all governance arrangements and all administrative processes can be treated as contractual relationships and that administrative design and implementation can be thought of as negotiating and enforcing contracts.

One way of describing contractual relationships involves the language of principal and agent. This language implies a hierarchical relationship, in which a nominal subordinate (agent) serves the purposes of a superior (principal). On the presumption that behavior is largely self-interested, principal-agent relationships are problematic (give rise to agency costs) only where (a) the efforts of the agent cannot be perfectly observed; (b) the interests of agent and principal diverge; and (c) agents pursue their own interests, that is, behave opportunistically.

One of the key goals of governance arrangements and administrative processes is to the minimization of agency costs. Of course, agency costs also include all resources used to reduce divergences of interest, that is, identifying collectively beneficial relationships, negotiating contributions, and devising procedures for monitoring performance and sanctioning defectors. Included here are a whole panoply of activities extending from the employment of security guards to the design and implementation of new or reconfigured accounting and reporting systems. Hence, minimizing agency costs means minimizing the sum of costs that result from opportunistic behavior plus the costs of avoiding or controlling that behavior (Zimmerman, 1995). Economic theory tells us that we find this optimum where the marginal costs of controls equal their marginal benefits.

Traditional or Weberian bureaucracies rely on rules to govern or prevent opportunistic behavior. In other words, principals specify in detail what agents must do (or must not do), carefully monitor their actions, and sanction all deviations accordingly. The problem with this approach is that agents often have better information about some things than do principals. Principals hire agents because of their superior expertise and to spare themselves the burden of being perfectly informed about every aspect of an organization's operations. In neither case will principals have the knowledge needed to specify in detail what the agent should do without thereby sacrificing performance. This means that rules are not always a wholly satisfactory solution to the principal-agent problem. It is this fact that makes the application of agency theory to the public sector especially important, for it is in the public sector that the opportunity costs arising from detailed rules often seem highest.

Organizational economists do not generally advocate more rules as a way to control opportunistic behavior. Rather, they stress two alternative approaches. One is to improve principals' abilities to monitor agents. This is often referred to as improving "transparency." For example, full accrual accounting gives a truer picture of resource use than does standard government accounting and thus helps make government operations more transparent. The second is to seek ways to align the incentives of agents with principals' interests. This is the preferred approach of organizational economists and managerial accountants. As the New Zealand Treasury (1987) observed, "Incentives matter.... Well designed policies will align the interests and actions of individuals with those of the nation."

The Role of Responsibility Budgeting and Accounting

Responsibility budgeting is the most common remote control system used by large-scale organizations in the private sector. It is a form of internal contracting in which: (a) units and managers are evaluated relative to the targets they accept, (b) only financial measures are used to measure and reward accomplishment or punish failure, and (c) financial success or failure is attributed entirely to managerial decisions and/or employee performance. While private businesses were quick to learn bureaucratic control from government, governmental organizations have been slow to adopt remote control systems.

The digression is relevant here because responsibility budgeting is as much organizational engineering as it is financial management and accounting. Organizational engineering is concerned with the following three elements:

- Administrative structure—the structure depicted in an organization chart showing the organization's administrative units and their relationships to each other. Under responsibility budgeting, work can be arranged into administrative units according to mission, function, and/or region.
- Responsibility structure—the allocation of authority and responsibility to individuals within the organization. Under responsibility budgeting authority and responsibility must be unambiguously assigned.
- The account or control structure—the system of measuring and evaluating performance. Under responsibility budgeting information on inputs, costs, activities, and outputs is critically important.

Under a fully developed responsibility budgeting and accounting system, administrative units and responsibility centers are coterminous and fully aligned with the organization's account structure, since the information it provides can be used to coordinate unit activities as well as to influence the decisions of responsibility center managers.

Under responsibility budgeting, two basic rules govern organizational design. First, organizational strategy should determine structure. Strategy means the pattern of purposes and policies that defines the organization and its missions and that positions it relative to its environment. Single mission organizations should therefore be organized along functional lines; multimission organizations should be organized along mission lines; multimission, multifunction organizations should be organized along matrix lines. Where a matrix organization is large enough to justify an extensive division of labor, responsibility centers should be designated as either mission or support centers, with the latter linked to the former by a system of internal markets and prices (transfer pricing).

The second basic rule is that the organization should be as decentralized as possible. Most students of management believe that the effectiveness of large, complex organizations improves when authority and responsibility are delegated down into the organization. Of course, authority should not be delegated arbitrarily or capriciously. Decentralization requires prior clarification of the purpose or function of each administrative unit and responsibility center, procedures for setting objectives and for monitoring and rewarding performance, and an account structure that links each responsibility center to the goals of the organization as a whole.

The biggest difference between government budgets and responsibility budgets is that government budgets tend to be highly detailed spending or resource acquisition plans, which must be scrupulously executed just as they were approved (Thompson & Jones, 1986). In contrast, operating budgets in the private sector are usually sparing of detail, often consisting of no more than a handful of financial targets. As we noted earlier, Sloan of General Motors (GM), one of the fathers of responsibility budgeting, believed it was inappropriate for corporate managers know the details of responsibility center operations. The notion that responsibility centers should be managed at arm's length, by the numbers, from a small corporate headquarters, reflects the effort to delegate authority and responsibility down into the organization. As the Organisation for Economic Co-operation and Development (OECD) report, *Budgeting for Results: Perspectives on Public Expenditure Management* (1995), explains, delegation of authority means giving agency managers the maximum feasible authority needed to make their units productive—or, in the alternative, subjecting them to a minimum of constraints. Hence, delegation of authority requires operating budgets to be stripped to the minimum needed to motivate and inspire subordinates. Under responsibility budgeting the ideal operating budget would contain a single number or performance target (e.g., a production quota, a unit cost standard, or a profit or return on investment target) for each administrative unit/responsibility center.

In responsibility budget formulation, an organization's policies, the results of all past policy (capital budgeting, see Thompson, 1997) decisions, are converted into financial targets that correspond to the domains of administrative units and their managers (Anthony & Young, 1994, p. 19). In responsibility budget execution, operating performance is monitored and subordinate managers are evaluated and rewarded. Operating performance targets must be expressed in financial terms. This makes it possible to make comparisons across unlike responsibility centers, thereby permitting the relative performance of managers to be evaluated and increasing the motivational efficacy of internal competition. It also has the effect of keeping higher levels of administration ignorant of operating details, thereby discouraging them from meddling in the affairs of their responsibility center managers.

Types of Responsibility Centers

Responsibility centers are usually classified according to two dimensions:

- The integration dimension—that is, the relationship between the responsibility center's objectives and the overall purposes and policies of the organization; and
- The decentralization dimension—that is, the amount of authority delegated to responsibility managers, measured in terms of their discretion to acquire and use assets.

On the first dimension, a responsibility center can be either a mission center or a support center. The output of a mission center contributes directly to an organization's objectives or purpose. The output of a support center is an input to another responsibility center in the organization, either another support center or a mission center.

On the decentralization dimension, accountants distinguish among four types of responsibility centers based on the authority delegated to responsibility managers to acquire and use assets. Discretionary expense centers, the governmental norm, are found at one extreme; profit and investment centers are at the other. A support center may be either an expense center or a profit center. If the latter, profit is the difference between costs and "revenue" from "selling" services to other responsibility centers. We note that the word "sells" is in quotation marks here because the organization as a whole has not sold anything to an outside party. Rather, the responsibility center providing the service records revenue in its accounts and the center receiving the service records an expense. Revenue and expense cancel out when the organization consolidates its books. Money rarely changes hands in interdivisional transfer pricing. Responsibility centers don't get to keep "their" profits. Only the organization as a whole earns a profit. Selling to and buying from outsiders are the only activities that can generate real profits or losses for an organization).

This is a very important practical point. In the U.S. federal government revolving fund agencies are prohibited from earning a "profit." Instead, they are generally directed to operate on a breakeven basis. The motivational effect of this ruke is to cause their actual costs to exceed standard cost in the majority of instances. In contrast, if they were directed to maximize "profit" and, assuming that they continued to base per unit user charges on historical fully distributed average costs, the effect would be to encourage them to save budget authority for their internal customers and dollars for the U.S. Treasury. It might also have the effect of ratcheting their unit costs down, instead of permitting them to creep gradually up as is now typically the case. Clearly, the breakeven policy does not make sense and probably reflects the failure to understand the simple point that selling to and buying from outsiders are the only activities that can generate real profits or losses for the organization. Interestingly, many revolving fund agencies are permitted to earn a profit for their parent organization when they sell outside the organization (e.g., U.S. Armed Services' product support for foreign military sales). Finally, both profit and investment centers are usually free to borrow, and investment centers are also free to make decisions about plant and equipment, new products, and other issues that are significant to the long run performance of the organization.

Discretionary expense centers incur costs. The difference between them and other kinds of responsibility centers is that their managers have no independent authority to acquire assets. Instead, the manager's superiors must authorize each acquisition. In the U.S. system, under detailed line item budgets, acquisitions must be authorized by Congress and signed into law by the president. But all discretionary expense center managers are accountable for compliance with an asset acquisition/resource requirements plan (expense budget), whether written into law or not. Once acquisitions have been authorized, discretionary expense center managers are usually given considerable latitude in their deployment and use. Managerial accountants generally believe that administrative units should be discretionary expense centers only where there is no satisfactory way to match their expenses to final cost objects.

In some cases, expense center managers are evaluated in terms of the number and type of activities performed by their center. Where each of the activities performed by the center earns revenue or is assigned notational revenue (transfer price) by the organization's controller, these centers are referred to as revenue centers.

In a cost center, the manager is held responsible for producing a stated quantity and/or quality of output at the lowest feasible cost. Someone else within the organization determines the output of a cost center—usually including various quality attributes, especially delivery schedules. Cost center managers are usually free to acquire short-term assets (those that are wholly consumed within a performance measurement cycle), to hire temporary or contract personnel, and to manage inventories.

In a standard cost center, output levels are determined by requests from other responsibility centers and the manager's budget for each performance measurement cycle is determined by multiplying actual output by standard cost per unit (see Thompson, 1998). Performance is measured against this figure—the difference between actual costs and standard costs.

In a quasi-profit (or pseudoprofit) center, performance is measured by the difference between the notational revenue earned (transfer price) by the center and its costs (Kaplan & Cooper, 1998, pp. 56-73). For example, let's say a Veteran's Administration hospital department of radiology performed 500 chest X-rays and 200 skull X-rays for the department of geriatrics. The notational revenue earned was $25 per chest X-ray (500) = $12,500 and $50 per skull X-ray (200) = $10,000, or $22,500 total. If the radiology department's costs were $18,000, it would earn a quasi-profit of $4,500 ($22,500 − $18,000).

In profit centers, managers are responsible for both revenues and costs. Profit is the difference between revenue and cost (or expense). Thus, profit center managers are evaluated in terms of both the revenues their centers earn and the costs they incur. In addition to the authority to acquire short-term assets, to hire temporary or contract personnel, and to manage inventories, profit center managers are usually given the authority to make long-term hires, set salary and promotion schedules (subject to organization wide standards), organize their units, and acquire long-lived assets costing less than some specified amount.

In investment centers, managers are responsible for both profit and the assets used in generating the profit. Thus, an investment center adds more to a manager's scope of responsibility than does a profit center, just as a profit center involves more than a cost center. Investment center managers are typically evaluated in terms of return on assets (ROA), which is the ratio of profit to assets employed, where the former is expressed as a percentage of the latter. In recent years many have turned to economic value added (EVA), net operating "profit" less an appropriate capital charge, which is a dollar amount rather than a ratio and is more generally consistent with the value-creating purposes of organizations (Carlton & Perloff, 1996, pp. 77-78, 334-341, 373-374; Kaplan & Cooper, 1998, pp. 265-270).

Formerly, in most large complex organizations in the private sector, individual production units were typically standard cost centers; staff units were typically discretionary expense centers. Indeed, only mission centers were allowed to be investment centers. The reasons for this are complex, but they go to difficulties associated with expensing intermediate and joint products. Mission centers in private sector organizations produce final products that are easily priced and that are expensed following generally accepted accounting practice. In contrast, support centers produce intermediate products and these were, until recently, hard to cost, let alone price, with accuracy. Attempts to do so were often either excessively arbitrary or prohibitively costly. Now, however, advances in information technology, managerial accounting, and organizational design have made it possible and, in some cases, beneficial to treat every responsibility center in an organization as an investment center (Thompson, 1998).

Paradoxically, public sector organizations are a mirror image of large complex organizations in the private sector. We know now how to treat support centers in most organization as quasi-profit or even investment centers (Lapsley, 1994; for additional public sector examples, see Anthony & Young, 1994, pp. 371-374; Kaplan & Cooper, 1998, pp. 245-251). But, because the final products of government's core mission centers are public goods that are passively enjoyed (Vining & Weimer, 1998), pricing final outputs remains for the time being and for the foreseeable future either excessively arbitrary or prohibitively costly. This means, for example, that, while it might make sense to treat military depot maintenance, spare parts management, or facilities support centers as investment centers, it will continue to be necessary to treat the armed forces' combatant commands as discretionary expense centers. Fortunately, as far as exhaustive expenditures are concerned, about 75% of the activities performed by the U.S. federal government fall into the support category and, for the most part, state and local governments are not in the business of supplying pure public goods (see Goldin, 1977).

Transfer Pricing

Under responsibility budgeting, support centers provide services or intermediate goods to other responsibility centers in return for a notational transfer price, organizations are structured to take advantage of specialized knowledge and local conditions, center managers make decisions and are held responsible for the overall financial performance of their centers. Sound transfer pricing is, therefore, the key to aligning the incentives of responsibility center managers with organizational interests.

Transfer pricing is also important to transparency within organizations. It helps to determine the costs of services provided by one unit to another, which is central to measuring performance relative to a financial target, and therefore plays a major role in establishing, as well as manipulating, the incentives facing responsibility center managers. Transfer pricing also reveals the internal costs of service decentralization where costs are incurred in transferring decision rights to others within an organization. When one subunit transfers tangible assets, knowledge, skills, and so forth, to another, both units calculate the cost as a means of revealing their liquid and tangible asset use internally and in external provision of service.

There are two common approaches to transfer pricing:

- Laissez-faire transfer pricing: buying and selling responsibility centers are completely free to negotiate prices, to deal, or not to deal; and
- Marginal or incremental cost pricing: the responsibility center selling the service is required to charge the buying responsibility center whichever is less of market or incremental cost.

(A third method is based upon fully distributed average cost of the service or product.)

However, the circumstances that justify large complex organizations—economies of scale and scope—render these simple transfer-pricing mechanisms problematic. Scale economies are usually the result of large, lumpy investments in specialized resources—technological knowledge, product specific research and development, or equipment. These investments tend to give rise to bilateral monopoly, a circumstance that provides an ideal environment for opportunistic behavior on the part of suppliers and customers. For example, once an intermediate product producer has acquired a specialized asset, customers may be able to extract discounts by threatening to switch suppliers. In that case, the supplier may find it necessary to write off a large part of the specialized investment. Or, if demand for the final good increases greatly, the intermediate product supplier may be able to extort exorbitant prices from customers. Hence, where the relationship between intermediate product supplier and customer is at arm's length, opportunistic behavior may eliminate the payoff to what would otherwise be cost effective investments. For example, the Report of the Commission on Roles and Missions of the Armed Forces (see Thompson & Jones, 1994) suggested that budget authority should flow through the combatant commands to the military departments. Were that the case, lacking a long-term credible commitment on the part of the Joint Chiefs and the combatant commanders, the U.S. Navy's investment in specialized assets like aircraft carriers would permit it to be exploited in peacetime. In wartime, of course, the tables would be turned.

The new economics of organizations tells us that vertical integration occurs because it can mitigate this problem, in part through the substitution of direct supervision for remote control (Williamson, 1985). For example, in a study of military procurement, Masten (1984) demonstrated that specialized investments are critical to vertical integration. Where intermediate products were both complex and highly specialized (used only by the buyer), there was a 92% probability that they would be produced internally; even 31% of all simple, specialized components were produced internally. The probability dropped to less than 2% if the component was unspecialized, regardless of its complexity.

Unfortunately, the problems that arise in arm's length transactions where there are few alternative suppliers/customers also arise where one attempts to replicate free market forces within the organization, allowing buying and selling responsibility centers complete freedom to negotiate prices (laissez-faire transfer pricing). Traditionally, economists have argued that services should be transferred at marginal or incremental cost to the buying responsibility center. But this can seriously distort the evaluation of support center performance and tend to eliminate incentives to improvement.

As a result, organizations face a serious dilemma. They can maximize short run performance by using marginal cost in internal transactions, thereby seriously distorting performance measurement and incentives, which will cause shortfalls in long-run performance. Or they can sacrifice short-term performance by relying on laissez-faire transfer pricing, thereby obtaining superior measures of the support center's contributions to organizational performance, and improve the chances of maximizing performance in the long term. Organizations can, promote short-run performance by using incremental cost pricing or they can promote long-term performance by using laissez-faire pricing, but they cannot do both simultaneously using either of these simple transfer pricing mechanisms.

In theory, bilateral monopoly can be governed quite satisfactorily by unbalanced transfer prices, multipart transfer prices, or quasi-vertical integration. Under unbalanced transfer prices, the selling responsibility center is credited with the full cost of the transacted item (often standard cost), plus an agreed upon markup, the buying center is charged its marginal cost, and the organization's accounts are adjusted to reflect the difference between the two. Unbalanced transfer prices are rarely used, however, where market prices are available. Under, multipart transfer prices, the service delivered is decomposed to reflect underlying cost drivers and priced accordingly (your home phone bill is an excellent example of a multipart tariff). Under quasi-vertical integration, the buyer invests in specialized resources and loans, leases, or rents them to their suppliers. Quasi-vertical integration is common in both the automobile and the aerospace industries, and, of course, it is standard procedure for the Department of Defense to provide and own the equipment, dies, and designs that defense firms use to supply it with weapons systems and the like (Monteverde & Teece, 1982). Other organizations that rely on a small number of suppliers or a small number of distributors write contracts that constrain the opportunistic behavior of those with whom they deal.

In still other cases, desired outcomes can be realized through alliances based on the exchange of hostages (e.g., surety bonds, exchange of debt or equity positions) or just plain old-fashioned trust based on long-term mutual dependence. Toyota, for example, relies on a few suppliers that it nurtures and supports (Womack, Jones, & Roos, 1990). They have substantial cross-holdings in each other and Toyota often acts as its suppliers' banker. Toyota maintains tight working links between its manufacturing and engineering departments and its suppliers, intimately involving them in all aspects of product design and manufacture. Indeed, it often lends them personnel to deal with production surges and its suppliers accept Toyota people into their personnel systems.

Toyota's suppliers are not completely independent companies with only a marketplace relationship to each other. In a very real sense, they all share a common purpose and destiny. Yet Toyota has not integrated its suppliers into a single, large bureaucracy. It wanted its suppliers to remain independent companies with completely separate books—real profit/investment centers, rather than merely notational ones—selling to others whenever possible. Toyota's solution to the bilateral monopoly problem appears to work just fine (Womack, Jones, & Roos, 1990). In fact, with the exception of unbalanced transfer prices, none of the solutions to the bilateral monopoly problem noted here presumes vertical integration. All that is required is full access to cost and production information (Milgrom & Roberts, 1992). All of these solutions to the transfer pricing/organizational design are potentially available to government organizations. Indeed, many of them were pioneered by federal acquisitions personnel or imposed by public utility commissions. They are not, however, widely understood or appreciated by public administrators and financial managers.

RESPONSIBILITY BUDGETING IN GOVERNMENT

The origins of responsibility budgeting and accounting in government can be traced to the Planning, Programming, and Budgeting System (PPBS) era in the U.S. Department of Defense (1961-1967). Responsibility budgeting and accounting was the centerpiece of Project Prime, perhaps the most promising of the organizational design and development efforts initiated under Secretary of Defense Robert McNamara. Project Prime was the brainchild by Robert N. Anthony (Juola, 1993, pp. 43-44), who succeeded Charles Hitch as defense controller in September 1965. Anthony saw the need for clarification of the purpose of each of the administrative units that comprised the Department of Defense, their boundaries, and their relationships to each other, and for an account structure that would tie the entire organization together. Anthony (1962) proposed that the Department of Defense:

- Classify all administrative units as either mission or support centers;
- Charge all costs accrued by support centers—including charges for the use of capital assets and inventory depletion—to the mission centers they serve;
- Fund mission centers to cover their expected expenses—including support center charges;
- Establish working capital funds to provide short-term financing for support units; and
- Establish a capital asset fund to provide long-term financing of capital assets and to encourage efficient management of their acquisition, use, and disposition.

The principal formal device by which a measure of intraorganizational decentralization was and is accomplished within the Department of Defense is the revolving fund. These funds involve buyer-seller arrangements internal to the Department of Defense. They have actually been in use for some time. The navy had a revolving fund as early as 1878. Modern-day revolving funds date to the 1947 National Security Act, which authorized the defense secretary to use them to manage support activities within the Department of Defense. Two kinds of funds were established under this authority: stock and industrial funds (since replaced by Working Capital Funds). Stock funds were used to purchase supplies in bulk from commercial sources and hold them in inventory until they are supplied to the customer—usually a military unit or facility. Industrial funds were used to purchase industrial or commercial services (e.g., depot maintenance, transportation, etc.) from production units within the Department of Defense. Both kinds of funds were supposed to be financed by reimbursements from customers' appropriations (Juola, 1993, p. 43).

Anthony's proposal would have expanded the scope of this device and enhanced its effectiveness by establishing rules for setting transfer prices prospectively rather than retrospectively and by making support center managers responsible for meeting explicit financial targets. Internal buyer-seller arrangements encourage efficient choice on the part of support centers, as well as the units that use their services, only if prices are set ahead of time and support centers charge all of their costs against revenues earned delivering services. Furthermore, their managers must be fully authorized to incur expenses to deliver services, and held responsible for meeting the stated financial goals of their centers (Bailey, 1967, p. 343).

Project Prime failed. One reason for its failure is that the U.S. federal government accounts for purchases, outlays, and obligations, but it still does not account for consumption. Full value from the application of responsibility budgeting can be obtained only where government adopts a meaningful form of consumption or accrual accounting (measuring the cost of the assets actually consumed producing goods or services). Because the U.S. government does not account for resource consumption, its cost figures are necessarily statistical in nature (i.e., they are not tied to its basic debit and credit bookkeeping/accounting records). Without the discipline that debit and credit provides, these figures are likely to be satisfactory only for illustrative purposes or where a decision maker must make a specific decision and a cost model has been tailored to the decision maker's needs. Another reason for the failure of Project Prime is that U.S. appropriations process does not perform the capital budgeting function satisfactorily, a problem that PPBS did not really address and certainly didn't fix. Besides which, the existing process procrusteanizes every operating cycle to fit the fiscal year.

Responsibility budgeting next surfaced in the United Kingdom, as part of the Thatcher government's Financial Management Initiative, announced May 17, 1982 (Lapsley, 1994; Pollitt, 1993). The Financial Management Initiative called for a radical change in the internal structure and operations of government agencies. Objectives were to be assigned to responsibility centers. Costs were to be systematically identified. They were to be measured on an accrual basis (i.e., matching resources consumed to services delivered) and include not only the direct costs of service delivery but overheads as well. This identification enabled those responsible for meeting particular objectives to be held accountable for the cost of the resources they were consuming

The scope of responsibility accounting and budgeting in the United Kingdom was further extended in 1988 by the Thatcher government's Next Steps Initiative. In the last 8 years, much of the British civil service has been reorganized into a set of executive agencies that have been given considerable administrative and fiscal flexibility and expected to meet annual financial performance targets. The heads of these executive agencies are no longer career civil servants. They are recruited from either the private sector (about 25%) or public sector, hired on short term contracts, with pay and tenure contingent on their success in meeting annual performance targets. By April 1996, there were 125 executive agencies in the United Kingdom, with 37 more candidates under consideration, covering about 75% of the British civil service (Roberts, 1997).

Following the launch of the Financial Management Initiative in the United Kingdom, other governments including Australia, Canada, Denmark, Finland, and Sweden have adopted responsibility budgeting and accounting. None, however, has moved as far or as fast as New Zealand and the United Kingdom. Moreover, New Zealand's reformers explicitly recognized their debt to agency theory (Boston, Martin, Pallot, & Walsh, 1996).

Responsibility budgeting and accounting was adumbrated in the United States arguably in the content of both the Chief Financial Officers Act, in calls for mission-driven, results-oriented budgets and, more recently, performance measurement and management under the Government Performance and Results Act of 1993 as implemented in part under the Clinton administration but particularly by the George W. Bush administration under the Office of Management and Budget. However, thus far it has had limited effect in the United States due to the reluctance of the Congress to take on a reform that is presently supported in principle by the executive branch.

There are two other explanations for this absence of interest in implementation. The first is that many students of the expenditure process reject the notion that remote control can be reconciled with the American legislative budgetary process. Some people even assert that it can be practiced only by responsible unitary governments on the Westminster model, although that claim is belied by the Swiss and Swedish examples (Arwidi & Samuelson, 1993; Schedler, 1995) and various state (Barzelay & Moukheiber, 1994, pp. 161-163) and local governments here in the United States (Kaplan & Cooper, 1998, pp. 245-251). It would not be easy to reconcile responsibility budgeting with the U.S. legislative process, but we do not believe that they are necessarily incompatible (Harr, 1989; Harr & Godfrey, 1991, 1992; Thompson, 1994). A second possible explanation for its failure to leave its mark on government accounting and budget practices in the United States is that, unlike most other countries, the United States has large, well-organized corps of government accountants, auditors, budgeters, program analysts, and teachers of government accounting and budgeting. All of these groups have vested interests in differentiating public from private practice, because that difference gives value to their expertise. A third reason seems to be that many people, in and outside of government, evidently believe that "public" necessarily implies Prussian-style bureaucracy. Where the purpose of the organization is in question or the technology is available to it make Prussian-style bureaucracy inappropriate, they will hear of no alternative short of full-scale privatization.

In the Clinton administration's second-term, government reform efforts attempted to advance the concept of performance-based organizations (PBOs) modeled after Britain's Financial Management Initiative (Green, Jones, & Thompson, 1999; see, however, Roberts, 1997). The main theme of this reform effort was the use of contracts to hold PBOs accountable for financial performance. However, this reform did not go far under the Clinton administration and was left for further implementation after the presidential election of 2000. This is no tragedy because the progress of this effort was glacial anyway. When legislation for the first PBO candidate, the patent and trademark office, was sent to Congress, it aroused an intense debate between the administration and the chair of the House Judiciary subcommittee on courts and intellectual property regarding the relative merits of the PBO model versus a corporate model. This debate was reproduced in various venues for successive PBO candidates—thus RIP for the PBO concept and practice.

However, as described in chapter 2 it is noteworthy that in the 1990s and 2000s both Congress and the executive called for increased performance measurement and management. Some progress was made during the 1990s under the leadership of the president's Office Of Management And Budget (OMB) in implementing agency long range strategic plans including performance measures that were articulated into annual plans and to some extent annual budgets. However, it was not until 2001 that performance-based criteria were developed and applied to agency budgets by OMB.

In 2001 under President Bush, OMB developed and applied the Performance Assessment Rating Tool or PART. PART required agencies to submit performance data on a number of dimensions of management to be evaluated by OMB. As noted in chapter 2, PART has been deemed successful in congressional review as implementing the spirit of several performance-oriented laws passed in 1993 and 1995 in the Government Performance and Results Act and Government Management and Results Act (GPRA and GMRA). Also, the Government Accountability Office

(GAO) has testified to Congress that PART has improved the integration of performance measurement in executive budgeting.

What this experience demonstrates is that performance orientation has been adopted in the United States, as elsewhere, and that progress in applying the concept is almost inevitably slow and incremental. But slow is better than no implementation so in this regard the U.S. experience is a positive example of an incremental rather than a comprehensive reform, and one that is adopted to fit the nature of the political environment in which management reform initiatives always will be examined and evaluated. Thus it is all over the world. So, while we might prefer a more ambitious evolution to different types of organizational structures such as those referred to below as hyperarchies or networked organizations, supported by appropriate accrual and responsibility-oriented accounting and budgeting systems, elected officials and public managers alike mostly prefer to defend inefficient bureaucracies (while simultaneously assailing them for their inefficiency and wastefulness) rather than to change them. This is understandable because the known is amenable to political manipulation while the unknown is uncertain with respect to its susceptibility to the prevailing political will.

FROM TRADITIONAL BUREAUCRACY TO NEW ORGANIZATIONAL FORMS, OR IT TAKES TIME TO IMPLEMENT BETTER SYSTEMS

Most large-scale organizations in the American public sector are organized like turn-of-the-century railroads. Operating responsibility is delegated on a geographic or site basis, rather than a line of business basis. Regional chiefs report to an agency head. Small armies of administrative staff specialists also report to agency heads. Their job is to gather and process quantities of data for agency heads to use to coordinate activities, allocate resources, and set strategy. These structures can be traced directly to the administrative system developed by the Prussian bureaucracy under Heinrich von Stein, Gerhard von Scharnhorst, August von Gneisenau, and Helmuth von Moltke. The Prussian system included administrative innovations such as detailed centralized resource requirements planning (discretionary expense budgets), control by rules and standard operating procedures, functional organizational design, vertical integration, decomposition of tasks to their simplest components, sequential processing, and administrative centralization and specialization of administrative staff functions such as reporting, accounting, personnel, and purchasing.

The Prussian administrative system was once widely emulated by forward-looking businesses and governments all over the world. In the

United States, among the first large-scale organizations to adopt this system were the railroads and the military departments. In industry early adopters of the elements of the Prussian administrative system consistently grew large as hierarchy and bureaucracy created massive economies of scale and scope. Economies of scale are produced by spreading fixed expenses over higher volumes of output, thereby reducing unit costs. Economies of scope are produced by exploiting the division of labor—sequentially combining highly specialized functional units in multifarious ways to produce a variety of products (Chandler, 1962; Rosenberg & Birdsall, 1986). In some cases the expansion of the early adopters occurred through the destruction of business rivals, in others by merger with them.

Not only did the Prussian administrative system make large, complex organizations relatively efficient; it seemingly made them inevitable. Only very large organizations could fully exploit the Prussian administrative system. Only they could capitalize on extreme task specialization or afford the throngs of staff experts needed to gather and process quantities of data for top management. Hence, for a long time it seemed that bigger organizations were necessarily better. And there seemed to be no natural limits to this conclusion. The planning and control system the General military bureaucracy under General Erich Ludendorff used to mobilize Germany's resources during World War I (the Kriegwirtschaftsplan) was merely an amplification of its peace-time arrangements. The centralized planning system, Gosplan, used in the Soviet Union to implement its long-term policies and strategic plans was an adaptation of the Kriegwirtschaftsplan.

Improvements in information processing, especially in the realms of accounting and finance, eventually limited organizational expansion, however. These innovations had the effect of increasing the relative efficiency of coordinating organizational activities and the flow of materials through arm's length relationships (as opposed to direct supervision), making it possible to avoid some of the opportunity costs inherent to rule-based governance systems.

The administrative system developed by Alfred Sloan and Donaldson Brown at General Motors in the 1920s demonstrated the maturity of these innovations. Sloan is best known for the multiproduct or M-form organizational structure, in which each major operating division serves a distinct product market. Short-run integration under Sloan's system was achieved via buyer-seller relationships between GM's five automotive divisions and the divisions making automotive components (e.g., Fisher Body or Delco-Remy). Longer-run integration was achieved via the capital budgeting system devised by in 1923 by Donaldson Brown, GM's chief financial officer

GM's operating divisions were managed entirely by the numbers from a tiny corporate headquarters, using the DuPont system of financial control, also devised by Brown. Under this system, each division kept its own books, and managers were evaluated in terms of a return-on-assets target. The operating division managers continued to rely on control by rules and standard operating procedures and detailed resource-requirements plans. Sloan, however, believed that it was inappropriate, as well as unnecessary, for top managers at the headquarters level to know much about the details of division operations. If the numbers showed that performance was poor, it was time to change the division manager. Division managers with consistently good numbers got promoted, ultimately to headquarters. The divisional form of organization is not only a device to resolve a span of control problem; it also allows each division or business to be remotely controlled by the numbers from a strategic apex.

The general device that allows for remote control is a control system that aligns the incentives of operating unit managers with the purposes and priorities of the organization as a whole. For a remote control system to operate effectively, financial and cost information needs to be relevant. Establishing reporting entities corresponding to segmented business activities is the fundamental rule of thumb to be followed in the construction of such a system. A division is both a reporting entity and a segmented business activity. An ideal type—and even typical—division is one headed by a general manager who reports to the strategic apex and enjoys full line authority over the middle line and operating core.

It is somewhat ironic that governments are beginning to embrace what may be termed "remote control" at the same time many well-managed businesses are abandoning it (Bruggeman, 1995; Otley, 1994; Bunce, Fraser, & Woodcock, 1995). These businesses have abandoned remote control because they are no longer compartmentalized the way they once were and it simply doesn't reflect the way they are now put together (Bruggeman, 1995; Bunce, Fraser, Woodcock, 1995; Otley, 1994). Arguably, de-compartmentalization is being driven by the information revolution, which is breaking down economies of scale and scope built upon functional specialization (Reschenthaler & Thompson, 1996). According to Michael Hammer, modern data bases, expert systems, and telecommunications networks provide many, if not all, of the benefits that once made internal specialization of administrative functions like personnel, finance, accounting, and so forth, attractive (Hammer, 1990, pp. 108-112). To the extent that the provision of these services requires specialized skills, they are increasingly contracted out to specialist firms. The people in the organization who actually do its real work perform the rest.

Hammer and others claim that jobs should be designed around an objective or outcome instead of a single function; that functional specialization and sequential execution are inherently inimical to expeditious processing; that those who use the output of activity should perform the activity and the people who produce information should process it, since they have the greatest need for information and the greatest interest in its accuracy; that information should be captured once and at the source; that parallel activities should be coordinated during their performance, not after they are completed; and last, that the people who do the work should be responsible for decision making and control built into job designs (e.g., Hammer, 1990).

De-compartmentalization has led to smaller, flatter organizations, organized around a set of generic value-creating processes and specific competencies. Some single-mission organizations are now organized as virtual networks, some multimission organizations as alliances of networks. Evans and Wurster (1997) refer to both of these kinds of organizational arrangements as hyperarchies, after the hyperlinks of the World Wide Web (p. 75). Evans and Wurster assert that these kinds of organizations, like the Internet itself, the architectures of object-oriented software programming, and packet switching in telecommunications, have eliminated the need to channel information, thereby eliminating the tradeoff between information bandwidth (richness) and connectivity (reach). Evans and Wurster describe virtual networks (structures designed around fluid, team-based collaboration within the organization) as deconstructed value chains, and alliances of networks (the pattern of "amorphous and permeable corporate boundaries characteristic of companies in the Silicon Valley") as deconstructed supply chains, in which "everyone communicates richly with everyone else on the basis of shared standards."

The system reported in chapter 2 used by IBM (International Business Machines Corporation) at its plant in Dallas, Texas, is an example of an existing virtual network designed to mimic a market-like, self-organizing system. IBM used and uses powerful computers to keep track of all information loops and lines, to chart all activities and operational flows, to keep track of progress made at each stage of each transaction, and to prod tardy participants into action—this is control built into job design with a vengeance. The effect of this system was to eliminate the separation between departments and give employees the power to act independently but, at the same time, to and coordinate their actions with other stakeholders and production process participants. As a by-product, the computer systems used to manage and coordinate keep all of the loops and lines also identify the resources going into a particular job, almost entirely eliminating the need for cost allocation. Moreover, this information is available both prospectively and retrospectively to anyone in the organization.

Some well-managed multimission organizations including Johnson & Johnson, 3M, and Rubbermaid also have organized themselves into loose alliances of networks, sharing only their top management, a set of core competencies, and a common culture (Quinn, 1992). The control systems used by these organizations are like those of centralized bureaucracies in that they collect a lot of real-time information on every aspect of operations, including nonfinancial information, but unlike the control systems of stove-piped centralized bureaucracies, which were erected on the premise that the exercise of judgment should be passed up the managerial ranks, this information is used to push the exercise of judgment down into the organization, to wherever it is needed, at the point of sale, at delivery, or in production (Simons, 1995). From top management's perspective, the primary purpose of this information is to provide them with insight into the integrity, competence, and morale of their network managers and employees so that they can allocate their best people to the most important jobs.

How far hyperarchy can go is an open question. Evans and Wuster (1997) claim that it will destroy all hierarchies, whether of logic or of power, "with the possibility (or the threat) of random access and information symmetry." If hyperarchy is where we are all heading, responsibility budgeting and accounting is at best an intermediate stage (Otley, Broadbent, & Berry, 1995). It is now apparent, as it really was not before, that responsibility budgeting restricts the upward flow of operating information within organizations—making decentralization a necessity as well as an ideal. In contrast, networks and alliances are information rich environments. For the most part, access to information is symmetrical in fully networked organizations—equally available to all the people in the organization.

Why not skip the intermediate stages and go directly to networked organizations? Some governments appear to be moving in this direction. The trend toward performance efforts and accomplishments reporting and the wide-spread acquisition of so-called enterprise resource planning (ERP) systems built around common data structures and centralized information warehouses that permit data to be entered and accessed from anywhere in the organization (SAP, PeopleSoft, Oracle, etc.). However, Kaplan and Cooper (1998, p. 25) have argued that organizations that try to move directly to a system where everyone communicates richly with everyone else on the basis of shared standards, without passing through a recommended period of experimentation with operational-feedback and cost-measurement systems, will almost surely fail.

We are less certain that this is the case. Nevertheless, we would point out that decentralization can work in an information-rich environment only where top management attends to top management functions—strategic planning, organizing, staffing, the intellectual, and cultural development of the organization—and refrains from meddling in the conduct of operations. This takes self-restraint, and self-restraint must be learned. For that reason, it may make sense for governments to experiment with responsibility budgeting rather than going directly to new modes of organization and control. Few have had much experience with decentralization and almost none with self-restraint (Johansen, Jones, & Thompson, 1997; Jones & Thompson, 1999).

CONCLUSIONS

In conclusion it must be reiterated that the purpose of matching institutional structure to strategic positioning is to install responsibility and control structures in public organizations that are appropriate given their operating environments and the customer-service strategy. The costs and benefits of alternative responsibility and control structures and methods must be thoroughly evaluated to make these choices. Where the organization's administrative and control structures are not aligned with its strategy, performance will be sacrificed.

A comprehensive understanding of the appropriate application of budgeting and management control techniques is necessary to implement matching institutional structure to strategic positioning. In our view, the employment of responsibility budgeting and accounting is a significant step forward in this regard for most public sector organizations. However, as noted, there are alternatives to this approach, and risks associate with its implementation. As with restructuring, reengineering, and the learning cycle, public sector decision makers are challenged to embrace comprehensive rather than marginal reform if they want more responsive, transparent and results-oriented government. Yet this expectation is unrealistic given how difficult it is to reform government. Therefore, the phases of reform presented in this book probably should be attempted slowly, one step at a time over a period of a decade or decades. Thus, at the level of national governments the real challenge is to sustain a reform agenda across presidential administrations. This has happened in the U.S. to a significant extent in with elements the Government Performance and Results Act and Government Management and Results Act during the period 1996 through 2007 largely due to the efforts of the Office of Management and Budget, for example, partially through the use of the Performance Assessment Rating Tool (PART). Therefore, what seems impossible at first glance may be achievable over the longer term given the willingness of presidential administrations to devote the efforts of their staffs to the task.

CHAPTER 8

CREATING THE QUICK LEARNING ORGANIZATION IN GOVERNMENT

Creating the quick learning organization requires rethinking of everything from the organization's goals to its work processes, market and strategic planning, and outputs and results. And as we have stressed and address more fully in chapter 9, rethinking organizational design must move from reforming bureaucracy incrementally to more ambitious creation of netcentric and hyperarchic means for creating knowledge and performing work. Also essential is analysis of how organizations learn to create, infuse and disseminate knowledge (Nissen, 2006). In our conception, rethinking stresses the importance of speeding up observation, orientation, decision, and action to reduce the cycle time within which organizational learning occurs. The crucial step in the entire reform process is thinking creatively about markets, constituents, clients, customers, stakeholders, services and products, and the organization of work in public organizations. Rethinking requires moving to "quick analysis" for organizational decision making and learning how to think creatively about hard problems using conceptual blockbusting and other techniques to speed analysis and feedback. Managers need to learn how to sort out real problems from symptoms, and how to manage people to solve real problems more quickly. Team management and group motivation through distinguishing real versus false problems is essential. The key to rethinking is learning how to apply and infuse public management reform conceptions to create the self-teaching, adapting and knowledge creating organizations that stimulate their employees to greater productivity, link incentives to performance and invest in human capital (Pfeffer, 1998; see also Dixit, 2002; Ichniowski & Shaw 2003; Lazear, 2000). Rethinking requires better, faster evaluation of service performance, using survey research and other techniques, and quicker assessment of how to improve service and market strategy, and product/service positioning relative to competitors.

Building a shared vision of the future can also increase organizational speed and flexibility. By getting employees at every level to adopt the organization's external goals and purposes as their personal goals and values, a shared vision helps employees to orient themselves to new situations and decide on a course of action that will serve the interests of the organization. How does this process work? In many Japanese firms, goals and purposes are inculcated by everything the organization does, from starting the workday by singing the company song, through wearing uniforms, sharing onerous tasks between workers and management alike, and dispensing rewards and incentives. On a day-to-day basis many Japanese firms try to get their employees to evaluate everything they do to in terms of the overall goals and purposes of the organization. Their employees still have individual jobs, but they are expected to use their intelligence and initiative to work within and beyond those jobs to serve the organization's interests.

In most cases with highly skilled professionals, it is necessary to do more than explain organizational values and goals to its managers and employees. A high degree of training is also needed to teach managers and employees what to do and how to do it. It is also worth mentioning that personnel stability helps organizations react to and anticipate change. Training will not pay off for the organization if the employees that are trained leave or, even worse, if management moves them willy-nilly around the organization. Moreover, strangers do not work well together; sometimes they do not work at all. If people do not know each other, they will not trust each other. They will not count on each other for support, and they may not even care what others think about them, in which case they are unlikely to contribute their intelligence and their initiative to the organization (Barzelay & Thompson, 2005).

As noted in the previous chapter, the shift from linear to integrated work arrangements encourages trial and error challenges to standard operating procedures. New kinds of learning and thinking are stimulated at different levels and functions within the organization. Many fast-cycle time theorists argue that all jobs should be designed around objectives or outcomes instead of single functions, that is, that functional specialization and sequential execution are inherently inimical to faster learning and doing (Hammer, 1990; Meyer, 1993, p. 49; see also Stalk & Hout, 1990). Meyer has argued that organizations should be made up of interdisciplinary task forces or project teams, and team members must be located in direct physical proximity to each other. Sequential execution is usually inimical to fast action, especially where task performance involves parallel activities, that is, multiple, interdependent activities that have to be carried out simultaneously. However, there is more than one way to coordinate parallel activities. For example, support agencies may be tied directly to the mission delivery parts of the organization using a single real-time, spatially structured information system that permits activities to be coordinated as they are carried out.

A number of organizations have experimented with a similar approach to the coordination of parallel activities. They use sophisticated information technology to chart all workflows within an organization, to keep track of progress being made at each stage of each internal transaction, and to prod tardy participants into action, thereby encouraging employees to take the initiative and to coordinate their activities amongst themselves. For want of a better term, this approach might be described as virtual proximity. According to *The Economist,* in the early 1990s virtual proximity, "helped IBM trim its workforce at the Austin plant from 1,100 to 423; increase its range of products from 19 to 85; cut the time taken to develop new products from more than two years to eight months; and shrink the average manufacturing cycle from 7.5 to 1.5 days" (1993, p. 80)

We now move to an analysis of how organizations learn to create, infuse and disseminate knowledge. This conception of the knowledge creating organization is integral to our conception of rethinking in the context of the fast learning organization. Much of the thrust of this chapter is based on the work of Peter Senge (1990; Senge, Cambron-McCabe, Lucas, Smith, Dutton, & Kleineret, 1994; see also Sergiovanni, 1992).

The period 1975 to 2007 has witnessed a redefinition of the relative roles of government, business, and the market in most countries worldwide, with the role of government in universal retreat. These changes are more than ones of fine tuning, modest realignment, or reaction to public debt pressures from financial markets; they involve, on balance, a reduced role of government as a planning and regulatory agent in the economy and the adoption of new approaches to governance. In this chapter we examine some of the forces driving these changes. We focus on the use of the learning organization paradigm developed to explain many of the obstacles to change in the public sector which prevented earlier—and more moderate—reform and laid the foundation for more radical change. We suggest that the public management reform is a response to these forces of change and represents an effort to convert government and public sector organizations into more effective learning organizations.

GREAT TRANSFORMATIONS IN THE ROLE OF GOVERNMENT

Karl Polanyi (1944), in his book *The Great Transformation* documented two great transformations in the role of government in the economy: the transformation from mercantilism to laissez-faire capitalism (1770s to 1830s), and the transformation from laissez-faire capitalism to the modern mixed economies and, in some instances, centralized command economies (1830s to 1970s). Since the mid-1970s, most OECD (Organisation for Economic Co-operation and Development) countries have entered a third great transformation which is resulting in significant change in the economic role of governments. What happened during this third transformation in the role of government in the economy is important in understanding the role of government as it has evolved to the twenty-first century.

We begin with a brief review and critique of the essentials of a public interest version of pluralist theory and, second, public choice theory. We explore the usefulness of these two widely used approaches in explaining both the growth in the role of government in the economy during the period 1830 to 1975 and the partial decline during the last 3 decades. We proceed with an analysis of forces of change that have impacted on the private and public sectors over the period 1975 to the present, and then examine why there is a convergence of forces driving the behavior of government and private sector organizations. This review raises the question: what organizational elements are necessary for government to succeed in the long term? This leads us to consider how the failure of government as a learning institution can explain many of the "failed" public polices of the past and many of the policy problems of the present without reliance on traditional public interest or public choice frameworks. Finally, we suggest that much of the public management reform practice, which represents an effort to rehabilitate government, essentially involves making governments more effective learning organizations.

MODELS AND PARADIGMS OF THE ROLE OF GOVERNMENT

Through the 1970s, political scientists and political economists predominantly embraced "pluralist" models to explain the evolution of the role of government in the economy. In pluralist theory, public policy emerges as a consequence of the interaction, negotiation, and brokering among interest groups within their own organizations, within larger coalitions of organizations, within political parties, and within government itself (Dunleavy, 1991, pp. 14-27). In these processes different interests are expected to emerge and counterbalance each other, and with time, the processes are expected to serve the "common" or "public" interest. Pluralist theory recognizes but arguably does not emphasize differences in motivation, focus, size, composition, cohesiveness, economic resources, preference intensities, organization, and strategic positioning of different interest groups. Rather, its focus is much more pragmatic.

Pluralist theory possesses an important underlying element of optimism, beginning with an assumed element of "civic culture" (Kelman, 1987a, 1987b). There is an implicit assumption that somehow the political process will result in the common interest being served in the long run. It may fairly be seen as a model that envisions people as slightly fallen angels capable of overriding or blunting the pursuit of self-interest. This is not to say that self-interest is not an *important* motivating force or that different interest groups are not perceived as varying widely in their influence on public policy. Nevertheless, pluralists seem to believe that, on balance, "democracies have political competition among groups with relatively equal political strength" (Becker, 1985, p. 344) and, even when interests are not equally balanced, pluralists "remain optimistic that stark influence imbalances will create systems of countervailing powers" (Dunleavy, 1991, p. 25)

From an economic perspective, and from the perspective of mainstream economics textbooks used widely through the late 1970s, the pluralist approach was represented, or embodied, in what we label a public interest or market failure paradigm. We believe that it is fair to propose that prior to the late 1970s the public interest paradigm reflected most academic thinking. Within this framework, government was viewed as an instrument to fix, buffer, or compensate for "market failure," or as an instrument superior to markets. In any case, the government was seen as an instrument to serve, or promote, the public interest. Polanyi captured the essence of the "market failure" approach when he analyzed the great transformations in Europe: first to laissez-faire capitalism and then, beginning in the 1830s, to the modern "mixed" economy. In that framework, as the public came to *perceive* that the market "failed" to provide socially and or economically acceptable results, alternative instruments or working rules (Commons, 1968) were sought: regulation, taxation, subsidy, public ownership, competition policy, self regulation, and civil law. In general, then, government was seen as a supporter and fixer: To the aggrieved interest group or groups, government could "fix" or, at least, take actions that would alter or buffer public consequences.

In addition to correcting for perceived market failure, the public interest/market failure model envisions governments establishing institutions, primarily legal systems, with well defined property rights that collectively provide for effective, efficient, and fair contract law, as well as public peace and order. Without these, transactions costs rise and markets cannot work efficiently: civil and/or criminal law must prevent or offer remedies for fraud and failure to fulfill understood expectations of contracts; otherwise markets fail. In addition, government intervention could go well beyond cases of market failure to promote broader political objectives. This was an interventionist prone model. The public interest/market failure model readily justified rapid expansion of government during and after the Great Depression, during World War II, which called for central economic direction, and during the period of post-World War II adjustment. There seemed to be abundant evidence to demonstrate the failure of market systems on a large number of dimensions. The performance of these government functions in centralized, large government bureaucracies were intended to mimic the performance of administrative functions in private industry, and large administrative organizations in government produced administrative economies without new, but less tangible and less immediately visible, costs. Those who could see market failure rarely envisioned, or gave much credence, to the potential problems of government failure.

The public interest model was vulnerable to criticism: It was pragmatic without any scientific argument for demonstrating why "good" should prevail. It was naive because it assumed that people who were expected to be naturally self-interest driven in all aspects of their private economic lives, suddenly became focused on the public interest or public good when they entered interest groups, when they entered the voting booth, or when they were elected to public office. It was open-ended in its definition of market failure, inviting intervention. It did not consider the "free rider" problem, the related problems of information and transactions costs, and the impact of these on individual and group behavior. It presented no theory to explain the administrative process of policy development and implementation. It gave little thought to behavioral motivation, communication, and learning problems of employees in the public sector responsible for implementing public policies. It was unable to easily rationalize the ever increasing number of examples of each of the rationalizations for public policy intervention used in the past to serve the interests of particular stakeholder interest groups to the disservice of the public. Consequently, it did not systematically address the question of public sector failure. That it did not provide systematic, historically valid explanations of many failed public policy interventions in the economic realm is perhaps its most serious deficiency. Research by economists and historians over the last 40 years reveals that while most acts of government intervention in the economy have been clothed in public interest arguments, those promoting the interventions often have been influenced by their self-interest.

Given these weaknesses, there remained some optimism in the pluralist model and the public interest version based on the view of democracy as a pragmatic process in which the public interest is sought by a "reasonable" electorate imbued with some sense of social or community welfare. Mistakes are to be expected. Ideas were seen as important, and "good" ideas were expected to prevail over bad ideas and mistakes over time. Growth in government was not taken as inevitable under public interest theory, and a contraction in government over time was consistent with its fundamental philosophy. This optimism was rooted in the belief that the electorate is ultimately composed of humans who are slightly fallen angels as opposed to apes recently down from the trees.

By the 1960s, the theoretical and empirical foundations had been developed for an alternative model: public choice. Since that time, the public choice model has come to dominate academic thinking, particularly among economists. The intellectual foundation for the public choice approach is found in the writings of Buchanan and Tullock (1962), Downs (1957, 1967), Olson (1965), and Niskanen (1971). Dunleavy asserted that the public choice literature offered a coherent picture of most aspects of the political process and provided a comprehensive theory of public sector failure. This theory was not taken up by academics alone. The key decision makers who directed the influential reform that is known as the New Zealand model freely admit that they were inspired and attempted to implement public choice thinking to transform their government in the late 1980s and 1990s. Thus, the public choice model may be viewed to have supported much of the application of New Public Management in New Zealand, Australia, the United Kingdom, and in other commonwealth nations.

The essence of public choice theory may be captured by identifying its key behavioral assumptions and considering their logical implications. Public choice theory envisions public sector failure as a natural and expected consequence of self-interest behavioral assumptions about individuals, interest groups, political parties, politicians, governments, and public administrators/employees. Public choice theory has eight key behavioral assumptions: (1) People are rational actors with defined, logically consistent preferences; (2) People are driven by self (or family) interest and are maximizers in the sense that they engage in activities which provide maximum net utility or "comprehensive net worth" as measured in non-pecuniary (psychic) as well as pecuniary terms; (3) The political process involves efforts by individuals and politicians, alone and in coalitions, to obtain economic rents through their ability to influence or control government in its initiation and implementation of public policy; (4) Coalitions are built to meet short and long term stakeholder needs with individual stakeholders being courted or marginalized depending on the importance of their inclusion for the success of the coalition, the cost of obtaining their support, and the likelihood they would join or support the coalition without formal solicitation or compensation; (5) Some stakeholders win and others lose in what is largely a zero sum exercise. Some stakeholders are well organized, focused, cohesive, possess continuity (permanence), develop and nourish contacts and networks in government, develop and maintain networks of related stakeholders, and understand political—writ large—processes (O'Toole & Meier, 2004). As a result, when necessary they can act in a timely, cohesive, and focused manner with the assistance of other stakeholders with related interests; (6) Some interest groups suffer fundamental disadvantages in the dynamics of collective action due to the free rider behavioral problem: The successful stakeholders almost always suffer less from the "free rider" problem; (7) Individuals within the government's administrative apparatus are driven by self-interest to expand and protect existing programs and develop new programs of intervention; and (8) Due to the competitive nature of the political process, in seeking rents through the intervention by the government, interest groups will often, collectively, wastefully from a social or allocative standpoint expend resources to influence public policy equal to the actual rents likely achievable.

Given the above, our view is generally that networks can be influenced by stakeholders and participants, but they cannot be "managed" per se. Rather, true networks of the type characterized by Evans and Wurster (1997) cannot be managed but instead evolve as entities relatively free of control and management by any party. However, there is a school of thought that views networks as manageable (see, for example, Kickert, Klijn, & Koppenjan, 1997; O'Toole & Maier, 2004), but we do not agree with this perspective.

The public choice theory of government is ultimately one that focuses on wealth redistribution. In its extreme form, there is an underlying assumption that individuals inside or outside government are incapable of altruism. The pursuit of self-interest is seen as the driving force in private and public affairs. In the phrasing of economists, every organization and individual is seeking economic rents. In this model, government economic activities are designed and implemented to prevent market solutions for resource allocation. Most individuals and groups turn to government as an instrument to assist them to receive or preserve economic rents (pecuniary and nonpecuniary benefits) that would otherwise not be available to them in noncoercive, competitive market settings.

Most importantly, the public choice model is pessimistic about the public sector in general: Public sector failure is expected and is explained in terms of public policy programs corrupted in design to serve the private interests of rent seekers, who are facilitated in their efforts by information cost related problems of losing stakeholders, and corrupted further in their design and implementation by the self-interest rent seeking motivations of elected and nonelected individuals and groups within government.

We can extrapolate from the public choice model and envision a society as having several common pools of wealth that may be tapped by interest groups. Each stakeholder and each interest group attempts to use the collective, coercive power of government to adopt and implement public policies which transfer wealth in its favor. A convenient framework for this analysis is to stipulate that societies possess at least six pools of common wealth: (1) a personal and business current wealth pool; (2) a public sector current real and financial wealth pool, net of natural resources; (3) a pool of natural resources which is owned in the public sector; (4) a human capital resource pool; (5) an environment pool which is a measure of the "quality" of the environment writ large; and (6) the wealth of the future generations. The wealth of future generations is largely dependent upon the use of the first five pools currently held.

These six common pools, or commons, are sources of possible wealth transfers. The process of government then is one by which stakeholders attempt to hold on to what they have or to obtain the transfer to them of parts of these wealth pools, which are either held privately by others or in common. To be explicit, this pursuit of "unearned" wealth is rent seeking, and as in the case of the traditional overuse of the commons problem (Hardin, 1968; Senge, 1990, pp. 294-298, 387-388; and Soden, 1988), rent seekers are attracted by the proverbial "free lunch" where the marginal private benefit and cost are less than the marginal social cost. In theory, stakeholders will compete for necessary government coercive support to allow them to tap these commons and, in some situations, may bid away economic rents. Also, most importantly, all rent seekers collectively will overuse the public goods available to them. This overuse is termed the "tragedy of the commons." Groups most vulnerable to losses in this framework all suffer information disadvantages. The young and the unborn who will share the cost of government debt obviously have no information and no direct representation. Consumers and taxpayers, individually and collectively, suffer information disadvantages related to the unavailability of information, the cost of obtaining information on potential losses, and problems of collective action related to the free rider phenomenon. The success, and thus potential costs, of rent seeking is limited only by the extent to which a society has a culture, institutions, and laws which compel accountability and transparency in stakeholder and government behavior. The problems are ultimately ones of overuse of commons goods, scale and information cost.

The public choice model is cynical as well as pessimistic. In its strongest form it suggests that humankind is incapable of altruism; people are selfish, and nothing more, or they are driven as some sociobiologists will argue by nothing more than the desire to preserve and enhance their gene pools. In its extreme form, public choice effectively denies any role for what Steven Kelman (1987a; see also Trebilcock, 1994, p. 41) calls "public" or "civic" spirit, except to the extent that self-interest is defined to include an interest in the welfare of others, an effort to make the concept even more open ended. Public choice also largely denies that ideas have power. Trebilcock has pointed to the movements to privatize, to deregulate, and to reform taxation by government as examples of policies which public choice theory, at times, is hard pressed to explain. To Trebilcock, and as he reminds us to J. M. Keynes (1936, pp. 383-384), at least some ideas seem to have some force in the long run relative to political interests. In this view democracy becomes a pragmatic system which tests ideas as well as interests. To public choice theorists, the political process tests only the relative acumen and strategic placement of different private interests, private interest coalitions, and bureaucrats. Trebilcock commented that, "politics, to an important extent, is partly about what are thought to be good ideas as well as what are thought to be politically salient interests" (p. 94)

The public choice paradigm also suffers a serious scientific methodology problem in that it does not allow a test for refutation of its fundamental precept that all behavior is self-interest driven. Once the concept of psychic or nonpecuniary benefits is introduced, and once it is taken as given that people have no incentive to do anything unless expected benefits exceed expected costs, it follows that anything they do must provide a net "gain"—otherwise, by definition, they would not bother to do it. Apparent heretical behavior is easily explained in this closed system. Public choice theorists point out that individuals may obtain recognition and status benefits from "belonging" to apparent nonprofit advocacy groups. They may experience utility through the "legitimization" of their own aesthetic, ethical, environmental, religious, sexual, or wealth distribution values when the government imposes those values on everyone through law. Consequently, any behavior which appears to be altruistic or for the community good can be explained in psychic benefit terms including banking points with the Almighty. Finally, we note that once the sociobiological concept of gene-pool protection is introduced, any environmental protection activity becomes explicable in self-interest terms. Similarly, public policies to reduce public sector deficits can be seen as contributing to the net wealth pool of future generation carriers of one's gene pool.

These problems aside, and clearly they are not small problems, the public choice model is powerful, and we would argue extremely useful, in providing a framework for thought that leads to a healthy skepticism about the real goals of interest groups and political coalitions which clothe themselves in public interest assertions. We must always ask what is under the cloth?

The public choice model does more than explain the genesis of public policies. Its theories on implications of information costs, coalition formation, free riding, agenda setting, and bureaucracy are all important contributions to the theory of political economy. Public choice theories on bureaucratic behavior that focus on self-interest rent seeking behavior of individuals within the bureaucracy, as well as those elected to office, to explain public sector growth and implementation problems have been widely heralded, although these effects have been recognized by theorists on organization behavior previously. Public choice argues government programs have grown, the sizes of bureaucracies have increased, and the publicly articulated objectives have rarely been achieved because of self-interest motivations of the implementers: Regulators want more to regulate, that is, to find new problems, the military wants a larger defense establishment, and social workers want more "victims" of family and society to nurture, preferably in smaller case ratios.

It should come as no surprise that those presenting the public interest case for intervention typically have pointed at *instances* of presumed "market process failure." Those who take a public choice approach typically have pointed to "public sector process failure" that usually refers to examples of presumed public policy design, choice, and implementation *process* failure.

From an analytical standpoint, one of the greatest problems with both frameworks is that they are presented as polar choices. We believe that it is possible to reconcile the two approaches to explain public policy and to augment these theories with a new approach that provides additional insight into public policy and public management reform process.

SERVING THE PUBLIC INTEREST AND PUBLIC CHOICE

It is clear that many government interventions in the private economy and the lives of citizens are inspired from the beginning by stakeholders who are rent seekers and who will benefit significantly. It also seems clear, to us at least, that many interventions have been primarily motivated by a widespread perception of market or institutional system failure. A few examples should suffice. First, in the nineteenth and twentieth centuries, the railroads never opposed government regulation to the extent that their owners' public governments would have suggested at the time. However, it is clear that the main political pressure for government regulation came from disgruntled railway customers who faced monopoly railroads. Second, while Theodore Vail and AT&T did support government regulation of telephone service early in the twentieth century, the reason they did so was out of knowledge that the public was going to insist on some type of government intervention, and independent regulatory commission regulation was much more attractive to Vail than the alternatives. Third, government intervention in the twentieth century that resulted in legislation to provide equal pay for equal work (not work of equal value) were primarily driven by a perception that the market failed, or, more properly, social values and institutions failed.

These three examples are useful in allowing us to develop a hypothesis we believe allows us, at least to some extent, to reconcile the two apparently contradictory perspectives on government intervention. We propose that while early intervention proposals are often, if not typically, motivated by public interest-market failure considerations, that stakeholder groups which initially seem to be likely to be affected adversely will, with time, turn government intervention to their advantage. Similarly, as illustrated by cases where large amounts of capital are at stake, public power projects for example and some social programs such as social security, where it is clear from inception that some groups will benefit more than others, the beneficiaries often will follow the "foot in the door" principle and turn the projects to their advantage in ways perhaps never anticipated by government.

In the case of work place equity, a similar pattern prevails, but with a twist. Here, from the beginning, the likely beneficiaries of government intervention were actively involved, but their concerns were widely shared, that is, this is a market failure problem. Having enjoyed success, those stakeholders then sought further gains, first to equal opportunity legislation, then to equal pay for work of equal value, and ultimately to preferential hiring in the form of employment equity. Without judging the merits of each of these stages of government intervention, it is fair to say that, progressively, each was publicly and politically more controversial and the subject of increased accusations of special stakeholder rent gains.

We could explore other examples but our point has been be made. The public choice model that explains the problems of collective political action by large, diverse stakeholder groups who suffer from free rider syndrome, may be more useful in explaining why the *process* of government intervention once initiated is more likely to serve to the disadvantage of losing groups than is the model in demonstrating the original rationale or impetus for government intervention. This is particularly true when the contributions of public choice (e.g., Niskanen, 1971) in explaining bureaucratic rent seeking behavior are considered as well as other problems of governments as failed learning organizations.

We believe that an understanding of these two perspectives on government involvement in the economy do provide useful insights into why governments overreached in economic interventions over the period of the second transformation. However, we do not believe that either of these paradigms, reconciled or not, is wholly adequate to explain perceived public sector failure and the current transformation. To develop an acceptable paradigm, a better understanding of the forces that have been having an impact upon both the private sector and on government during the past thirty year period is required, as well as a better understanding of learning processes in government and, consequently, its problems in adapting to change. In the next section we examine some of these forces and their implications for development of a more complete model to explain public sector market intervention and its effects and, ultimately, the need for creating the learning organization in government.

RETHINKING THEORY ABOUT GOVERNMENT BEHAVIOR

As with earlier periods of change in the relationship of government and the market, there is a clear pattern. The third great transformation, however, is differentiable from the previous two because of its near universal nature, the "reformist" driving forces, the time frame, and its transparency. The two previous transformations tended to be less focused in their change, to be spread much more temporally among countries, and to be documented after the fact. In the case of the current change, the fundamental forces are all quite similar, virtually all industrialized and advanced developing countries are affected—though the rates and extent of change vary, and the time window is very short: 1970 to 2007.

The pattern of change has included: privatization, contracting out, economic deregulation, reduction or stabilization of tax rates, greater use of payroll and excise taxes, freer trade, and—more recently—significant reductions in public sector employment. The pattern of policies on social (environmental, workplace health and safety, product safety, municipal land use and rent level, and employment practices), private law, fisheries, financial, cultural industries, and competition regulation is much more mixed. Government, it appears, will continue with very substantial regulatory agendas in the latter areas; however, the adoption of reformed approaches—such as the use of incentives and more attention to costs relative to benefits—is already apparent in many countries.

The new pattern of government management, however, goes well beyond these elements. The way the government manages the affairs of the government—and the culture of government itself—is in transition even in the areas in which government is not in retreat. This pattern of new behavior or new culture began to emerge in the late 1970s, and in its maturing form may be thought of as the public management reform movement, but more about this later.

Pressure for reform, fundamentally, derives from public perception of public sector failure. We believe, that the increased visibility or transparency of problems is a more important force during this transformation than during earlier periods and weighs heavily in accounting for the short time frame in which change is occurring. Furthermore, the sensitivity of the public to public sector failure has been heightened by income stagnation, high unemployment, and increased visibility and concern with mounting public deficits of the type present in the U.S. in the 2000s. These failures have become increasingly visible to the public due to the information/communications revolution. While rapid technological, social, and economic changes have occurred in the past, the failures of government were not so quickly, so closely, so measurably, so visibly, so pervasively, and so selectively observed by and analyzed for the public at large. The communications/information revolution has dramatically reduced the information cost disadvantages often faced by stakeholders likely to be losers from public policies in place or proposed.

The reduced costs of obtaining and disseminating information and the related new and relatively inexpensive methods of communication have improved the ability of losing stakeholders and stakeholder groups to organize and act in cohesive, timely, and effective ways. More recently, the Internet system further reduces the costs and increases the effectiveness and efficiency of these communication and organizational activities.

To some extent this process is a natural continuation of the development of comprehensive special interest data bases which began in the 1970s and has been related to the continuous improvement in the performance capacity and dramatic reduction in cost of computer hardware and software and telecommunications. While these changes initially were developed and mastered by special interest rent seeking groups and political parties, the capacity has become increasingly available to broader based stakeholder groups as well. They are reflected in the organizational and lobbying successes of diverse groups with concerns about long-term environmental, natural resource, tax, and debt implications of existing and proposed policies and related public management.

The effectiveness of these mechanisms was highlighted in 1995 by the experience of Intel with its flawed Pentium chip. In the past its policy of largely ignoring the problem might have worked. In this case, however, the Internet system was used as a vehicle for different potential losing consumer stakeholder groups to communicate and mount concerted actions which resulted in a policy reversal by Intel within a few days.

We propose that this increased ease and reduced cost of information dissemination and joint action has contributed to the pressures on government by stakeholders who have incurred loses or are at risk of loss. It is fair to argue that most special interest stakeholder groups have always had the lobby vehicles available to be effective participants in the political processes. These groups have also benefited from the changes in information management of the last 2 decades. The future, however, promises further improvements in the abilities of losing groups—particularly those composed of individuals who perceive particularly remote and tenuous loses—to organize and act in cohesive, timely, and effective ways. In any case, with the changes in the information economy which we have discussed, the burden of effective response by potential or actual losing stakeholders from intervention is reduced at each stage of the political and administrative process. It is, therefore, an important factor in understanding the shifting roles of government and the market in the third transformation.

Along with the reduced costs of information and communications (organization) for stakeholders who previously faced high information/transactions costs has come a new mind set. The new mindset is one of increased skepticism about government, that is, a deeply rooted cynicism. This change in mental frame may well have developed in the 1960s and 1970s related to the post-Vietnam era of disillusionment with the apparent failure of U.S. government to either win or end an unpopular war. This disillusionment was then reinforced by the Nixon Watergate scandal (just as corporate wrongdoing of the ENRON type in the 1990s and 2000s eroded confidence in the private sector). Prior to Vietnam and Watergate, it may be argued that the public's mental framework toward governments in their paternalistic and market correcting roles was much more positive and trusting. This change in cognitive framing also may have been affected by the influence of the ideas and empirical work of the public choice school, which as noted is uniformly cynical about the role of government in serving the rent seeking activities of special interest stakeholders to the disadvantage of policy losers who face high information and organization costs that deter effective reaction.

Thus, the Vietnam war and Watergate episodes and revelations in public choice theoretical and empirical work may have contributed to lowering the cost of information about political issues and political systems and encouraged action by providing a new frame of reference for voters and stakeholders to use in accessing and evaluating declining cost, increasingly available information: they know what questions to ask and where to, economically, look for information.

The end of mercantilism and rise of laissez-faire capitalism, Polanyi's first transformation, does in some ways parallel our current experience. Governments were demonstrated by Adam Smith in the *Wealth of Nations*, not to work very efficiently or in the public interest—as he defined the public interest. Smith did not need a public choice model to explain government failure, though he certainly understood the concept of pursuit of self-interest and the problems of agency. We recall that Smith was no admirer of the large charter companies with their close ties to the government, and he foresaw—wrongly, or prematurely—the decline of large corporations with too many layers of management of questionable motivation: Where was the eye of the shop master? Smith did see pressures emerging from the new merchant class in the private sector. He wrote in a period of change; and he was surrounded by governments and large organizations that he saw as failed planning and regulatory institutions: failed learning organizations.

In the past, both government and business failure could continue undetected and unpunished for long periods. Eventually business management failure would result in recognition to the extent that annual reports were released and market values of shares ultimately declined. Public sector failure was, typically, not similarly recognized, measured, and penalized. The forces driving change in the public and private sectors typically were not related by the public, except to the extent that some type of private sector failure might lead to demand for public sector intervention.

More so than in earlier periods in world history, many of the forces driving public sector reform today are the same as those driving private sector reform or failure. To develop this point, we draw on some models created primarily to explain organizational effectiveness in the private sector: Some of the same models that explain success and failure of private organizations can serve to explain the success and failure of the public sector generally, and its operating organizations specifically. Our belief is that governments, for systemic reasons, have lacked the ability or will to learn or adapt fast enough in a period of rapid change such as that experienced during last 20 years.

In the next section we identify some of the recent forces for change in the private sector. In the current period, what is happening in the private sector directly impacts on the public sector, the general public's perception of government, and the nature of demand for change.

PRIVATE SECTOR EXPERIENCE

During the period 1975 to 2007, private sector organizations have been under intense pressure to change the way they do business. We briefly review some of those pressures for change and their effects, because we think that it is necessary to understand the changes in private sector management in order to understand the reasons for some of the more important pressures that have caused the transformation in government and business relations.

The stability in relations and status of big labor, big business, and big government that prevailed in most industrial countries in the West during the post-World War II (Galbraith, 1956, 1967) period began to collapse in the 1970s (Reich, 1991). Global competitive pressures began to force fundamental change in the way the private sector functioned. They developed as a result of declining global and domestic transportation costs and dramatic improvements and innovations in the speed and efficiency of passenger and commercial transportation, making integrated global operations efficient from a transportation of people and goods standpoint; improvements in telecommunications, which facilitated low cost, global communications; the opening of the American market to European countries and Japan for political reasons; the subsequent, and simultaneous, economic recovery of Europe and Japan from World War II, and thus, the development of the resources and incentives for their businesses to seek foreign markets; the opening of the American market to other Asian competitors under the evolving rules of the World Trade Organization (WTO). Other factors that must be considered include the following:

1. The general opening of markets as a result of trade liberalization through the WTO;
2. The development of techniques by businesses to circumvent non-tariff barriers to trade;
3. The maturity of Japan, China, Korea, and Taiwan as international competitors;
4. The increasing political and economic stability and market orientation (reduction of political and economic risk) of many third

world countries, making them more attractive sources for manufacturing—particularly China, India, Thailand, Malaysia, and Indonesia.
5. Technological change driven by the computer revolution and its global availability;
6. Related advances in information systems technologies;
7. The achievement of the full benefits of economies of scale by a large number of global firms in a large number of industries;
8. The decline in firm size required to enjoy production economies of scale in many industries, along with increasingly sophisticated global marketing and distribution systems;
9. The declining cost of capital and its dramatically increasing productivity and particularly substitutability for labor due to advances in computer and information technology;
10. A tendency for the cost of labor to rise in some industrialized countries due to increased employer borne, payroll taxes;
11. The end of the need for large, vertically integrated firms with large, permanent bureaucracies in many industries due to the preceding and, in general, declining transactions costs;
12. Economic deregulation and privatization;
13. Redefinition of industries by technology;
14. Increased efficiency and competitiveness in financial markets with much more aggressive roles being played by institutional investors seeking value;
15. Better informed industrial consumers and retailers taking advantage of new information technologies to pressure manufacturers;
16. The revolution in competitiveness in retailing and service industries; and
17. The "quality" revolution leading customers to expect quality goods and service as a norm.

The effect of these changes on industry was to increase competition dramatically. In Robert Reich's (1991) terminology, business organizations had to discard 150 years of "volume" orientation in favor of becoming "value" oriented. Traditional oligopolistic industries facing traditional industry-wide unions with traditional big government support and protection could no longer continue business as usual. We want to expand briefly on the increasing competitiveness, rates of change, and discontinuities faced by private sector management that result from these and related forces. The period for business has been characterized as one of traumatic and discontinuous change.

Advances in, along with major reductions in the cost of, computer hardware and software joined by related advances in telecommunications, information systems technology, and transportation, allowed organizations to restructure and effectively substitute capital for labor across the board. The cost of capital was falling very rapidly relative to labor and the ease of substitution was rising very rapidly, particularly for less skilled workers in manufacturing at first, but later in service activities.

Transportation, communications, and information system, as well as other changes identified above, drastically reduced the transactions costs related to outsourcing of goods and services by private sector companies: the calculus of choosing to rely on in-house production (within the hierarchy) or contracting through markets shifted sharply in favor of markets (Bradley, Hausman, & Noland, 1993; Malone & Rockart, 1995; Malone, Yates, & Benjamin, 1987). And, inevitably, organizations are less efficient than markets (Gibbons, 2003). While Hamel and Prahalad (1994) focused thinking in management in 1988, business already was developing an appreciation of the advantages of concentrating on core competencies and had begun seeking opportunities to contract out to the extent that rapidly falling transactions costs allowed.

These changes, along with increased stability and manufacturing capability in emerging third world countries in Southeast Asia and a general move to free trade and free trade groupings allowed management increased flexibility in shifting production abroad; competitive pressures compelled prompt responses. The opening of China, India, and other Asian nations as major manufacturing sources for lower and medium technology intensive goods has further increased competitive pressures. Companies were compelled to concentrate on higher order functions such as design, planning, control, testing, and marketing while contracting internationally for everything else. They profitably contracted out many of these functions as well.

By the mid-1990s, the implications of these changes are reflected in the observations of four leading writers on business strategy: Mintzberg, Hamel and Prahalad and D'Aveni. Their private sector observations will have relevance for our later discussions on the public sector.

Mintzberg (1994), in his book *The Rise and Fall of Strategic Planning*, examined the decline in the use of strategic planners and strategic planning departments in a large number of major business organizations during the 1980s and 1990s. His central hypothesis is that the rate of change in markets is so fast that traditional approaches to strategic planning are no longer sustainable: planning must be continuous and incremental. The rate of change and the frequency of discontinuities are so great that corporate strategic planning as such often runs the risk of imposing greater costs than benefits on organizations. In his view the process has often failed and frequently the failure has been dramatic. Often failure is reflected in the discouragement of learning. Mintzberg's analysis focused on planning as decentralized action and informal learning within the context of a strategic vision closely tied to the core competencies of an organization. A strategic plan becomes only a flexible framework that is always in the process of adaptation to changing economic and political environments.

Hamel and Prahalad (1994), in their book *Competing for the Future*, and in a number of *Harvard Business Review* (Hamel & Prahalad, 1989, 1990, 1993) articles that preceded it, examined a broad range of management issues. Two are particularly important to us. First, they place an emphasis on continuous organizational and individual learning. Second, they offered the view that while business organizations must identify, develop, and fully exploit core competencies (those which will likely provide sustained competitive advantages and make substantial contributions to stockholder value, and have clear strategic intent), they must go further and find ways to compete against themselves. They cannot rest on competitive advantages of the moment or they will be displaced by aggressive competitors: Static competitive analysis is a formula for bankruptcy. They, like Mintzberg, see traditional cookbook strategic planning and competitive conditions analysis as extremely risky. The external threats are so great that organizations must anticipate change and create change conditions themselves on a continuing basis. Thus Intel cannot wait for a competitor; it must drive down the price of Pentiums itself, and bring on the next generation of chips as a replacement long before a competitor produces one. In short, the tempo of competition is increasing to the point that business organizations must continuously reinvent themselves, reinvent their products, and discover latent needs which consumers have yet to imagine, much less articulate. If existing competitors fail to concentrate not only on consumers' existing needs but on latent needs as well, a new competitor will. High quality products and service are now part of the baseline to compete—a requirement for getting a seat at the competitive table. Technical efficiency and flexibility in production, distribution, information systems, and organizational design are taken for granted. Readers of Hamel and Phahalad are always listening for the sound of Schumpeterian waves or creative destruction breaking in the background and wondering which organization will be the next victim of either the direct impact or the undertow.

D'Aveni (1994) went a step beyond in his book *HyperCompetition*. D'Aveni, borrowing heavily, and acknowledging his debt, from Joseph Schumpeter and the Austrian School of Economics' concepts of competition and strategy, argued that competitive pressures in today's markets are destroying nongovernment protected competitive advantages of firms at rates which will force most industries, over a relatively short period of time, to face industry competitive results comparable to that old favorite, but rarely seen, competitive "norm" model of economists: perfect competition. In effect, the consumer can look forward to high quality and the lowest possible price with fast rates of technological improvement as the norm in industry; while industry can rarely expect to enjoy economic rents for any but the briefest periods of time. While he probably exaggerates the ability of firms to undercut or circumvent government-created legal protections for intellectual property, his general thesis is well supported by analysis and by his examples. Sustained economic rents for firms and resource suppliers not protected by government become impossible in this hypercompetitive world.

The same competitive pressures that impacted on business have had a derivative effect on resource markets—particularly labor markets. Market pressures have forced reexaminations of virtually every aspect of business conduct. A value test has to be applied to each line of business, each division, each department, and each resource input, including each employee or group of employees. In hypercompetitive industries, firms cannot carry employees who do not produce competitive value outputs equal to or greater than their costs: cross-subsidization becomes competitively impossible over time. Similarly, and as all management students are increasingly aware, the company or organization man or woman, the average worker who spent 30 to 40 years grinding up through the ranks with lifetime employment as a reward is increasing rare and will soon be of interest only to organizational anthropologists.

Blue collar manufacturing workers lost bargaining power as they found themselves caught up in the maelstrom of: (1) the declining cost of capital and its increasing capabilities, substitutability, and productivity; (2) increased ease of outsourcing and producing abroad; (3) increasing numbers of low cost nonunion competitors domestically; and (4) relatively inexpensive—and often well-trained—foreign labor. Service sector workers lost bargaining power caught in the crunch of: (1) new technology; (2) displaced blue collar workers; (3) some foreign competition; and (4) new, poorly educated, labor force entrants. Except in the public sector, the power of labor unions was increasingly undermined by these market forces and by accommodating public policy. The emergence of a "just-in-time" part-time labor force, accounting for over 10% of the labor force in North America in 1995 and which has grown larger by the mid-2000s, with minimal bargaining power and claim to few fringe benefits further reduced labor bargaining power on issues of compensation, work rules, and health and safety.

White collar, middle management faced the same value squeeze as new technology-driven management and information systems capital, which also was declining rapidly in cost as it rose in its range of uses and productivity for analysis and control, made the middle managers increasingly redundant. Not all labor has been adversely affected by these pressures. The distribution of income and wealth has moved toward greater inequality in many countries during this period of transition. Households in the top 20%, typically, have gained significantly. Knowledge workers, as they have come to be called, have tended to benefit with real income gains, at times substantial. Unfortunately, for the majority of workers in most industrialized countries the new competition has meant often declining and, at best, stable real income levels over the period since 1975. High levels of individual and family anxiety and stress follow. We now see hypercompetition in labor as well as product markets.

These changes in the private sector product, service, and labor markets were bound to have an impact on the way the public viewed the performance of the public sector and its expectations of the public sector. We now examine some of these expectations and related effects.

THE CHANGING PUBLIC SECTOR

Collectively, the changed circumstances of the private sector have played an important role in explaining the shift in the role of government in the economy during the third transformation. These have, moreover, combined with a number of other forces. In this section these are explored. The following forces have played important parts in the drive for value and change in government, and, therefore, the nature and scope of its role in the economy:

1. The power of ideas: the development of the public choice framework, as well as academic and other studies that revealed public intervention in the market to have often led to the transfer of wealth to special interest groups and the promotion of inefficiency, with attendant costs to consumers and taxpayers;
2. Public perceptions of government—public policy—failures in the 1960s, 70s, and 80s;
3. The media/communication/broadcasting technological revolution and globalization, and the private media's financial incentive and ability to identify and publicize public sector failure world-wide as well as to provide information, inexpensively, to stakeholders who are or who potentially may be losers under existing or proposed public policies.

4. The growth in social regulation since the 1970s which, unlike economic regulation, has been generally opposed by business, is expensive, and has been viewed by small business as unacceptably intrusive and in some cases leading to relocation of manufacturing facilities outside of the U.S., Europe, Japan, Australia, and other developed nations;
5. Relatively stagnant productivity growth and stagnant, or negative, growth in real incomes for large portions of the population in North America in the period following 1972 until the economic boom of the 1990s, leading many to question the value and cost of large government;
6. Rising taxes accompanying stagnant incomes prior to the 1990s high tech boom, which caused government to be increasingly seen as a threat to economic welfare;
7. Perceptions of unreasonable use of economic power by organized labor groups which might be gaining due to government cooperation as other groups slipped behind;
8. New technologies which led to the emergence of new interest groups ranging from Greenpeace and the Sierra Club to the new business lobby groups, which saw government increasingly as a barrier to their ability to meet legitimate constituent or consumer needs;
9. Increased private sector competition and performance globally, and the emergence of e-Business, which established new standards for customer service and value, often with an individual customer orientation;
10. The decline of organized labor (in the United States to a proportion of the private sector labor force below levels of the early 1930s), which had always been a major supporter of activist government;
11. The technological revolution in computerization and telecommunications and their implications for economies of scale, and organizational size, management, and control, contributing we argue to the end of the golden age of bureaucracy and mass production;
12. The ascendancy of the new institutional economics with its emphasis on transactions costs and the dichotomy between market and hierarchical approaches, the modern theory of the firm, with its view of the firm as a nexus of transactions, and the managerial concept of concentration on core competencies—all with implications for public sector contracting out;

13. A broad consensus on the apparent failure of modern public welfare programs;
14. TThe rise of interest groups driven by religious, social, and/or cultural agendas, which prefer smaller government and expanded roles for local governments;
15. A decline in the perceived economic importance of the large nation government as freer trade and multicountry trade groups increased in importance;
16. The globalization of business along with technological change (computerization), the declining cost of capital relative to labor, and the increased ease of substitution of capital for labor combined to increasingly place traditional blue collar manufacturing industry workers and many service sector workers at an economic disadvantage and under threat;
17. Perceptions by key stakeholder voting groups that big government had engaged in excessive transfers of wealth and opportunity to "preferred" groups, at a real cost to themselves and increasingly threatening in time of perceived limited quality job opportunities;
18. The realization by some groups, including many manufacturing and service sector workers, that their real incomes might continue to decline in face of competition from the developing world and the realization they lacked the leverage to induce governments to transfer increased wealth to them from other groups, thus leaving them with the possibility of increasing their real disposable after tax incomes only by inducing governments to contract the size and/or the cost of government, without reducing their own entitlements and, thereby, reducing taxation levels;
19. The high technology boom and bust of the 1990s which created and then eliminated so much wealth and opportunity in developed nations, leading to outsourcing to developing nations and skepticism about the long-term health of the economies of the western world;
20. A related association by some lower and middle income class groups of stagnating real incomes with intrusive, inefficient and high cost government;
21. The rising costs of health care and the perceived inability of governments to cover the long-term costs of the social safety net of public services, for example, social security and Medicare and Medicaid in the United States and expensive health care and retirement programs in Western Europe.

22. The elimination of the Soviet global threat and, thus, a lessening in the 1990s of the need for big government to address national security problems, particularly in the United States.
23. The shrinkage of the workforce as a result of demographic changes in the developed world and the perception that expensive governments would have to be supported in the future by a dwindling labor force.
24. The emergence of networks and new technologies as means for organizational, governmental and private sector problem solving on a global basis.
25. The advent of the Global War on Terrorism (GWOT) signaled by the traumatic attack on the United States of September 11, 2001 and attacks elsewhere in the developed and developing world by Muslim fundamentalists leading to frustration among the public over the strategy and tactics used to fight this war, the costs of war, and the inability of governments to win it or bring the main perpetrators of GWOT to justice.
26. The use of networks and the application of the principles of net-centric organization in warfare. As noted in chapter 9, we believe that it takes a network to fight a network war (see also Arquilla & Ronfeldt, 2001) and by its actions in developing the Global Information Grid system, the U.S. Department of Defense and the leadership of allied nations clearly agree with this perspective in terms of devising means for effectively prosecuting the Global War on Terrorism.

These are some of the key forces which collectively have driven the post-1970s transformation in the roles of government and business in national and global economies. With an understanding of the two leading paradigms to explain government involvement in the economy and an understanding of the forces driving business and government during this period, we now turn to the development of a new framework.

THE LEARNING ORGANIZATION FRAMEWORK IN THE PUBLIC SECTOR

We have elaborated on the strengths and weaknesses of the public choice and public interest paradigms and have attempted a reconciliation of the two paradigms of thought. It is possible, we believe, to develop a more benign and more managerially/operationally based model of reasons why governments tend to have difficulties in early on diagnosing problems correctly, selecting policy directions, designing effective and efficient programs, implementing those programs, and avoiding what is commonly called public sector failure.

There is a management literature which suggests that successful business organizations are those which are flexible and are particularly effective in adapting to change. Senge chose to call these "Learning Organizations." In his book *The Fifth Discipline* (1990), he provided a framework for understanding why some organizations succeed while others fail. While not the focus of his work, Senge et al. (1994). did include numerous examples of public sector failure and his *Field Book* provides one study of problems of the public sector as viewed by an Australian public administrator.

We believe that governments and managers in making and implementing public policy are always at greater risk of slipping into failure than are private organizations and their managers; effective, output oriented management in the public sector may, as often is argued, be more demanding than in the private sector for positions of comparable scope. The circumstances or factors which make for certain failure for business organizations as effective learning organizations are commonly encountered in public sector settings. Governments may be seen as particularly susceptible to certain individual and organizational learning disabilities. It is important to note that developing a model of failure of governments as learning organizations does not displace the public choice or public interest models; however it does complement those models and, unlike public choice, holds out the possibility that there may be ways to improve the performance of government in the economy. This explains, in part, the relative success of the some public management reform initiatives.

Most managers would surely agree that to be effective over time an organization must have the ability to adapt to change. To do so, they must achieve some reasonable level of competence in five learning disciplines. These are: (1) the possession of a shared vision throughout the organization; (2) the use of systems thinking; (3) a desire for and a sense of personal mastery by staff; (4) the utilization of valid mental models about people and activities within the organization and about the environment, institutions and people outside the organization in thinking by staff; and (5) capacity for and willingness to engage in team learning. In addition Senge and followers have identified "system archetypes" and common "learning disabilities" which tend to be found frequently in failed organizations. In the following section we develop this framework with particular application to public sector organizations and management reform.

APPLYING THE LEARNING ORGANIZATION MODEL IN THE PUBLIC SECTOR

Many observers and critics of organizational learning or lack thereof have focused their analyses on the private sector although they use a large number of examples of learning disability and failure from the public sector. There are special problems which arise in applying learning disciplines in the public sector relative to the private sector. To some extent many of these problems are problems of scale and are faced in all large, bureaucratic organizations. Nevertheless, the problems are compounded by special aspects of the public sector. We believe that it is fair to conclude that, in large measure, the failure of governments to become effective learning organizations contributes significantly to the failure of the public sector and to the current transformation in the role of government. Godfrey and Ross have noted that: "governments are difficult soil for learning organizations to grow in" (Senge et al., 1994, p. 493).

Senge identifies five disciplines which he maintains are essential for organizational learning. We explore each of these in the context of public organizations. We also examine some of the special "learning disabilities" and system archetypes (generic structures) which are frequently encountered in ineffective organizations.

Shared Purpose and Vision

Purpose explains why organizations exist, while vision is the "What or Where To Go." Strong visions shared widely in an organization are viewed to be compelling and overriding needs by most organizational theory experts. Shared visions provide common concern and commitment.

> "Shared vision is vital for the learning organization because it provides the focus and energy for learning. While adaptive learning is possible without vision, generative [creative] learning occurs only when people are striving to accomplish something that matters deeply to them. (Senge, 1990, p. 206)

A shared vision, to be effective, becomes an incentive and elicits voluntary commitment as opposed to commanding compliance. It elicits voluntary risk taking and experimentation, encourages maximum sustainable productive behavior as opposed to minimal acceptable productive behavior, and encourages taking the long term view.

On occasion governments do present unified visions; unfortunately, these usually seem to occur mainly when crises arise: wars, depression, "excessive" inflation, and problems related to public debt. Obtaining support for a particular unified vision by members of the executive, legislative (when they are separate), regulatory (when independent), and administrative/bureaucratic elements of government is especially challenging. Democratic governments have problems with vision, and totalitarian governments often have visions which the world might be better off without.

We do not want to exaggerate the importance of the vision problem. However, we do want to point out why the problem is so severe within government. Achieving a unified vision in government and one that changes marginally and predictably is complicated by:

1. The focus of government is on the process of obtaining, using, and retaining power—not in offering serious vision;
2. The multiplicity of articulated and nonarticulated goals;
3. The large number of stakeholders, many (most) of whom are rent seekers and many of whom will be in conflict;
4. The existence within government of many conflicting stakeholders who have departmental or ministry bases;
5. Changing leadership politically, and in the American case, at the heads of the bureaucracies—which raise questions of commitment and continuity;
6. The agency problem with management in the public sector (Jensen and Meckling, 1976);
7. Shifting coalitions—the general problem of coalitions;
8. Time horizons—the opportunity window to the next election unless there is a crises;
9. At any level of government, there must be sensitivity to interests of stakeholders at other levels of government, to regional interests that cross party lines, to special issue stakeholders, and to values, myths and symbols of importance to various groups; and
10. An employee problem which is considered shortly.

If a government lacks a shared vision and purpose, if there is not a shared vision of current reality and a common construction of future reality, then there will be problems in motivating people, in inducing a shared commitment and capacity to act effectively and efficiently, and to innovate. In broader terms, there will be a missing synergy necessary for fostering productivity growth, cost control, risk taking, experimentation, and innovation.

The problems of the bureaucracy restrict a government's ability to reach with a vision, even if it does have one. The problem of the bureaucracy is aggravated by three other related factors: (1) even if there is a shared vision, staff are aware it may change by, or after, the next election; (2) the risks of "buying in," thus become much greater; (3) purpose for the bureaucracy is found in presenting politically acceptable alternatives, implementing policy, and avoiding unnecessary embarrassment or alienation for the government—these are not dynamic functions.

Finally, there is a tendency in private sector organizations for a "diversity of visions [to] grow until [they] exceed the organization's capacity to harmonize diversity" (Senge, 1990, p. 43) This diversity problem, and the problem of setting priorities that it creates, may be more severe in government with each stakeholder holding its own vision.

A Systems Approach

If government can overcome the vision problem, it then faces the most important discipline of all. It faces a dynamic which induces the analysis of problems in pieces, not as wholes. A fundamental problem for business organizations is a failure to see problems as elements of system failures; the problem in government is even more serious. Public policy problems by nature of their "publicness" tend to be complex with interconnected elements and interests. There are many classic examples from the public sector including the Cold War and its escalation and de-escalation processes.

While public policy issues tend to be "systems" problems, the public policymaking process tends to favor nonsystems approaches. The public tends to want simple, linear—cause and effect, good and evil answers. Public choice theory reveals that it is not in the interest of a rational citizen/voter to spend the necessary time mastering the details, much less the systems nature, of policy problems. The media finds it easier, and often necessary due to time constraints, to focus on narrow problem definition and possible quick fixes. The media tends to present "symphony of sound bites" analyses and solutions. The "emotional," "real people," or "traditional value" representations, while important, can distract attention from the complexity of issues. One consequence is for the media and voters to focus on symptoms.

Within the political system, often there is little to be gained politically by addressing core or system problems. System problems may be large and may impinge on interests, values, or mental models of current or future coalition stakeholders and may be financially expensive to address: to the politician, the proverbial "can of worms" and reminder of the virtue of "letting sleeping dogs lie." The reluctance to address issues broadly may be reinforced by the knowledge of potential gains to be made fixing blame rather than fixing problems. There is, as well, a timing problem. In politics the long term is the time to the next election, which is more likely to be time sufficient to deal with symptoms or immediate effects, not systems type problems.

Compartmentalization in government also discourages systems approaches in spite of efforts to overcome the problem with interdepartmental and intergovernmental task forces. Public sector departments tend to be more rigidly divided up into fiefdoms, and turf battles are more common than in the private sector where they are significant as well. Individual departments either do not see or do not want to see the whole picture. An individual's department can become the centre of her universe. We are often looking at a zero sum game in government among departments. This environment discourages cooperation and encourages competition. Learning, as a consequence, in any one department will be independent of other departments. The view of external stakeholders that they "own" the interest of certain departments or ministries simply accentuates the compartmentalization problem. Put together, the effect is that employees within the bureaucracy frequently lack incentives to think in systems terms. Still, the effect on policymakers and employees extends even further.

We believe that all systems tend to be characterized by "naturally" reinforcing and "naturally" balancing tendencies. In many systems growth and contraction tend to accelerate. This is true of systems as a whole and of parts or variables. Forces of growth or of contraction seem to feed upon themselves. Examples are found in business cycles, compound interest, house and land market price movements, stock market movements, and organizational and individual success or failure. In a virtuous loop: "We are on a run," or "the sky is the limit." In a negative or vicious loop: "Can things get worse?" "Is there a bottom?" An individual skilled in systems analysis tends to look for and seek to understand reinforcing elements which may be at work in a given situation.

An individual skilled in systems analysis also knows that, typically, as reinforcement processes accelerate, balancing forces of resistance begin to develop, a plateau is approached or a pattern of oscillation emerges. In economics, the principle of diminishing returns in the short run and increasing (and decreasing) returns to scale and scope in the long run are well understood. In economic, environmental/ecological, animal-predator, and almost all other system situations, self regulating and self correcting forces tend to come into play in time. An important part of a systems approach involves seeking, identifying, and appreciating the roles, timing, and importance of balancing forces.

The nature of the political process described above tends to undermine the examination of reinforcing and, especially, balancing force dynamics.

In public policy, the failure to examine balancing system dynamics can lead to unnecessary or inappropriate economic interventions with quick fixes that ultimately backfire. The appeal of quick fixes in the public sector is explained by other factors as well. Quick fixes often fail and backfire with unintended consequences, mainly because they involve attacks on symptoms. The quick fix problem often results from related behavior patterns: (1) an undue fixation on events; and (2) a need to present an "illusion" of being in charge.

Elected policymakers and public managers often have an undue fixation on recent high profile events, that is, where media coverage is extensive. Many politicians and the public want simple problem definition and quick fix solutions. The political clock, the government need only get to the next election, tends to encourage attention to symptoms and meets the need for government to get credit for having done something before the next election. Interest group and media pressure demand proof that something is being done; accordingly, the system requires that snap shots be taken and dealt with. Unfortunately, low leverage decision-making results from treating symptoms. Individual or organizational failure will not necessarily result from failure to address long term or system problems, and the public seems to have a much shorter memory for failure then do stockholders or boards of directors.

Related to the event focus is political pressure to present the illusion of taking charge. Image, particularly for the political leader, but for government in general, demands the illusion of taking charge, for example, to be present at a disaster site such as in New Orleans after Hurricane Katrina did its damage. However, the reality of the system of policy formulation and implementation typically inhibits effective taking charge. Organizational effectiveness (better problem/opportunity definition processes, shorter response times, superior decisions, and superior implementation) requires that those closest to the problem have the power to make decisions and deal with a problem; unfortunately, such empowerment and discretion will rarely be allowed do to fear of loss of control: the localness problem we explore later.

Another method for avoiding systems approaches involves the use of tactics to shift the burden or responsibility. People can avoid identifying fundamental or potentially embarrassing problems and seeking relevant system solutions by shifting the burden somewhere else. One variant of this system failure archetype was explored above: the quick fix. As a pattern of quick fixes is adopted, the burden of and interest in identifying and resolving the fundamental problem fades. The result may be alternating improvement and deterioration in the problem symptom. A second variant involves "crises heroism" in which crises are regularly dealt with by organizational "crises actors" who are viewed as responsible for handling-

-and owning—the problems. A third variant involves shifting the burden to interveners.

Government is increasingly being compelled to address the problem of direct and indirect incentive effects of programs. To the extent that government intervention and programs either build a belief that society and government are to blame for the problems of individuals or groups or businesses, or that government agents are responsible for finding solutions, the act of intervening clearly has the potential to build dependency and undermine self-sufficiency (build "addiction loops") while possessing, as well, the potential, at times, to lessen dependency. Thus, many acts of intervention have the potential to carry with them systemic second order responses which will serve to negate many of the expected first order effects and lead to new public demands for further intervention.

A final variant of the "shifting the burden" rationale involves attribution of blame: The enemy is out there! There is temptation and ease in "shifting the blame" or "shifting the burden" in the public sector—fundamental system problems need not be addressed. In government, the enemy is out there in the past administration (inherited the problem), other levels of government, other political parties, agencies, labor, the courts, bureaucracy, unions, stakeholder groups, the media. Since major change is difficult, "the enemy is out there" is handy and natural. In some ways this is an extension of the stereotypical politician's basic approach to accountability: pass the buck. For the civil service employee, all of this is encouraged by the "I am my position" mental model and compartmentalization that we discuss shortly. Much of this behavior is apparent to have resulted after the attacks of 9/11/2001 and the disaster of Hurricane Katrina in the United States for example.

Systems thinking and approaches are also undermined by the presence of organizational "Tragedy of the Commons" problems. There is a mini-tragedy of the commons problem within organizations where individuals and departments draw excessively on common resources which are not priced properly. They, thus, excessively draw down or exhaust the resource pool. If there are common pools of resources within organizations without individual ownership, adequate accountability for use, or proper internal pricing, then there will be an incentive for each individual or department to draw excessively on those common reserves. In a very real sense a short run focus in decision making can be seen as drawing on the long run resources of the organization and, thus, on a commons. At a broader public policy level, policy solutions to problems may have resulted in commons problems because of underpricing and inadequate accounting of public goods and services.

Finally, time and lags in timing discourage systems viewpoints. From a systems standpoint, public policy and administration suffer from several learning disadvantages related to recognition, learning period election cycle, and implementation/effect lags.

The public sector, as a system, is especially vulnerable to problem recognition lags—particularly, as we have observed, where problems are elements of a system. Phrases common in government (and business as well) reveal the problem: "We can get by to the next election" and, "If it isn't broken, don't fix it." Classic time and communication problems are typical of large bureaucracies as messages move from source to the ultimate decision makers. The problem is accentuated by the realization that to recognize a problem is to risk being forced to act upon it. It is better to allow others to own the problem. Thus, some situations must deteriorate significantly before recognition that action is required. Problems of the environment, education, infrastructure, and debt all fall here.

As well, the electoral cycle, the changing agenda or composition of key issues, and changing actors undermine learning by the consequences of experience. Arguably, the managers in the public sector, relative to those in the private sector, may tend to be more removed in time and space from the effects of policies and fail to see, directly, the repercussions of decisions: they do not witness the outcomes and have responsibility for the effects, an important part of learning experiences.

Implementation and effect lags discourage action for some of the same reasons. Action and effect are often not closely related in time. After implementation, there may be further delay or deterioration before there is improvement. In most programs there are always delays after a decision is made and funding is provided related to capital purchase, installation, staff hiring, training, and placement.

The preceding are the more important of the system characteristics or frameworks that Kim (1993), Forrester (1961), Senge (1990), (Senge et al., 1994), and others have diagnosed, and which they see as particularly dysfunctional in organizations in preventing learning and adaptation to change. The public sector system is susceptible and vulnerable to most of these. These system frameworks, however, are problems in the public and private sector, and are dysfunctional for all organizations under pressure to produce value efficiently in the short and long term. Unfortunately, each is part of the system that tends to come with government. They do not reflect self-interest motivation or a conspiracy as is implied by public choice administrative theory; they are simply dangers faced by all organizations. In some very real sense, failure by individuals to take systems approaches reflects a failure of another learning discipline: personal mastery.

Personal Mastery—Initiative and Innovation

Governments fail a third test of learning organizations: They provide little incentive for personal mastery by employees. Senge argued that business organizations will not succeed if the employees do not enjoy success themselves. Personal mastery is the discipline of continually clarifying and deepening personal vision, of focusing energy, developing patience, seeing reality objectively, and having the self-generated incentive to take initiative. Unfortunately and understandably, many incentives exist within the bureaucracy to "satisfice" and produce a minimally acceptable level of productivity--adequate to ensure progress through the ranks. This contrasts with the ability of learning organizations to motivate employees to reach for maximum *sustainable* individual and group productivity and innovation levels which lead to continuous growth, or ratchet effect, in individual and organizational potential.

Government functions tend to become routinized—standard forms and standard procedures. Rules and procedures provide for control and direction. There is fear of localization of function: empowering people is dangerous due to unclear or changing purpose and vision—or too politically risky. In an unaligned, weakly visioned organization, empowerment can be counterproductive: the dark side of "localness" of decision making.

Further, various government and civil service rules and regulations have been designed to prevent nepotism, discrimination, political preference and bias: The rules of the bureaucracy were constructed to ensure meritocracy and fairness and to protect against arbitrary dismissal. They also minimize discretion and suspect initiative. The rules ensure standard and uniform treatment of consumers or clients: a standard product or volume. Ironically, as they also have observed, given the intangible nature of many government services, providing incentives for initiative and interest in productivity gains needs extra attention, not less.

In general, any interest in personal development or mastery by individuals within government, which will contribute to potential organizational change, is dampened by the knowledge that, once entrenched, rules, regulations, and values will change slowly; and they will face political tests before facing effectiveness or efficiency tests. The former, of course, is a far less predictable test.

We believe that reconciling the requirements of rules and the expectations of service to be the heart of the problem. Historically, the English "public/civil service" tradition emphasized "quality outcomes-delivering a service," while the "European" view focused on "quality of process—how well the organization conforms to regulations, rules, and policy dictates of functionaries.... Designers and critics of government ... want perfect service and perfect adherence to the rules. But in a fast-changing world, this is not an option.... Empower the frontline staff to deliver, and orient them to customer service, and ordinary common sense will recognize that some of the rules will cease to be relevant" (Godfrey, 1994, p. 495). Further, there is some awareness that there may be no resources or commitment of capacity to allow proposed innovation or change. Unlike industry, resources will not necessarily be found for high yield or high profit proposals. Moreover, there may be no overriding purpose in these areas and no bonuses.

There are additional reasons why governments fail in promoting personal mastery: First, employment and advancement, typically, reward education, written test performance, years on the job, and at times ethnic, physical, age, or gender characteristics. Complicated and rigid pay and classification systems are problems in mobility and reward. Salary increments tend to be automatic and promotion possibilities limited. Overall performance continues to play too limited a role. Thus, salary and advancement constraints discourage personal mastery and team learning. There is an incentive to identify with the box a person fills: "I am my position—that is all!"

These rigidities contribute to compartmentalization. The size and complexity of organizations and constraints on rewards encourage locking into the domain of the job and department, and avoiding risk taking. Mistakes will stand out, and risks of going out on the limb are great, so individuals become their positions to the book and "cover your assets" becomes the modus operandi. All these forces reinforce the tendency to see the enemy as all around and to be prepared to shift blame. These forces in the system tend to weaken the drive for personal mastery, to take a systems view, to build team linkages, and, as we discuss later, look for leverage opportunities. In this sense they undermine the need for a "creative tension" in individuals: The need to continuously consider the relationship between the way things are done and the way they might or should be done.

Second, problems arise related to the time dimension of work. The time dimension is less clear on some work, but totally event response oriented on other work—thus there is an incentive, in their view, to become less time sensitive. Third, the big career risk is the risk of failure: thus, do only what is safe. And, fourth, the ever present atmosphere of possible public investigation of even small details of day-to-day operations by a large number of different audit entities within and outside government for their own political advantage, inhibits personal growth, and experimentation. Thus, doing more of the same and building larger bureaucracies may reflect following the old, safe course as much as a desire to pursue self-interest by building empires.

Team Orientation

In the absence of organizational vision, systems thinking, and a culture that provides incentives for personal mastery, team or group learning becomes tenuous, at best. Team learning requires alignment, complementarity, harmonization of individual efforts, and commonality of direction. The complexity and interconnectedness and systems nature of many problems and interests in modern organizations require team approaches. The lack of purpose or vision and the lack of continuity in vision and purpose, even when it exists momentarily, hamper team learning. Perhaps even more so than in industry, the public sector participants are not a team but are resource competitors in what we previously observed is often viewed as a zero sum game. Empowering individuals without common vision and group alignment is a formula for chaos. Organizational success requires team learning. There must also be insightfulness, innovation, and coordination in relation to other teams. In government agencies that capture the essence of the team concept, successful organizations achieve team learning where the team IQ is greater than the mathematical sum of individual IQs of the members.

We can envision a relatively simple model to demonstrate the typical outcome. There is a public bureaucracy made up of members subject to the constraints discussed on personal mastery. There is a competitiveness element, but in the context of a zero sum game. There is little recognition of the concept of a growing pie. The focus is on compartmentalization and the department's and individual's shares of the pie. Thus, "I am my position no matter, and my interest is in maximizing that position," easily becomes the norm. This attitude creates distrust, "the enemy is out there." This leads to resistance and distrust of shared visions: "Are we being co-opted?" This also leads to a tendency to shift blame and minimize risk taking. Dialogue and cooperation, therefore, are difficult given the priorities of public sector workers and their perceptions of how the system works. The existence of complex hierarchical structures further deters team building.

There is also a dark side to teams, particularly in organizations with tight cultures: the problem of groupthink and a related unwillingness to engage in critical, collective inquiry or dialogue. Argyris (1991, 1993; and Argyris & Schon, 1978) identified problems associated with inducing constructive, critical dialogue as the most fundamental for learning in organizations. It is not clear that problems of group think—or nonthink—are more severe in government than in large private organizations. However, it is at least equally dysfunctional in government (Whyte, 1989).

When all of this is considered, we are left with some unanswered basic questions: (1) About our ability to define a typical team in the public sector in the same way we do in the private sector; (2) About whether public sector teams can interact, challenge, and change ways of doing things as effectively; (3) About whether differences can be readily bridged and dialogue and cooperation motivated; and, (4) About whether individuals can be convinced that there is a meaningful potential for long term payoff from team learning. That these remain unanswered questions serves to partly explain public sector failure in the past. One question answered clearly from organizational analysis is that team learning can be effectively undermined by dysfunctional mental models.

Mental Models

In government and in private industry, as well as in interpersonal and inter-group relations, mental models can facilitate or retard cooperation and effectiveness of performance. Mental models are the ways we cognitively and socially construct reality (Berger & Luckman, 1980). Through mental models, images, assumptions, frameworks for organizing thought, that people make sense of the world. Mental models reflect assumptions about human behavior, family values, what is normal, the market, time horizons, religion, styles of human interaction, and much more. Within organizations, mental models, and the organizational metaphors that embody them constitute integral elements of organizational cultures. The mental models are, typically, reflected in the language and metaphors used by individuals within organizations. It is through mental models that individuals and groups stay aligned with reality and the possible or, in the extreme, become fundamentally out of touch with reality.

In government, is it "them and us," or "them versus us?" "Them versus us" is a natural tendency in the public sector. Rarely, in the past, did employees identify themselves as driven by the need to meet client/customer needs, of delivering services to identifiable customers and of being customer oriented. There are too many mental models and stereotypes in the same departments, different departments, different levels of government, and, among outside stakeholders that collectively and individually inhibit organizational success.

When business deals with business, there tends to be a common sharing of values and culture. Even in dealing with consumers, there is a common playing field. However, when business deals with government mental models become a serious problem. The mental models held by business of government are probably less dysfunctional for business, as learning organizations and in dealing with government, than are the mental models of many in government of business in preventing government from dealing effectively with business and other stakeholder groups. Unfortunately, the mental models of the private sector probably reinforce the sense of defensiveness and concern held by employees and managers in the public sector and hardens their stereotypical mental models of the private sector. Consequently, distrust, conflict, and debate readily substitute for understanding and dialogue.

Prior to drawing conclusions about the full implications of the preceding discussion on the five learning disciplines as applied to government, we address two other critical concepts that emerge in the learning organization literature: leverage and localness.

Leverage and Localness

Leverage means seeking out the small change or instrument that delivers a relatively large impact: the right little effort as opposed to the wrong Herculean effort. In a public sector context, leverage is about what House (1990) and others refer to as governments thinking "smaller and smarter." Contemporary lexicon refers to best practice or smart practice. In a learning organization the pursuit of leverage becomes part of organizational culture. Since people seem to pursue leverage in their own personal affairs and since it might reasonably be seen as a reflection of what W. E. Deming has referred to as the "intrinsic motivation" in people to take pride in their work, to experiment, and to improve, it is obviously there to be tapped by the intelligent learning organization.

Usually, achieving maximum leverage requires understanding systems and motivation. Given the forces that we have described in the government process, do government and individuals within government have the freedom and incentive to identify and utilize the policies and policy instruments which possess the highest leverage potential and to apply them so as to achieve maximum leverage? Our previous discussion would suggest that the freedom and incentive have been limited in the past.

Public management reform as it has evolved over the last 30 years has provided evidence that freedom and incentive to seek out and to use leverage can be dramatically increased. The most compelling evidence is found in the search for and application of new and newly rediscovered regulatory instruments designed to encourage maximum voluntary compliance by regulated firms in lieu of traditional command and control instruments. Given limited program resources and given sufficient statutory flexibility, regulatory agencies can be directed to devise compliance strategies that achieve maximum voluntary compliance from a fixed regulatory agency budget. Some governments have prepared operating manuals to focus the attention of all agencies on the pursuit of leverage in all compliance programs.

Localness is ensuring that decisions are made at the lowest level possible in an organization. Flattening organizations, restructuring, empowering, and devolution all have localness as a major objective. Again we return to the reality that the forces for positive change impacting on government administration are the same, or very similar, to those impacting on the private sector. In management theory, localness supplements leverage in that every individual is motivated to practice the learning disciplines and seek high leverage opportunities for change on behalf of themselves and of the organizations. Local decision making in smaller organizations lessens likelihood of alienation of employee from the organization and its objectives; responsibility, cooperation and appreciation of tragedy of the commons situations are more likely. The more localness, the potentially more effective and efficient the organization, and the less potential for alienation and loss of responsibility and accountability.

Localness also implies learning from mistakes and looking at systems. Unfortunately, localness without shared vision and personal mastery is a negative force. The challenge is to balance independence and governance/control. But this has been the challenge for the last decade in the private sector as well. The problem of localness is found in the tension between the drive for localization, empowerment, devolution on the one hand, and the need of an organization to achieve coordination, synergy between units, and collaborative efforts toward common organization-wide objectives, on the other. Bluntly: there is often a tension or outright conflict between localness and control.

The preceding discussion has focused on the characteristics of learning organizations. We are led by that analysis to the conclusion that governments and organizations within government have been, and are, seriously disadvantaged as learning organizations. This raises the question: Can government organizations be rehabilitated and developed into effective learning organizations? We believe that the public management reform tradition that has emerged, formally, only very recently, is a reaction to the events of the third transformation and proposes to add elements to public administration which are constituent in the learning organization paradigm, although clothed in a slightly different fashion.

PUBLIC MANAGEMENT REFORM AND THE LEARNING ORGANIZATION

There exists a large literature on processes by which private sector organizations can become more effective learning organizations. Indeed, much of the work in organizational change, team building, total quality management, and reengineering involves organizational learning; unfortunately, many of these efforts have failed in the private sector (Hammer & Stanton, 1995). A review of our preceding discussion of the five characteristics of learning organizations, as well as a review of the literature on methods developed and used by consultants and business organizations, suggests just how difficult it will be for government in its operations to become an effective learning organization. On the other hand, voters can compel government, writ large, to learn or change through the ballot box. As elections in the united governments and elsewhere suggest, the importance of this kind of learning cannot be underestimated: voters can redefine strategic intent for government. This is apparent in the period 1980 through 2006.

From a managerial perspective, we are optimistic that within government effective learning organizations can be developed: There are many opportunities for change. At a fundamental level, these are attitudes, values, and methods of doing things which directly facilitate the processes of change for individuals and groups within organizations. Much of the existing literature and the training programs on learning organizations concentrate on these. Programs on techniques to assist individuals and organizations to better understand learning processes and common individual and organizational barriers to learning; to develop improved communication and dialogue processes; to identify, analyze and—at times—alter existing mental models; to build strategies and incentives for systems thinking; and to promote team learning and functioning are currently found in industry and in the public sector. These changes progress slowly and face the obstacles we discussed previously; progress varies widely among organizations and is difficult to measure. At a public policy level, changes have been mandated by legislative or executive directives, by budget policy, and by either a sensed need by public administrators for survival or a sense that the time was right to allow the kind of changes and policies they had long desired as good managers. These are the changes which are highly visible to policy analysts, to politicians, and to the general public, and to which we now turn our attention.

As we have noted, some of the same forces that have been driven organizational change in the private sector over the last 20 years are now driving change in the pubic sector. In the same sense, the changes that have allowed many private sector organizations to thrive in the new environment can benefit public administration. It is no longer accepted that large bureaucracy and hierarchy are desirable, much less necessary for efficiency and effectiveness. The same forces that have driven private organizations to think in terms of concentrating on core competencies and ways in which these competencies can be leveraged to divest or contract out for everything else makes as much sense in government as in industry—it is not the answer. Milward argues that creating hollow (or wholly virtual organizations we might add) will not lead to more productive government (Milward, 1994). Changes in computer and information technology that have led to dramatic reductions in transactions costs have facilitated and invited increased reliance in public service provision on contracting or other market oriented methods.

In this changed environment, the real issues become: (1) Which are the core competencies of government today? (2) Is its strategic intent clear? (3) Can governments effectively determine when core competencies match strategic intent and when there is a mismatch, and when there is a mismatch to evaluate and objectively chose among their alternative options? This is the crux of the problem: Even when the strategic intent is clear, the core organizational competencies often are not clear, are mismatched, or do not exist. The public management reform process attempts to addresses these questions and problems while developing proposals to allow governments and organizations within government to become more effective learning organizations, and, thus, more effective in adapting to change. To this extent it is directed at reducing public sector failure.

It should be noted that government in the past often took on functions because of the assumption of the absence of nongovernment alternatives. In the same way many large private organizations often did things in-house because of the assumption they could not be done outside as effectively, efficiently and/or profitably. One of the benefits of the experience with the modern government of the post-World War II period is that many alternative options have been identified and technology has made some increasingly feasible and attractive. Additionally, time has allowed the public to view many generic public policies in more systemic ways and to understand that some have failed and others have had unintended and at times costly and dysfunctional consequences.

Contemporary public management reform practice represents an effort to rehabilitate government, a roadmap to allow it to respond to the flaws which the learning organization model reveals, and a practical, managerial response to the crises in the role of the government in the economy presented by the third transformation. Ultimately, it is that crises to which the governments must respond. The crises of government in the third transformation is driven by a demand by the public that it receive more value from the public sector, a demand by taxpayers that taxes not rise and ideally fall in a period of static real incomes for many taxpayer households, a demand by business for tax reductions due to the pressures of global competition; demands by the public at large that government activities cease to be a drain on the growth of real incomes and real wealth of current and future generations, and a general challenging by the public of many institutions, of which governments obviously are only one, and how they do business. Further, the demand of financial markets that public deficits be brought under control by contraction of public sector expenditure eventually must be heeded.

Public management reform practice with its emphasis on performance appraisal and efficiency; the disaggregation of public bureaucracies into agencies which deal with each other on a user-pay basis; the use of quasi-markets and contracting out to foster competition; cost cutting; and a style of management which emphasizes, amongst other things, output targets, limited term contracts, monetary targets and incentives, and freedom to manage (Rhodes, 1991, p. 11) reflects fundamental change in the way governments govern and, consequently, in the choice of governance instruments. Public management reform practice has as its basic theme delegating authority, replacing rules and regulations with incentives, developing budgets based upon results, exposing government operations to competition, searching for market rather than administrative solutions, and, whenever possible, measuring the success of government in terms of consumer satisfaction.

Contributors to the public management reform movement have explained that the time is right for changes in government and governance. If taxes have reached levels which the public finds unacceptable; if further increases in the finance costs of public debt are resisted by the financial community and by taxpayers; and further reductions in public services and entitlements are resisted by voters, then by a process of elimination, this leaves as the only viable option the provision of the same, or more, or better quality public services at less cost, that is, a dramatic enhancement in the efficiency and productivity of the public sector. A dramatic reduction in public services is, obviously, another option but not one that appears to be supported by the public or powerful interest groups except in meaningless lip service through the media.

The public management reform practice solution is to borrow from the learning of the private sector over the previous 20 years, the new institutional economics we discussed earlier, and the new information technology. Fundamentally, it envisions governments "steering," or planning and directing, more and "rowing," or doing less. Governments must increasingly ask themselves: What should we be doing and how can we do it most effectively and efficiently? Second order questions then include: (1) How can governments overcome "agency" problems related to the management of government employees? (2) Under what circumstances, and to what extent, should governments rely on the private (market) provision of public services?; and (3) What types of institutional planning and control arrangements are optimal when a private supplier is used in any given situation?

We note many of the proposals for reforming government made have been made in previous studies of government in the United States and elsewhere (Jones & Thompson, 1999; Thompson & Jones, 1994). There also is a wealth of practitioner examples and recent knowledge emergent from the new institutional economics and from the writings of a number of management theorists, as well as the experience of many organizations in the private sector over the last 20 years that supports reform.

Nevertheless, we have argued and provided examples (Jones & Thompson, 1999) to demonstrate that in the short term there are limits to the financial savings possible from rethinking how governments and public managers can do their work (Thompson & Jones, 1994, p. 86). However, the long term the benefits are potentially huge.

Finally, it is clear that the public management reform practice does not call for more public sector market intervention and is wary of comprehensive planning. As Mintzberg (1994) has demonstrated, comprehensive strategic planning in business and in government has the potential of, and a demonstrated record of, preventing learning and discouraging innovation. In the past, public and international organizational demands for comprehensive plans and strategies may have had unintended consequences in that plans and strategies were generated which required, or provided incentives for rigid adherence by public managers. In the extreme situation, public managers often have become focused on the rules and output targets of the plan. Thus, concepts of clear purpose and strategic vision are more appropriate for the learning organization in government than are traditional strategic plans. With respect to strategic planning, we have suggested that a new type is needed, one that learns, decides, has strong absorptive capacity and acts more quickly to environmental contingency and change (Nooteboom, 2000; Zahra & George, 2002).

CONCLUSIONS

The model of government as a flawed learning organization in its role as an intervener in the economy adds many insights into past government performance not provided by either the public interest or public choice models. It adds a rational, benign explanation for public sector failure. It suggests that failure can be reduced.

In our view, the adoption of a quick learning organization approach to dealing with many of the problems of government in devising and implementing public policy and complementing it with public management reform practice as indicated in this book is an important step forward. Indeed, what becomes possible is the rehabilitation of the public sector for itself and for the taxpaying public and the reframing of public sector programs and management in a positive context as opposed to the largely negative and cynical context which the public choice framework has produced—and the public has readily accepted—and the relatively open ended public interest framework. It also provides an administrative avenue for positive change. As a result, it fits constructively with the philosophy that, in large measure, attempts to convert, to the extent possible, government bureaucracies into quick learning organizations, particularly those driven by new operational and mental models, and new tools. Among these tools is increased use of new information technology. As we note in the next chapter there is significant evidence that, without any doubt, computers increase performance and productivity where employees have been trained properly to use them (Brynjolfsson & Hitt, 2000). Also, quick learning organizations are more reliably adaptable to highly contingent environmental circumstance (Weick & Sutcliffe 2001).

The conversion of governments to quick and effective learning organizations is also dependent, however, on the conversion of politicians, public sector employees, and the public. This is a difficult challenge in a period of crises, employment reductions, compensation freezes, rollbacks, and distrust. The failure to respond assertively will be even less attractive to public managers and, in the long run, probably to the public itself. The real challenge is for politicians and public managers to find new managerial and organizational solutions if governments are to survive what we have termed, after Polanyi, as the third transformation.

Creating the quick learning organization requires an must benefit from creative reassessment of everything about the organization from its customers and sponsors, its strategic plan and implementation strategy, the manner in which services and products are produced and delivered, how customer satisfaction is evaluated and the results examined to change what the organization is doing to better serve its clientele. Creative thinking requires comprehensive knowledge about both how the organization functions under the status-quo and how markets and customer preferences and behaviors are changing. Creative thinking must be supported by the culture of the organization from top to bottom. Experimentation with new ideas and methods has to be encouraged. Nurturing and coaching teams of thinkers to try to define better ways of doing business is critical. Organizational leadership must not only be supportive; it must lead. It is no good for employees to experiment with reengineering, for example, if the results of their efforts are ignored by executives. Government executives need to be perceived as open to new ideas and experimentation to pilot test new ideas. Public managers and employees must be rewarded for creativity and this attention needs to broadcast throughout the organization so that by example other employees are stimulated to think creatively about what they do, why they do it, and how what they do can and should be improved. This is the product of the quick learning organization.

CHAPTER 9

MOVING FROM BUREAUCRACY TO HYPERARCHY AND NETCENTRICITY

Enabling the Quick Learning Organization Using IT and Modern Technology

This chapter focuses on the inherent contradiction between the basic building block of most nonmarket productive relationships—hierarchy—and the vision inspired by the architecture of modern information technology, especially the World Wide Web, of a more egalitarian culture in public organizations. As noted earlier, Evans and Wurster (1997) have argued that, in the future, all knowledge-based productive relationships will be designed around fluid, team-based collaborative communities, either within organizations (deconstructed value chains), or collaborative alliances like the "amorphous and permeable corporate boundaries characteristic of companies in the Silicon Valley" (deconstructed supply chains). They assert that, in these relationships everyone will communicate richly with everyone else on the basis of shared standards and that,

---

From Bureaucracy to Hyperarchy in Netcentric and Quick Learning Organizations: Exploring Future Public Managment Practice, 231–259
Copyright © 2007 by Information Age Publishing
All rights of reproduction in any form reserved.

like the Internet itself, these relationships will eliminate the need to channel information, thereby eliminating the tradeoff between information bandwidth and connectivity. "The possibility (or the threat) of random access and information symmetry," they conclude, "will destroy all hierarchies, whether of logic or power."

Evans and Wurster (1997) lay it on a bit thick. Nevertheless, we ignore such visionaries at our peril. The World Wide Web, together with the canon that two heads are better than one, has created something immensely interesting and potentially transformative. The genius of the World Wide Web is, as Evans and Wurster explain, that it is (a) distributed (so that anyone can contribute to it), and (b) standardized (so that everyone else can comprehend the contributions). Random access and information symmetry jeopardize the power of gatekeepers of all sorts: political leaders, managers, functional staff specialists, and even experts to determine *what* information counts as evidence and what beliefs are sufficiently *warranted* to count as knowledge. In other words, they threaten nearly everyone with a vested interest in existing institutional arrangements. One does not expect folks to surrender position or power without a struggle. Furthermore, homo sapiens' need for leaders is evidently instinctive, deeply rooted in our simian brains (Heifetz, 1993). The need for hierarchy buttresses the status quo, even where the powerful are neither wise nor unselfish.

To understand the conflict between hierarchical arrangements and the vision inspired by contemporary technology and the possible outcomes of this conflict, we will look closely at three cases based upon recent encounters with e-government in the United States: the 2004 presidential election, and the American military's development of a worldwide information grid. These two cases were selected because they are at the leading edge of e-government owing both to the scale and scope of the activities in question and the resources lavished upon them.

THEORETICAL CONSIDERATIONS FROM THE ECONOMICS OF ORGANZATION

The basic idea behind the new economics of organization is that the comparative advantage of governance mechanisms boils down to a question of information or transaction costs "and to the ability and willingness of those affected by information costs to recognize and bear them" (Arrow, 1969; Coase, 1937). Hence, the circumstances which create market failures: public goods, natural monopolies, externalities, moral hazard and adverse selection, and so forth, the problems that justify government action in a capitalist economy, are all fundamentally information failures.

Markets could deliver public goods, for example—if information technology existed that would permit free riders to be profitably excluded from enjoying them as explained in the previous chapter. Monopolies could be compensated to behave like competitors—if information costs were lower. And, bargaining between self-interested individuals could eliminate externalities, without the intervention of government—if transaction costs were zero. Much the same logic applies to the choice between organizations and markets and the kinds of governance mechanisms used within organizations.

A corollary to this basic Coasian insight is that information costs—typically search, bargaining, logistics, and/or enforcement costs—can be reduced by carrying them out through formal mechanisms of governance: organizations rather than markets or government rather than private organizations. Reduction does not imply elimination, however. This fact implies a second, perhaps, less obvious corollary to the basic Coasian insight: the conditions that wreck markets will also impair organizations and governments. Consequently, as Robert Gibbons (2003) explains, the organizations we observe tend to be less efficient than the markets we observe, even though they are more efficient than the markets they replace; the government agencies we observe tend to be less efficient than the private organizations we observe, even though they are more efficient than the private organizations they replace.

Gibbons' corollary to the basic Coasian insight is illustrated in Figure 9.1, which plots the declining efficacy of markets, organizations, and government as transactions difficulty increases. At the critical values of transaction difficulty shown by the dotted lines, markets and organizations and organizations and governments are both equally efficacious; to the right of first vertical dotted line, organizations are more efficient than markets; to the right of the second, government is more efficient than private organizations.

The evidence seems to support Gibbons' corollary. Where the production of privately consumed goods and services—steel, banking, even telecommunications—is concerned, private organizations are usually observed to be more efficient than state-owned enterprises. Finally, it also might be noted that Gibbons' corollary is entirely consistent with the observation we made in chapter 8: reducing the cost of information should increase the efficacy of markets relative to organizations and of nongovernmental organizations relative to government. Because, improved communications technology, logistics, and IT (information technology) have all reduced the cost of information, it is reasonable to infer that both sets of vertical dotted lines shown in Figure 9.1 have shifted to the right.

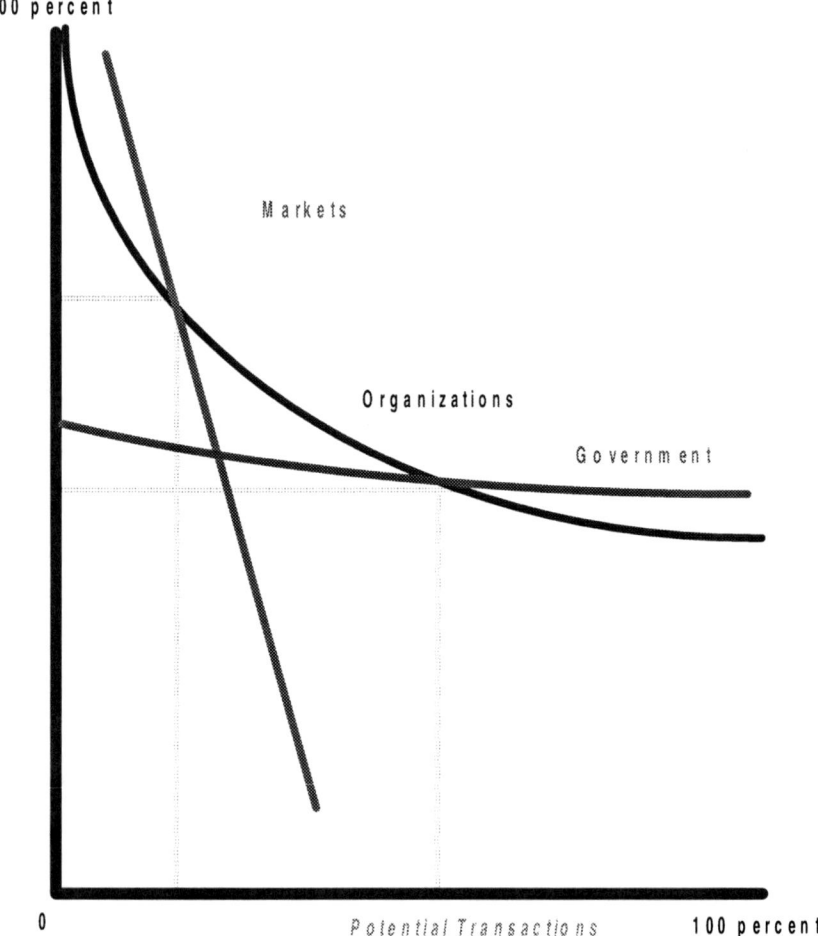

Source: F. Thompson (2006, p. 67).

Figure 9.1   The relative efficacy of alternative governance mechanisms.

This observation most emphatically does not mean, however, that the most efficient technology, let alone set of social/institutional relationships, must necessarily win out in the end. Technological development is not a coldly rational, self-regulating economic process, which proceeds automatically along a singular path. Even if one sets aside the contested nature of efficiency, the evolution of social constructs is precisely analogous to natural selection, a process that is inherently path dependent, a fact made patently obvious by English spelling in the first case and the platypus in the second. For our purposes we accept Paul David's (1985) definition path-dependence in the following manner: "A path-dependent sequence of economic changes is one of which important influences upon the eventual outcome can be exerted by temporally remote events, including happenings dominated by chance elements rather than systemic forces" (p. 332) In other words, economic arrangements are partly a function of systemic change; but they are a function of random, fortuitous events as well. Moreover, systematic forces include culture, position, and power—people, institutions, and competing values—and not merely payoffs.

Moreover, the evolution of social constructs is not entirely a Darwinian process but is at least partially a Lamarckian one. Human agency intervenes at every stage to order arrangements to suit felt needs and wants. We shape economic arrangements, social relationships, and technological developments at the same time they shape us.

Instead, we would stress the normative power of these observations: not that Y will cause X, but that if you want Y, you should do X. Brynjolfsson and Hitt (2000) provide compelling evidence that computers do increase performance: where both are compared to industry averages, an 8% increase in IT assets is associated with a 1% increase productivity. They emphasize, however, that the payoff to IT investment varies substantially across firms, even in the same industries. Measurement error may explain some of this variation. IT measurement focuses on tangible assets —hardware and, in some cases, software. Intangible assets—investments in human capital, business process reengineering, and organizational culture—are usually overlooked, although in successful IT projects, systems implementation and deployment typically account for 75% of total project costs. In explaining this phenomenon, Brynjolfsson and Hitt stress not the level of effort given to IT systems implementation and deployment but the manner in which systems are implemented and deployed. They argue that if we want the high productivity that IT promises, it is not sufficient to invest in computers and software, our organizations must also adopt a specific relational architecture, set of processes or routines, and culture.

Brynjolfsson and Hitt refer to this pattern of practices as the digital or netcentric organization. They insist that IT and digital organization are complements: firms that simultaneously adopt the digital organization and invest more in IT have disproportionately higher performance. They imply that adopting any of the seven practices of highly effective netcentric organizations in isolation may actually hurt performance, although their evidence speaks only to a couple of the practices and to investment in computers. Five of the characteristics of digital or netcentric organizations are often found in high performance organizations, especially those operating in hazardous environments that call for high reliability on the part of their members (Weick & Sutcliffe 2001). These organizations consistently maintain focus and communicate goals, foster information access and communication throughout the organization, link incentives to performance, hire the best people, and invest in human capital (Pfeffer, 1998; see also Asch, 1990b; Dixit, 2002; Ichniowski & Shaw 2003; Lazear, 2000).

Moving from analog to digital processes and distributing decision-rights to frontline personnel are the practices that truly distinguish the netcentric organization from more traditional bureaucracies. The first is inconceivable without computers; the second is a recipe for disaster where people lack a clear sense of mission and the motivation, capacity and information needed to accomplish it. It makes sense that implementing either of these practices in isolation could degrade organizational performance. The architecture that distinguishes the netcentric organization from more traditional bureaucracies was, perhaps, first clearly articulated by Hammer (1990) in his rules for business process reengineering:

- Jobs should be designed around missions and goals rather than functions (functional specialization and sequential execution are inherently inimical to efficient processing);
- Those who use the output of an activity should perform the activity; the people who produce information should process it, since they have the greatest need for information and the greatest interest in its accuracy;
- Information should be captured once and at the source;
- Parallel activities should be coordinated during their performance, not after they are completed;
- The people who do the work should be responsible for making decisions and control built into their job designs.

Moving from analog to digital processes means reconfiguring processes to exploit the power of IT to perform a variety of tasks rather than merely using IT to perform steps in existing processes. This is not a new problem nor is it necessarily an easy one. First the technology must be ready. Then someone must grasp its full potential and figure out how to configure work to extract every advantage from it. Here the early history of the moving assembly line in the American automobile industry is instructive. Its development required two fundamental technological advances that took decades to achieve: tougher metals, which were needed to make jigs and bits for high-precision cutting, turning, boring, milling, and stamping machines, and small-scale electric motors, which were needed to run them. High-precision manufacturing machines were needed to produce interchangeable parts and small-scale motors to liberate workflow from the tyranny of a single central source of motive power and the need to transmit it via belts, shafts, and gears. These were necessary, but not sufficient, conditions for the invention of the moving automobile assembly line. Both were put in place when Ford Motor's Highland Park plant was designed in 1910. It was not until 1914, however, that its managers and engineers fully grasped the potential of interchangeable parts and machines run by small-scale electric motors and reorganized automobile manufacturing accordingly, doubling the plant's productivity at a stroke. The actual reorganization took only a few months. Recognizing the possibilities inherent in the new technologies and figuring out how to take advantage of them took years. It then took additional decades for the processes pioneered by Ford to become widespread throughout automobile industry and to be adopted in other industries. Given this story, it is, perhaps, no surprise that the industry that has most fully exploited the power of IT is the IT industry itself.

Every social construct has precedents. Hammer's rules reflected not only the promise of IT but also the assumptions underlying Toyota's system of flexible production, which had invited considerable attention from students of organizational design in the late 1980s and early 1990s. Toyota's system was intended to reduce work-in-progress inventories and manufacturing cycle time and increase product quality, thereby increasing economic value added by conserving both plant and equipment and working capital. The Toyota system of the 1990s embodied the view that nobody but the frontline worker adds value, that frontline workers can perform most functions better than specialists, and that every link in the value chain should be perfect (Womack, Jones, & Roos, 1990). This system, which had also been pioneered by IBM and Bell Labs in the United States, featured several of the elements of netcentric organizations: multidisciplinary teams, whose members work together from start of job to completion of a project, the devolution of power down to teams that do an organization's work, and a more equal distribution of knowledge, authority, and responsibility. With the addition of computers and digital processes and the system was complete.

To support the importance of sustaining multidisciplinary teams, teamwork and equal distribution of knowledge as a critical element of Toyata's netcentric-oriented organizational success, when this system was weakened, Toyota began to experience uncharacteristic problems in sustaining production quality. Preserving the company' reputation for quality became a significant issue in July, 2006 when Toyota announced the need to recall vehicles due to various problems. The issue became a national scandal when Japanese police accused Toyota executives of concealing product defects over an eight year period ("In Japan, Quality Problems Wound Nation's Pride," 2006b). At the same time another Japanese corporate giant, Sony, recalled a large number of faulty computer laptop batteries and admitted to production quality control failures. These incidents led to a national debate in Japan in 2006 over the issue of whether the quality of industrial production, quality control, worker incentives, and even the quality of Japanese school systems, had weakened substantially.

Explanations for these lapses in quality of production and control ranged from criticism of deterioration in the work ethic of Japanese workers to the influence of introduction of Western-style management methods. Thus it was reported:

> Some have also begun to blame the decline on recent American-style management changes, like performance-based pay, the end of traditional lifetime job guarantees and increased use of temporary workers in order to cut costs. Many economists and corporate managers now say these changes, adopted in the 1990s as Japan groped for ways to revive its floundering economy, sapped employee morale and frayed the sense of teamwork that underpins a commitment to quality. ("In Japan, Quality Problems Wound Nation's Pride," 2006b, p. 14)

For example, in 1993 Fujitsu adopted a performance-based pay system (PBP). However, by the mid-2000 the firm abandoned the system, returning to an emphasis on group performance. Thus, computer systems and netcentric methods work only in tandem with employee education and training, and proper systems of motivation. Indeed, by the mid-2000s many American firms and public sector entities had phased out performance-based pay systems and the academic community had thoroughly debunked the efficacy of such approaches, finding that PBP had damaged worker productivity due to the introduction of compensation inequities of various types ("In Japan, Quality Problems Wound Nation's Pride," 2006b, p. 14).

With these lessons in mind we may observe that the power of netcentric organization to transform productivity is dependent on a number of variables, including good human resource management. The role of new technology in enhanced productivity is highly evident as was first demonstrated in the computer industry. Many of the characteristics of netcentric organizations were already common practice in this industry by the 1990s. Owing to their technological expertise, its leaders were themselves well positioned to grasp the possibilities inherent in the technology and to figure out how to reconfigure basic business processes to take advantage of them, although actually doing so often took many years. IBM's Business Continuity and Recovery Services facility in Dallas, Texas, as noted earlier in chapters 2 and 7, was an early example of a complete netcentric organization. It explicitly mimicked the self-organization of markets. Everyone was either a customer or provider, depending on the transaction, which transformed the facility into a network of voluntary exchanges and substantially boosted productivity.

Can government copy the netcentric model, organizing itself into alliances of networks, sharing top management and core competencies, investing in multidisciplinary teamwork and a common culture, and using computers to chart activities and operational flows? Can it use real-time information on operations made possible by modern IT systems to pass the exercise of judgment down into the organization, to wherever it is most needed, at service delivery, in production, or to the client? Can government abandon its hierarchies, its need to push operating decisions to the top of the organization, or its stove-piped functional organizations? Can it consistently maintain focus and communicate goals, foster information access and communication throughout the organization, link incentives to performance, hire the best people, and invest in human capital, as well as computers and software? The benefits are there, but so too are the costs. Adopting the netcentric organization is problematic in several ways, two of which are crucial: lack of understanding that certain practices matter and that these practices must be adopted together, as part of a complementary system, and the unwillingness of the people at the top to share authority.

NETCENTRIC LESSONS FROM THE 2004 PRESIDENTIAL CAMPAIGN

Electoral campaigns may seem a trivial test of netcentric principles. But American presidential campaigns involve millions of volunteers, thousands of professionals, and billions of dollars. Moreover, for many elected officials, campaign leadership is the only executive experience they ever get. Lacking other executive experience, what they learn on the campaign trail strongly influences administrative practices in office. Political campaigns are also endowed with certain of the characteristics that facilitate the adoption of netcentric architectures: a clear focus and shared sense of purpose, open communication throughout the organization, and bright, intrinsically motivated participants.

A survey of candidates' Web sites in the presidential primaries clearly demonstrated that most simply used the net as an alternate channel for information available via other media. Use of this channel undoubtedly facilitated communication with the ten to 12% of the population that relies of the World Wide Web for news and with reporters, who tend to be fairly net savvy. Many reporters find it easier to take information from press releases on the Internet than from faxes and to use the Web to search through position papers for inconsistencies and to compare and contrast the stances of the candidates. There were two salient exceptions to this generalization, however: Howard Dean's use of the Web to identify likely supporters and to ask them for money and the Bush campaign's use of the Internet to get out the vote on Election Day.

The Dean campaign was remarkable for its ability to raise funds from small donors (< U.S.$250.00). Democrats have customarily relied more heavily on very large donors—wealthy individuals, trial lawyers, and teachers' unions primarily—and federal matching funds than have Republicans, who have relied primarily on direct mail campaigns to raise funds. The Dean campaign was so good at raising money that it could afford to forgo federal matching funds (along with the spending limits they entailed) and eventually announced that it would no longer accept large individual and corporate donations. While the Dean campaign failed (many of its IT workers were recruited for John Kerry's presidential campaign, where they ultimately substantially contributed to the Democrats' success in matching Republican campaign spending), Howard Dean was later elected Chairman of the Democratic Party. Under Dean, the Democratic Party has raised $2 for every $3 raised by the Republicans, despite its incumbency advantage. As Chairman, Dean has relied on the precisely the same organizational and IT know-how that carried him a surprise lead early in the race for the Democratic nomination for the presidency for his successes—his failures have largely been the result of an inability to keep his feet out of his mouth, also just as before.

Openness has been one of the keys to Dean's success in the use of the Internet for campaign purposes. The Republicans and, initially, the Kerry campaign merely solicited e-mail responses to their press releases and position papers. Most messages received an automatic reply appealing for support. In contrast, Dean's campaign network classified and posted the comments to the Web and invited responses from viewers. They also asked viewers to copy comments to friends and to invite them to link to Meetup.com. This had the effect of creating an extensive community of online participants; according to the *Toronto Star* ("Web Plays Wild Card in U.S. Election," 2004, p. 27), over 13,000 in April 2003, 61,000 in July, and 110,000 in October. Meetup.com peaked in February 2004, with 189,000 participants.

Furthermore, potential active supporters identified themselves through their willingness to participate in the online community. Only then did the Dean campaign solicit their support. Not surprisingly, the response rate to Dean's solicitations was between 4 and 10 times higher than his competitors'. Of course, this meant that the Dean campaign organization had to mobilize and train a large number of individuals to monitor traffic on the Web, identify potential supporters, and tailor appeals for support to them. It also meant that the campaign had to use its computers to chart volunteer activities and communications traffic so that it could afford to pass the exercise of judgment down into the organization to the volunteers communicating directly with the other members of the online community. As Democratic Party Chairman, Dean has installed this same system. Perhaps its most astonishing feature is that most volunteers supply their computers and work from their own homes, schools, or offices.

The Republican effort to get out the vote on Election Day was every bit as fascinating. The problem both parties face is insuring that likely supporters actually vote. Both parties maintain extensive databases on registered voters, paying special attention to party members and independents, especially identified supporters and those with characteristics that would predict their support at the polls. They also try to determine who has voted and who has not and to encourage those who have not to do so. This means reminding voters with absentee ballots to mail them in, monitoring polling places to identify those who have not voted and phoning or visiting the laggards to persuade them to vote. In presidential elections, special attention is usually given to potential supporters who vote intermittently in by elections.

Forty years ago this process relied heavily on local organization and local knowledge. Data, which are now typically supplied in digital format by county clerks and frequently updated, often in real time, and warehoused by the national party organization, were laboriously coded by hand on note cards maintained at the precinct level. While a few well-organized patronage machines could rely on street-level adherents to know their constituencies so intimately they could predict not only who would vote but also how, most simply maximized turnout, leaving it to the fates to sort things out. The electoral advantages that accrued to large-scale, centralized data base management transformed this process. When voter data was combined with modern political/market research, including push polling, and the use of giant call centers, national campaign managers could determine which voters to target to maximize the vote count in their favor given the volunteer resources available. This had the result of reducing overall turnout vis á vis earlier times, but of increasing the predictability of outcomes. It also resulted in the centralization of the process. In 2004 the Democrats relied on this basic process, using the Internet to transmit orders to volunteers in the field and to check on results.

In contrast, the Republicans used the Internet to transform the process. They made data on voters, their intentions and their propensities, information from the phone banks and polling places available to local volunteers and relied upon them to interpret the data and to use the Internet to coordinate their own efforts. To participate in this process all interested volunteers had to do was enter their zip codes on a Web page: the system provided a targeted list of neighborhood voters, a map showing the locations of their residences, estimates of the time required to visit them, and a set of talking points. The rest was up to the volunteers. In other words, the Republicans used the Internet to distribute information and decision-rights to frontline personnel and depended upon them to figure out how to leverage the resources available locally. As a result, Republican volunteers were consistently faster off the mark and responded more appropriately to the emerging situation than their more centrally directed Democratic counterparts. The final result was the largest voter turnout in any American national election in recent history. And, while this is by no means certain, many serious analysts now attribute the Republican margin of victory to their success in getting out the vote on Election Day. Moreover, this success evidently reversed what started out to be a clear win for the Democrats.

Zack Exley, director of online communication and organization for Kerry-Edwards 2004, was subsequently reported to have said in reference to the Republican voter mobilization campaign, that, "The right is beating the left at what used to be our game: grassroots politics, real democracy. Ironically, we were a little more 'command and control,' which doesn't really reflect the way the Democratic Party works" (Exley, 2004)

THE NETCENTRIC EXAMPLE OF THE U.S. DEPARTMENT OF DEFENSE GLOBAL INFORMATION GRID

The search for consensus as to which practices matter is dramatically reflected in the U.S. defense department experimentation with netcentric warfare. One might be inclined to skepticism. Military organizations have earned a reputation for conservatism. In part this is a necessary consequence of their need for resiliency and reliability in the face of severe harm. Moreover, Fountain (2001a) has described the failure of an early experiment carried out by the U.S. Army's 9th Mechanized Division (HiTech) at Ft. Lewis, Washington, with a network enabled information system. The failure of this experiment was at least partly due to the unwillingness of its senior officers to abandon hierarchy or to push their operating decisions down into the organization. Nevertheless, Hughes (1998) reminds us that the very first netcentric organization may well have been the Defense Advanced Research Project Agency's ARPANET project. Started in the late 1960s, the project was characterized by a flat, collegial, meritocratic management style as contrasted with a vertical, hierarchical one; the resort to transdisciplinary teams of engineers, scientists, and managers in contrast to reliance on discipline-bound experts; the combining of diverse, or heterogeneous, physical components in a networked system instead of standardized, interchangeable ones in an assembly line; and a commitment by industry to change-generating projects rather than long-lived processes. (p. 5)

The U.S. defense department and the uniformed services are seriously trying to figure out how to utilize the power of IT to increase the agility of combat forces and the speed and effectiveness with which the military is deployed to achieve political ends without combat. The backbone of this initiative is the integration of the Department of Defense communications and computer systems into the Global Information Grid or GIG.

The GIG is a distributed network that is designed to spread processing power across a network of thousands of processors, servers, and routers located around the world. The diverse computers that make up the network will be linked together via a communications system that automatically routes and relays information from source(s) to destination(s) through any available medium or node. The GIG's communication system will use technologies pioneered by the Defense Advance Research Projects Agency's packet radio project as well as landlines, both of which rely on the Internet's open-systems standards and protocols to facilitate interoperability among its component elements. This communications network will allow the computers in the grid to exchange information, share workloads, and cooperatively process information to provide users with information about local operating conditions such as the status information on the enemy, friendly forces and neutrals, and terrain and weather information. Information will be supplied by users, local and regional sensors and processed by intelligent agents to help them figure what they need and to get it when they need it. Information and related services will be available to any and all "net-ready" users, meaning connected to the GIG, with an adequate interface to enable the acquisition and presentation of information. For example, a rifleman's processor could be a thin client dedicated to supporting a human-computer interface (with voice recognition, heads-up display, speech synthesis, and communications). It need not have its scarce computing capacity tied up providing other information-related services. Computing resources to support a user can reside anywhere on the grid.

When the GIG is complete, everyone in the American military will be able to communicate with everyone else on the basis of shared standards. The architectures of object-oriented programming and packet switching in telecommunications will eliminate the need to channel information, thereby eliminating the tradeoff between information richness and reach, or so its advocates claim.

The grid is designed to be scalable to several levels or tiers of networks. At the highest level, it will comprehend all sensors, information processors, and users from satellites in geosynchronous orbits on down—all the military's processors, servers, and routers, the communications grid, and stored data and metadata registers and catalogs. Metadata describe and classify the information to which they are appended, including its source, description, intended use, pedigree, and security classification. Hence, they allow users to convert data into useful information. The next tier might be a wide-area network comprehending a regional command, the next a medium-area network comprehending all the combat and support teams conducting operations in an area, and finally a local-area network comprehending the participants of a combat team or rapid reaction force.

As with most high-tech organizations, the GIG will rely on quasi-market mechanisms to link customers and providers (sensors, weapons platforms, and intelligent agents, as well as people), and to ensure that users have access to the information and services (bandwidth, etc.) that they want when, where, and how they want it. Depending on the transaction, a user may be either a customer or a provider. Department of Defense policy envisions that users will post all of the information they collect or produce so that it can be immediately available to those who need it. In addition to tracking the progress of transactions and providing management for the system of exchange, the GIG's infostructure will supply:

- Metadata posting and collection;
- Searchable catalogs advertising the availability of services and information on the GIG. These catalogs will contain information that describes the capabilities of the service, the necessary inputs to use the service and the outputs of the service;
- Discovery mechanisms to locate and identify information to support user tasks, including flexible access control mechanisms to facilitate information visibility and availability (while hiding information where there is an explicit need for security beyond that afforded by the network);
- Agent-based mediation services to translate, fuse, and aggregate data elements into information to meet the needs of diverse users ranging from individuals to teams and organizations, and to sensors and/or weapons systems.

These software agents will use metadata to package information for users. They are supposed to filter and deliver the right information to the right automatically. That is to say, these agents will be made aware of the user's situation and information needs to provide relevant information without a specific user request. Software agents are intended to multiply the resources available to users by gathering and transforming raw data into actionable information to support operations, in the same way that users would, were the agents unavailable, thereby freeing them from routine information processing chores and allowing them to devote their attention to operations.

The GIG relies on workload sharing and packet switching for resiliency. The grid will operate reliably despite the destruction of many of its components or communication nodes because data and workloads can be stored and processed throughout the network and information is automatically routed through its undamaged nodes via surviving radio transmitters and landlines. Moreover, according to David Alberts and Richard Hayes (2003, p. 197) automatic packet-switching network protocols and algorithms could protect communications nodes in ways never before conceived through cover, concealment, and deception. For example, network-level protocols could make every node look the same (in a traffic analysis) as every other node, thereby limiting an adversary's ability to identify and target high-value nodes such as command and control centers. Similarly, network-level protocols could, if the system detects an attack, change its waveforms to mimic a radar site or even the radio signals of an enemy unit. Finally, The Department of Defense is developing hard to intercept and detect waveforms for ground-based communication networks.

It is a cliché to say that the World Wide Web like its namesake, is full of bugs and dirt. To defend against information attack, capture, or corruption the GIG will rely on commercial technology for conducting secure transactions, such as Internet protocol security, secure socket layer, public key infrastructure and key distribution mechanisms, strong encryption algorithms, intrusion detection systems, and inexpensive biometric systems (fingerprint readers and retinal scanners). To protect against hackers, spyware, computer viruses, or massive denial of service attacks, the GIG will rely on approaches such as sandboxing, codesigning, firewalls, and proof-carrying code. However, as even its champions acknowledge, these approaches have yet to be implemented, tested, or standardized.

Based upon most contemporary press coverage, the Iraq War represented the apotheosis of netcentric warfare. A more balanced discussion of events, written by Joshua Davis, appeared in *Wired Magazine*.

> The war was a grand test of the netcentric strategy in development since the first Gulf War. At least, that's the triumphal view from the Pentagon briefing room. But what was it like on the ground?... I tracked the network from the

generals' plasma screens at Central Command to the forward nodes on the battlefields in Iraq. What I discovered was something entirely different from the shiny picture of techno-supremacy touted by the proponents of the Rumsfeld doctrine. I found an unsung corps of geeks improvising as they went, cobbling together a remarkable system from a hodgepodge of military-built networking technology, off-the-shelf gear, miles of Ethernet cable, and commercial software. (Davis, 2005)

Nevertheless, Davis was favorably impressed with the system cobbled together. Known as "Geeks" to the soldiers in the field, the system tracked every friendly unit, weapons platform, and soldier in the theater and plotted their positions in real time on a digital map, together with all known enemy locations, plus a lot more: battle plans, intelligence reports, maps, online chats, radio transcripts, photos, and video. Soldiers accessed this system through a portal known as the Warfighting Web, which ran over the military's Secret Internet Protocol Router Network in much the same way as the public Internet.

Geeks facilitated the major operational innovation of the Iraq War: swarm tactics. In the earlier Gulf War, coalition forces advanced in a traditional linear formation, with each unit assigned sole responsibility for a specific portion of the front or held in reserve. Coordination was achieved and fratricide avoided through careful attention to the boundaries assigned the attacking units. Then, as each unit advanced, it would sweep its assigned corridor clear of adversary forces. If it met with unexpected resistance, higher command could redeploy neighboring or reserve units to overcome or in some cases seal off an exceptionally obstinate foe. Unfortunately, maintaining a continuous front is costly both in terms of manpower and equipment. Resources must be spread out all along the line and in echelon behind it. Moreover, units advancing in linear formation often cannot move any faster than their slowest element; they sometimes have no option but to engage forces blocking their assigned line of attack, battling on the periphery rather than going for the heart of the enemy's defenses; and they are easy to locate and, therefore, attack.

In the Iraq War, allied units were spread out like polka dots over the battle-space and charged with the destruction of enemy command, communications, and control centers, along with denying them supplies. When allied units encountered strong fixed defensive positions, they often merely noted the locations and by-passed them. Dangerous enemy offensive units were engaged and, through self-coordination of local air, land, and sea forces, overwhelmed. This was possible because Geeks allowed soldiers to keep track of each other, even when they were out of one another's sight, and to come together rapidly and stealthily from all directions. Of course, dispersed attack formations avoid many of the drawbacks of a linear formations: forces are much more likely to be used to good effect, thereby saving on resources; the swarm can move forward as fast as its fastest elements—speed and surprise tend to degrade the efficacy of an adversary's response (Coram, 2002); dispersed forces are hard to attack and nearly impossible to attack successfully when they move faster and concentrate firepower more accurately than their opponents. The worth of dispersed formations in desert warfare is not a new discovery. German General Erwin Rommel used dispersed formations and swarm tactics against the British Army in North Africa during World War II, typically taking personal command at the most decisive spot of the operation. Although these tactics were evidently effective, visitors from the German General Staff were often nevertheless appalled by Rommel's flagrant disregard for sound principles of war.

The allied swarm used Microsoft Chat to coordinate action—concentrate, attack, and disperse, combine and recombine—of myriad, dispersed, maneuver units. When a problem developed, a soldier would radio a Tactical Operations Center, where the problem would be typed into a chat session and addressed by anyone online—from experts at the Pentagon to the AWACS overhead or combat teams nearby. According to Davis, not only did technology change the way allied forces maneuvered, it also changed the way they thought.

On the negative side, several observers have noted that allied forces lacked a system of systems (Boyne, 2003; Cordesman, 2003). Many of the information systems available at the outset of the Iraq War remained service specific. As a consequence, a network had to be quickly improvised from these systems under difficult circumstances. Not surprisingly, this improvisation worked best between the highest levels of command. The net was probably weakest at the battalion level and below. But even platforms that were relatively well integrated into the net, U.S. Air Force fighter planes and bombers, had problems with interoperability, communications, and data flow, as well as in procedures and computer support. These problems often showed up in an inability to redirect aircraft in midflight away from targets that had been destroyed or to surviving targets in a timely manner. As Anthony Cordesman explained:

> The U.S. and its allies simply [did not] have a fully effective and reliable set of sensors, processors, and methods to support netcentric warfare with reliable battle damage assessment or to provide such data quickly enough to support near-real-time allocation of force assets for either tactical or targeting purposes. (p. 280)

Network communications problems also sometimes hindered the ability of logistical units to synchronize their movements with the combat teams they supported, causing delays in re-supply. Indeed, orders from higher commands often simply out ran the ability of lower level combat and support units to interact and coordinate with each other. These problems were evidently due to doctrinal and training failures as much as to technological and equipment failures, although Davis noted that one Army analysis of information problems during the Iraq War focused on the need for improved energy sources to replace batteries.

The GIG is supposed to provide the information and telecommunication services needed to fix these problems, except perhaps for battery life. It will enhance the ability of soldiers to make sense of the situations they find themselves in and support collaboration, both of which are essential to promote a high level of shared awareness and to create the conditions needed for effective self-synchronization. However, the GIG will not fix what Cordesman (2003:) describes as the tendency of bandwidth creep "to push information to virtually all potential users and to centralize decision making and review" (p. 280). He concluded:

> It is far from clear that today's problems are truly bandwidth problems as distinguished from a failure to create efficient systems that limit the need for bandwidth, and equally unclear that careful review has been made of where the flow of information should stop, of how much information can really be used, and of the need to delegate and limit information flow. (p. 280)

The champions of netcentric warfare within the defense establishment go much further. They argue that dramatic changes must be made in the military culture, architecture, decision-making processes, and operating routines to exploit the full promise of IT. In turn, these changes—expanding lateral information flows; increasing connectivity and interoperability, collaboration, and experimentation, forming and deploying small, agile, specialized teams; and devolving much (but not all) command authority downward—call for equally dramatic changes in the way military units are configured, trained, and equipped.

One of the key change agents in this process is the defense department's Command and Control Research Program, currently directed by David S. Alberts.[1] The Command and Control Research Program has produced a series of reports dating back to the mid-1990s outlining the changes the military must embrace to enter the information age (see Table 9.1). The most recent report in the series, *Power to the Edge: Command and Control in the Information Age* (Alberts & Hayes, 2003), reiterates the conclusions of its predecessors but goes much further in emphasizing the importance of flattening command hierarchies and of devolving power down to combat and logistic teams.

Although the Command and Control Research Program has not referenced this literature, the organization they prescribe is essentially Brynjolfsson and Hitt's digital or netcentric organization (see Table 9.1).

Table 9.1. Characteristics of Industrial Age and Information Age Organizations

Mass Military	Netcentric Military
Centralized expertise and coordination	Dispersed expertise and self coordination
Vertical integration and channeled communication	Horizontal integration and extensive communication
Large formations	Small formations
Many layers	Few layers
Specialized functional units	General purpose units
Extreme division of labor	Extensive cross-training
Narrow skill requirements	Broad skill requirements
Low training requirements	Very high training requirements
Mass and firepower	Speed and precision
Ponderous	Flexible/Agile
Sequential action and maneuver	Continuous action and maneuver
Heavy reliance on resources held in reserve to deal with the unexpected	Capacity to redeploy quickly
Limited situation awareness	High degree of shared situation awareness
Formal relations with subordinates, supporting units, and suppliers	Long-term, trust-based relationships
Low emphasis on social learning and information sharing	High emphasis on social learning and information sharing
Slow to adapt	Quick to adapt

Source: Alberts and Hayes (2003, p. 45).

To those who have learned about the U.S. military from old war movies, this looks like an impossible stretch. To those more familiar with the modern military, however, Alberts and Hayes can be understood as saying merely that the armed forces as a whole should look more like the Special Operations Command, with its joint headquarters, exercises and training, tactics and doctrine, its relatively high degree of interoperability and equipment standardization, and its tailored task forces, composed of units that are brought together to accomplish a given mission or accomplish specified objectives, and are then reorganized or reconfigured to take on new responsibilities. Further, Alberts and Hayes' combat and logistics units would look like special forces units: relatively small, highly skilled, multidisciplinary teams, with a lot of rank, but not many levels of command (Alberts & Hayes, 2003). This would still be a big stretch, but almost by definition not an impossible one.

At the same time that Alberts and Hayes call for the devolution of power to the edge, they are cognizant that authority, and accountability are essential features of any system of command and control. Organizations that fail to allocate responsibility for performance, to align responsibility with authority, or to hold individuals accountable for their exercise of responsibility and authority are predestined to muddle and the pursuit of sectarian interests. There point is that is possible to move from a "concept of command that is tied to an individual commander to a concept of command that is widely distributed" (Alberts & Hayes, 2003, p. 45)

Rather than issuing detailed orders about what to do, when to do it, where to do it, and how to do it or even specifying objectives each unit is to achieve, and leaving the details of when, where, and how to the units, Alberts and Hayes would have headquarters assign missions to the units involved, but leave decisions about how they are to be achieved to the units involved to workout for themselves—they refer to this decision-making process as self synchronization. They assert that effective self-synchronization requires headquarters to provide a clear and consistent understanding of command intent; appropriate rules of engagement, and sufficient resources. These measures would high guide but not dictate details to subordinates. In addition, effective self-synchronization requires quality information, shared situational awareness; and competence at all levels of the task force and 360-degree trust—in information, subordinates, superiors, peers, and equipment.

> The Network Centric Warfare concept of self-synchronizing forces is a statement of the requirement for massive improvements not only in flexibility but also in adaptability. The elements of such forces will need to be extremely competent and inspire confidence in the other force elements about that competence. They will also have to trust one another, recognizing the value of synergistic efforts and their ability to rely on one another to achieve them. They will need to be supported by networks that allow them not only to share information but also the tools that they need to develop situation awareness and situation understanding. They will also need to task reorganize on the fly. (Alberts & Hayes, 2003, p. 144)

To get from here to there, they rely on two critical assumptions. The first is that GIG will be constructed pretty much on time and on schedule. The second is that the American military will continue to experiment with netcentric warfare/organization, that its basic principles will be vindicated, and that this vindication will lead to consensus as to which practices matter, the recognition that these practices must be adopted together, as part of a complementary system, and, ultimately, to the willingness of people at the top of the uniformed services to share authority.

So far, development and deployment of the GIG has remained pretty much on schedule. This success largely reflects the military's willingness and ability to lavish resources on what is essentially an unproven concept. Few if any other organizations could afford to be so extravagant. The one area in which the GIG is admittedly behind schedule is in protecting the space-based segment of the GIG from attack, especially its resiliency in the face of information attack. This is not now a primarily a money problem. Rather, it seems that the military has so many platforms under development that there simply are not enough skilled aerospace systems engineers to go around. Since many of the platforms under development for the military reflect the assumptions of an earlier era, one might conclude that this constraint is a harbinger of more serious conflicts to come.

Out point here is that the U.S. defense department's resource allocation process, like most budgetary processes, is incremental in nature. It is better at preserving the human, material, and technological capacities of existing institutional arrangements and functional communities than at creating new ones. That conclusion holds a fortiori where it is necessary to scrap the old to bring into being the new. For the next few years, the American military can continue to pursue parallel tracks to the future, what Alberts and Hayes refer to as the modernization track versus the transformation track, but at some point migration paths from one track to the next must be put in place. Alberts and Hayes (2003) seem to agree, they argue that:

> [C]apabilities are usually a product of DoD's stovepiped planning, budgeting, and acquisition processes (all of which are material-dominated) and a requirements process that is backward looking. While power is currently distributed, being vested in the Services and Agencies, this power topology is clearly antithetical to jointness and far from the warfighter edge. Over the years, there have been numerous attempts to improve the system to make it more joint and responsive to warfighters' needs. To date, these efforts have been only marginally successful because they have not fundamentally transformed these processes into edge-oriented ones. The adoption of an edge-oriented approach to the main function of DoD, the conduct of military operations, demands that these supporting processes be transformed as well. (p. 284)

In other words, it is not certain that we get from here to there. The Air Force, which has thought long and hard about the need to make the transition to a space and air force, still has not figured out how to change its resource allocation process to make it actually happen (Barzelay & Campbell, 2003). What Alberts and Hayes (2003) propose looks a lot harder.

FROM THE NEW ECONOMICS OF ORGANIZATION TO NETWORKS

To make sense of these three stories, the idea of a value chain, one of the central organizing concepts in the contemporary management literature, is useful. A value chain is simply an arrangement of activities or tasks undertaken to add or create value. Economists presume that governance arrangements make value chains more efficient. That is, they are a means of managing the sum of transaction—search, bargaining, negotiation, and enforcement—and holding costs. This is an oversimplification, but it is often a useful starting place in the analysis of institutional arrangements.

As we have seen, the traditional transaction cost framework posits two polar types of institutional arrangements:

- The market, which at the limit is a completely deconstructed value chain
- The hierarchical, vertically integrated organization, which at the limit is a completely self-contained value chain

Of course, most real value chains are composed of both markets and organizations.

There is often a tacit presumption in this sort of analysis that the mass production of manufactured goods is the normal mechanism through which organizations create value. Under this mechanism, the lion's share of the value created derives from the production or fabrication process, a repetitive or cyclical process. Consequently, most of the costs incurred in creating value vary directly with the rate and/or volume of output. These presumptions imply a particular division of labor, one in which like activities or tasks are grouped together and performed sequentially and each node in the value chain or network is an event signifying completion of a discrete task. Hence, value chains are typically portrayed as linear networks of activities in which events follow sequentially from one to the next until the process culminates in the enjoyment of the good or service in question. A complex value chain might have many tributaries, but its flow is unidirectional. Except where so-called overhead services contribute to the value chain, its activities can be coordinated via simple push-pull mechanisms, with communication concentrated at the links in the process.

There is another important tacit assumption in this sort of analysis: information is very costly and must be carefully husbanded. Consequently, this presumption further implies that the main issue confronted in the governance of value chains is vertical integration, not only to maximize economies of scale, but also to minimize overheads through economies of scope.

In one of the most widely accepted formulations incorporating this perspective, two attributes of primary and intermediate products or services suffice to answer the question of how their place in the value chain should be governed: excludability and exhaustibility. Both nonexcludability and nonexhaustibility give rise to divisible prisoner's dilemma games, which often preempt efficient voluntary governance arrangements and, where that is the case, call for coordination by fiat or hierarchy.

The main normative prescription that flows from this perspective is that goods or services that are characterized by excludability and exhaustibility, so-called pure private goods, ought to be supplied via voluntary exchange, that is, markets. Goods or services that are both nonexcludable and nonexhaustible, so-called pure public goods, ought to be subject to hierarchical control. It is usually further presumed that a public-goods value chain involving final goods and services that benefit a large share of the citizenry should be managed by the state or one of its subsidiaries. This formulation logically suggests two additional patterns: excludable, nonexhaustible goods and services, so-called toll goods, and nonexcludable, exhaustible goods and services, so-called commons goods, externalities, or spillovers. Under the old structure-conduct-performance paradigm the former called for some form of administered contract (at the limit, government regulation of price and entry) and the latter an M-form organizational design or, at the limit, government process controls to increase the spillover when a good or decrease it when a bad. Table 9.2 depicts the traditional normative logic of vertical integration.

Because value-creation strategies are usually conceived along product-market lines (single product, differentiated products, multiple products) and because the M-form structures provide a general manager for each product line (rather than for regions or functions), the M-form is broadly endorsed as the mode of organizing and managing large, multiproduct organizations whose products are by definition heterogeneous. The broad outline of the M-form structure is one where substantial decisional authority is decentralized to agents, within the context of well-specified rules determining how agents will be rewarded for their efforts. According to this perspective, the management process mainly involves acquiring and deploying assets and, to influence this process, principals must establish a consistent set of delegated decisions, performance measures, and

Table 9.2. The Traditional Logic of Vertical Integration

Service Characteristics	Excludable	Nonexcludable (Economies of Scope)
Exhaustible (constant or increasing costs)	Market	M-form organization
Nonexhaustible (economies of scale)	Administered contract	Hierarchy

Source: Thompson (2006, p. 74).

rewards. Organizational units in such a setup participate in quasi-voluntary value chains linked by transfer prices. Managerial rewards are based on economic quantities of interest to principals, such as returns on capital employed (holding plus embedded transaction costs).

The final assumption of the structure-conduct-performance approach to transaction-cost oriented value-chain analysis is that the coordination of interdependent cooperative activities is easier under an organizational hierarchy than in markets. In turn, the coordination advantages of organizations supposedly derive from the internal homogeneity of their systems of internal contracts: communication systems, including budgets, incentive regimes and authority structures. A corollary of this assumption is that organizations that rely on a small number of suppliers or distributors can write contracts that will, at some cost, constrain the opportunistic behavior of those with whom they deal.

There is a fair amount of evidence supporting the logic of this formulation. Arguably, for example, the main thrust of the regulatory reform movement of the 1970s and 1980s and the privatization of state-owned enterprises was to align governance mechanisms with the characteristics of the goods and services produced. In the private sector, mergers and acquisitions that conform to the dictates of this formulation are usually successful. Those that do not conform almost inevitably destroy stockholder value. Finally, in a study of defense businesses, Masten (1984) showed that nonexhaustibility (economies of scale) and nonexcludability (economies of scope) directly influenced vertical integration. Where intermediate products were both complex and highly specialized (used only by the buyer), there was a 92% probability that they would be produced internally; even 31% of all simple, specialized components were produced internally. The probability dropped to less than 2% if the component was unspecialized, regardless of its complexity.

Nevertheless, it is increasingly apparent that the principles of hierarchy, levels of graded authority, and a firmly ordered system of super- and subordination and formal contractual mechanisms are at best imperfect solutions to the problems caused by divisible prisoner's dilemma type games. A better way to conserve on transaction costs is through the elaboration of trust-based, relationships of mutual dependency. These can be reflected in intraorganizational cooperation or take the form of interorganizational alliances. For example, Toyota's legendary just-in-time manufacturing process, which produces dramatic reductions in components, work-in-progress, and finished goods inventories and thereby holding costs, does not depend on vertical integration. Instead, Toyota relies on a few suppliers that it nurtures and supports. The members of the Toyota alliance have substantial cross-holdings in each other and Toyota often acts as its suppliers' banker. Toyota maintains tight working links between its manufacturing and engineering departments and its suppliers, intimately involving them in all aspects of product design and manufacture. Indeed, it often lends them personnel to deal with production surges and its suppliers accept Toyota people into their personnel systems.

Toyota's alliance members share much more than a marketplace relationship with each other. In a very real sense, Toyota and its suppliers share a common purpose and destiny. Yet, Toyota has not integrated its suppliers into a single, large bureaucracy. It wants its suppliers to remain independent companies with completely separate books—real profit/investment centers, rather than merely notational ones—selling to others whenever possible. Toyota's solution to the cooperative games created by spillovers and toll goods appears to work just fine. Note that the means of reinforcing trust-based alliances often includes the exchange of hostages-surety bonds, the exchange of debt or equity positions, or quasi-vertical integration. Quasi-vertical integration is common in both the automobile and the aerospace industries, and, of course, it is standard procedure for the U.S. Department of Defense to provide and own the equipment, dies, and designs that defense firms use to supply it with weapons systems and the like.

Moreover, modern information technology has made it economically feasible in a number of cases to exclude users and to design and apply demand-based multipart tariffs to deal effectively with problems of nonexhaustibility, thereby deconstructing vertically integrated value chains. Under multipart transfer prices, the service delivered is decomposed to reflect underlying cost drivers and priced accordingly (your home phone bill is an excellent example of a multipart tariff). Even where sequential value chains remain bounded by a single organization, these innovations often allow intraorganizational exchanges of services, tangible assets, knowledge, and skills to be governed by laissez-faire transfer prices, in which the buying and selling units are completely free to negotiate prices and to deal or not to deal.

Formerly, in most large complex organizations in the private sector, value chains were typically governed by centralized resource-requirements planning systems. Even where transfer prices were used, the financial performance of a processing unit that contributed directly to a value chain was typically measured against a standard unit-cost target; staff units were not a direct component of the value chain and were typically treated as discretionary expense centers. Only final product-market lines were evaluated in terms of return on investment or economic value added. The reasons for this are complex, but they go to difficulties associated with expensing intermediate and joint products. Consequently, attempts to find the costs of intermediate and joint products or to price them were often either excessively arbitrary or prohibitively costly. In contrast, final products have always been relatively easy to price and expense following generally accepted accounting practice. Recent advances in information technology, managerial accounting, and organizational design have made it possible and, in some cases, beneficial to treat every responsibility center in an organization as an investment center, including those providing overhead services. Our basic point is that there is more than one way to skin a cat, to cite a familiar value chain problem.

More significant, given our purpose, is the fact that technology, primarily information technology, but also the technology of social cooperation (mechanisms, processes, doctrines), has rendered traditional mass production methods obsolete by removing value added from the fabrication stage of many value chains. For many final goods and services, direct labor costs at the fabrication stage are now trivial and raw materials and components do not add value at that stage of the process. This means that most of the costs incurred in creating value do not vary directly with the rate and/or volume of output, but have other drivers. Moreover, modern fabrication technologies are largely available to any producer willing to make the necessary investment.

In a typical modern hi-tech value chain, most of the value is added in product development and design, logistics, materials handling, delivery, postdelivery servicing and maintenance and in customer relations. In other words, overheads and purchased services and components account for 90% of costs. Consequently, value is now defined more in terms of the quality and heterogeneity of goods and services, their availability when and where they are wanted and convenience of use, and consumer awareness and knowledge of product or service attributes, than in terms of cost or price.

This transformation reflects the fact that mass production entailed costs as well as benefits. These costs took the form of mismatches between individual tastes and preferences and product characteristics. The classic illustration of this phenomenon is Henry Ford's dictum that customers could have any color Model T they wanted, as long as it was black (blue in Canada). This potential misallocation of resources arising from the mismatch between tastes and the product homogeneity induced by mass production is directly comparable to the problem of providing public goods in a jurisdiction where people have different preferences for the good (i.e., where people cannot vote with their feet and zoning does not achieve efficient sorting) but face an identical tax price. In that case, where the quantity of the good provided is democratically determined (i.e., it reflects the preferences of the median voter), as we have seen, half of the citizens get more of the good than they want (they would rather not buy as much of the public good as they are made to) and half less (i.e., they would be willing and able to buy more). Technological changes mean that in many cases it is no longer necessary to bear these costs to obtain the benefits of productive efficiency even where value chains are concerned with manufactured goods.

Elsewhere the standard model of the value chain, based as it was upon the technical and social imperatives of the mass-production of manufactured goods, was probably never the best way to think about value creation. The delivery of services, for example, has generally involved at least some accommodation to the needs of the individual recipient. Treating service delivery, especially government service delivery, like manufacturing almost necessarily meant trying to fit it into Procrustean bed. Much the same could be said about the building and construction trades. Consequently, it may be argued that what has changed in recent years is that manufacturing has simply become more like other value creating activities.

If true, these facts ought to change the way we think about value chains in some fundamental ways. Instead, of linear networks of sequentially dependent activities, it may make more sense to think of value-chains as parallel networks involving reciprocally interdependent relationships through which activities are simultaneously carried out. Consequently, critical paths or PERT networks are better metaphors for these value chains than are directed or linear graphs. This is the case because holding costs can often be minimized by parallel processing where all the participants in the value chain have full access to information about every aspect of the process. The activities and tasks that comprise a value chain and the technologies used to perform them still determine its optimal arrangement and its governance structure, but the main coordination problems to be solved nowadays typically involve horizontal rather than vertical integration.

Unfortunately, the logic of horizontal integration is not very well developed or understood, in part because students of management have not fully appreciated the need to rethink the problem of coordinating activities when information costs are low or of organizing to create value via parallel processes. Organizational economists have been especially resistant to rethinking received doctrine. Fortunately, however, we have some empirical knowledge about managing projects, which is the closest analogue we have to the more general problem of horizontal integration (See Table 9.3).

The logic of transactions or information cost implies that networks are neither a distinct kind of relationship, nor necessarily superior in performance to other kinds of value chains, nor even uniquely more difficult to sustain than value chains comprehended by single organizations. "The principles of hierarchy," "levels of graded authority," and "a firmly

Table 9.3. The Logic of Horizontal Integration

Project Characteristics	Developmental Process	Known Process
Multiple Core Competencies Required	Alliances (voluntary collaborations involving multiple-organizations)	Systems management (hierarchical coordination involving multiple-organizations)
Multiple Personal Competencies Required	Teams (voluntary collaborations within a single organization)	Project management (hierarchical coordination within a single organization)

Source: Thompson (2006, p. 81).

ordered system of super- and subordination" are inimical to democracy. They are also increasingly inimical to high performance. Nowadays, it seems clear that high performing entities are more likely to be designed around team-based collaborations that successfully spread authority and responsibility throughout the organization and thereby mobilize the collective intelligences of their members.

CONCLUSIONS

We believe that networks represent a means to move from bureaucracy and hierarchy as means for coping with complex problems to consensus decision making through the use of netcentric systems and quick learning in organizations. In this regard, as we argued in chapter eight, we believe that networks can be influenced by stakeholders and participants, but cannot be "managed" per se. True networks of the type defined by Evans and Wurster (1997) cannot be managed. Instead, they evolve spontaneously as entities relatively free of control and management by any party. We acknowledge that there is a school of thought which views networks as manageable (see, for example, Kickert, Klijn, & Koppenjan, 1997; O'Toole & Meier, 2004), but we do not agree with this perspective.

With respect to how hyperarchy, netcentricity and quick learning can facilitate organizational decision making and action through the use of new technology, for our purposes it is reasonable to conclude that there is a hierarchy of technologies, from easy to hard, low risk to high risk, low payoff to high payoff that may be used to achieve desired results:

- Standardized component
- Standard formulation
- Innovative formulation

Table 9.4. From Inputs to Capability

Equipment	Operating software	Process design	Organizational design	Capability for use

Source: Thompson (2006, p. 82).

There is also a hierarchy of applications that goes from redeployability to asset specificity, or from a primary focus on dealing with process design factors to a primary focus on dealing with process context factors including mission and purpose, organizational constitution, culture and design, the basis of strategic thinking, and capability of assets for use.

As indicated in Table 9.4, the first two kinds of applications are what we usually think of when we talk about technology; the last three sometimes get lumped together under the rubric of business process reengineering, although there are disciplines concerned with each of the three sets of applications—process engineering, organizational design, and change management or knowledge management—which focus upon the development, stabilization, and operation practice. However, the basic payoff from investment on the left side results from investment on the right side. Second, the focus of this chapter has been on the use of information technology to improve communications and business efficiency for government departments and agencies.

Governments at all levels are grappling with these issues. The issue that must soon be faced is: what do the new technologies mean for the democratic process itself and for the prospect of enhanced citizen engagement? Democracy may be easier to achieve in the workplace than in society. Work is central to our lives but government and its functions are not, which implies an important relational distinction. At work, participation in governance is a benefit, in society writ large it is a cost. For democracy to work as it should, this cost must be bourn but, the incentives to participate are so widely dispersed in society that the absence of participation is understandable, if regrettable. This fact explains why governments so often fail to manage their business affairs properly, why corruption is prevalent in democratic and quasi-democratic political systems, and why public organizations are so resistant to management reform.

NOTE

1. Dr. Alberts is Director of Research and Strategic Planning, Office of Assistant Secretary of Defense for Networks and Information Integration.

REFERENCES

A guide to better buying. (1986, October 18). *The Economist*, p. 71.
Alberts, D. S., & Hayes, P. (2003). *Power to the edge: Command and control in the information age.* New York: Harper & Row.
Alchian, A. (1959). Costs and outputs. In *The allocation of economic resources: Essays by Moses Abramovitz and others* (pp. 23-40). Stanford, CA: University Press.
Anthony, R. N. (1962, June). New frontiers in defense financial management. *The Federal Accountant, XI,* 13-32.
Anthony, R. N., & Govindarajan, V. (1995). *Management control systems* (8th ed.). Chicago: Irwin.
Anthony, R. N., & Govindarajan, V. (1998). *Management control systems* (9th ed.). Chicago: Irwin/McGraw-Hill.
Anthony, R. N., & Young, D. (1988). *Management control in nonprofit organizations* (4th ed). Homewood, IL: Irwin.
Anthony, R. N., & Young, D. (1994). *Management control in nonprofit organizations* (5th ed.). Homewood, IL: Irwin.
Argyris, C. (1991, May-June). Teaching smart people how to learn. *Harvard Business Review,* 99-109.
Argyris, C. (1993). *Knowledge for action: A guide for overcoming barriers to organizational change.* San Francisco: Jossey-Bass.
Argyris, C., & Schon, D. A. (1978). *Organizational learning: A theory of action perspective.* Reading, MA: Addison-Wesley.
Arquilla, J., & Ronfeldt, D. (2001). *Networks and netwars.* Santa Monica, CA: RAND.
Arrow, K. (1969). *The organization of economic activity: Issues pertinent to the choice of market versus non-market allocation. The analysis and evaluation of public expenditure: The PPB System.* Washington, DC: U.S. Government Printing Office.
Arwidi, O., & Samuelson, L. (1993, June). The development of budgetary control in Sweden: A research note. *Management Accounting Research, 4*(2), 93-107.

Asch, B. J. (1990a, February). Do incentives matter? The case of navy recruiters. *Industrial and Labor Relations Review, 23*, 27-39.

Asch, B. J. (1990b, February). Do incentives matter? The case of navy recruiters. *Industrial and Labor Relations Review, 43*(3), S89–106.

Asian Development Bank. (1997). *Review of the bank's technical assistance operations.* Manila, Philippines: Author.

Asian Development Bank. (2003). *The strategic management of capacity building for decentralisation and deconcentration in the Kingdom of Cambodia. Contextual analyses* (Vol. 1) [Draft Report]. Manila, Philippines: Author.

Asian Development Bank. (2004a). *Training needs assessment and training and development plan for DOLA staff* [Draft report]. Manila, Philippines: Author.

Asian Development Bank. (2004b, November). *Results-based management in the public sector.* Manila, Philippines: Author. Retrieved from www.adb.org/projects/rbm

Asian Development Bank. (2005a). *Managing for development results.* Manila, Philippines: Author. Retrieved from www.managingfordevelopmentresults.org/2ndRoundtable.html

Asian Development Bank. (2005b, October 17). *Mainstreaming MfDR in support of poverty reduction: Draft technical assistance project paper.* Manila, Phillippines: Author.

Asian Development Bank. (2005c, September). *Results-based country strategies and programs.* Manila, Philippines: Author.

Asian Development Bank. (2005d). *Country strategy and program update: Indonesia.* Jakarta: Author.

Asian Development Bank. (2006). *Managing for development results ADB.* Retrieved September 12, 2006, from www.adb.org/mfdr

Asian Development Bank and World Bank. (2005, March 31). *Decentralization in the Philippines: Strengthening local government finance and resource management in the short term.* Manila, Philippines: Author.

Bailey, M. J. (1967). Defense decentralization through internal prices. In S. Enke (Ed.), *Defense management* (pp. 337-352). Englewood Cliffs, NJ: Prentice-Hall.

Bao, L. (2003). Intergovernmental tax competition and its effectiveness during an economic transition. *Asia-Pacific Tax Bulletin, 9*(5), 146-149.

Barzelay, M. (2001). *The new public management.* Berkeley: University of California Press.

Barzelay, M., & Armajani, B. J. (1992). *Breaking through bureaucracy: A new vision for managing in government.* Bekeley: University of California Press.

Barzelay, M., & Campbell, C. (2003). *Preparing for the future: Strategic planning in the U.S. Air Force.* Washington, DC: Brookings Institution Press.

Barzelay, M., & Moukheiber, C. (1997). Listening to customers. In J. L. Perry (Ed.), *Handbook of public administration* (2nd ed., pp. 154-173). San Francisco: Jossey-Bass.

Barzelay, M., & Thompson, F. (2005). Case teaching and intellectual performances in public management. In I. Geva-May (Ed.), *Thinking like a policy analyst* (pp. 83-108). New York: Palgrave-Macmillan.

Bauer, J. (1998). *The state of LGU development in the Philippines.* Unpublished manuscript.

Becker, G. (1985). Public policies, pressure groups, and dead weight costs. *Journal of Public Economics, 28*(2), 371-400.
Behn, R. (2004, January). *The Behn report*. Retrieved from http://www.ksg.harvard.edu/TheBehnReport/January2004.pdf
Berger, P. L., & Luckman, T. (1980). *The social construction of reality: A treatise in the sociology of knowledge.* New York: Insington.
Bhatta, G. (2006). *International dictionary of public management and governance.* Armonk, NY: M. E. Sharpe.
Bird, R. (2004). Administrative dimensions of tax reform. *Asia-Pacific Tax Bulletin, 10*(3), 134-150.
Blackburn, J. D. (Ed.). (1991). *Time-based competition.* Homewood, IL: Irwin.
Blunt, P., & Turner, M. (2005). Decentralisation, democracy and development in a post-conflict society: Commune councils in Cambodia. *Public Administration and Development, 25,* 75-87.
Borins, S. F. (1997). What the new public management is achieving: A survey of commonwealth experience. In L. R. Jones & K. Schedler (Eds.), *International perspectives on the new public management* (pp. 49-70). Stamford, CT: JAI Press.
Boston, J. (2001). The challenge of evaluating systemic change: The case of public management reform in New Zealand. In L. R. Jones, J. Guthrie, & P. Steane (Eds.), *Learning from international public management reform* (Vol. 11A, pp. 103-132). Oxford, England: JAI Press.
Boston, J., Martin, J., Pallot J., & Walsh, P. (1996). *Public management: The New Zealand model.* Auckland, New Zealand: Oxford University Press.
Bower, J. (1970). *The resource allocation process.* Boston: Harvard Business School Division of Research.
Bower, J. L. (1990, July-August). Business and battles: Lessons from defeat. *Harvard Business Review,* 48-53.
Bowornsak, U., & Burns, W. D. (1998). The Thai Constitution of 1997: Sources and process. *University of British Columbia Law Review, 32*(2), 227-247.
Boyne, W. (2003). *Operation Iraqi freedom: What went right, what went wrong, and why.* New York: Forge Books.
Bradley, S., Hausman, J., & Noland, R. (1993). *Globalization, technology, and competition: The fusion of computers and telecommunications in the 1990s.* New York: Harvard Business School.
Brillantes, A., Montes, R., & Sonco, J. (2005, August 1). Devolution-plus. *Newsbreak, 6.*
Bruggeman, W. (1995). The impact of technological change on management accounting. *Management Accounting Research, 6*(3), 241-252.
Brynjolfsson, E., & Hitt, L. M. (2000, Fall). Beyond computation: Information technology, organizational transformation and business performance. *Journal of Economic Perspectives, 14*(4), 23-48.
Buchanan, J., & Tullock, G. (1962). *The calculus of consent.* Ann Arbor: The University of Michigan Press.
Buchanan, J. M. (1969). *Cost and choice: an inquiry in economic theory.* Chicago: Markham.
Buentjen, C. (2000). *Fiscal decentralization in Indonesia—The challenge of designing institutions.* Unpublished manuscript.

Bunce, P., Fraser, R., & Woodcock, L. (1995). Advanced budgeting: A journey to advanced management systems. *Management Accounting Research, 6*(3), 253-265.

Buschor, E. (1994). Introduction: From advanced public accounting via performance measurement to new public management. In E. Buschor & K. Schedler (Eds.), *Perspectives on performance measurement and public sector accounting* (pp. VII-XVIII). Berne/Stuttgart/Vienna: Paul Haupt.

Carlton, D. W., & Perloff, J. M. (1990). *Modern industrial organization.* Glenview, IL.: Scott, Foresman-Little, Brown Higher Education.

Chandler, A. (1962). *Strategy and structure: Chapters in the history of industrial enterprise.* Cambridge, MA: MIT Press.

Chandler, D. A (1993). *History of Cambodia.* New Haven, CT: Silkworm Books.

Cheema, G. S., & Rondinelli, D. (1983). *Decentralization and development: policy implementation in developing countries.* Beverly Hills, CA: Sage.

Clark, K. B., & Fujimoto, T. (1991). *Product development performance: Strategy, organization, and management in the world auto industries.* Cambridge, MA: Harvard Business School Press.

Coakley, T. P. (1992). *Command and control for war and peace.* Washington, DC: National Defense University Press.

Coase, R. (1937). The nature of the firm. *Economica, 4,* 386-405.

Cohen, J., & Peterson., S. (1999). *Beyond administrative decentralization strategies for developing countries.* West Hartford, CT: Kumarian Press.

Commons, J. R. (1968). *Legal foundations of capitalism.* Madison: University of Wisconsin Press.

Cooper, R., & Turney, P. B. (1990). Internally focused activity-based cost systems. In R. S. Kaplan (Ed.), *Measures for manufacturing excellence* (pp. 43-61). Cambridge, MA: Harvard Business School Press.

Coram, R. B. (2002). *The fighter pilot who changed the art of war.* Boston: Little Brown & Company.

Cordesman, A. H. (2003). *The Iraq war: Strategy, tactics, and military lessons.* Washington DC: Center for Strategic & International Studies.

D'Aveni, R. (1994). *Hypercompetition.* New York: Free Press.

Davis, J. (2004). Corruption in public service delivery: Experience from South Asia's water and sanitation sector. *World Development, 32*(1), 62-63.

Davis, J. (2005). Untitled. *Wired Magazine, 7*(2), 28.

Davis, V. (1973). The politics of innovation: Patterns in Navy cases. In R. G. Head & E. J. Rokke (Eds.), *American defense policy* (3rd ed., pp. 393-401). Baltimore: The Johns Hopkins University Press.

Demski, J., & Feltham, G. (1976). *Cost determination.* Ames: Iowa State University Press

Dixit, A. (2002). Incentives and organizations in the public sector: An interpretative review. *Journal of Human Resources, 37*(4), 696-727.

Dixit, A., & Nalebuff, B. (1991). *Thinking strategically: The competitive edge in business, politics, and everyday life.* New York: Norton.

Downs, A. (1957). *An economic theory of democracy.* New York: Harper and Row.

Downs, A. (1967). *Inside bureaucracy.* Boston: Little Brown.

Drucker, P. (1953). *The practice of management.* New York: Harper & Brothers.

Drucker, P. (1969). *The age of discontinuity: Guidelines to our changing society*. New York: Harper and Row.
Drucker, P. (1993). *Post capitalist society*. New York: Harper Business.
Drucker, P. (1994). The age of social transformation. *Atlantic Monthly, 274*(5), 53-94.
Dunleavy, P. (1991). *Democracy, bureaucracy and public choice: Economic explanations in political science*. New York: Harvester/Wheatsheaf.
The Economist. (1993, February 27), pp. 14-15.
The Economist. (1993, December 11), p. 80.
Evans, P. B., & Wurster, T. S. (1997, September-October). Strategy and the new economics of information. *Harvard Business Review*, 71-82.
Exley, Z. (2004, December 14). Statement on 2004 election strategy, *New York Times*, p. 22.
Ezzamel, M., Hyndman, N. S., Johnsen, A., Lapsley, I., & Pallot, J. (2004). Has devolution increased democratic accountability? *Public Money & Management, 24*(3), 145.
Fallows, J. C. (1981). *National defense*. New York: Random House.
Financial Action Task Force. (n.d.). *What is the FATF*. Retrieved from http://www.fatf-gafi.org/document/57/0,2340,en_32250379_32235720_34432121_1_1_1_1,00.html
Forrester, J. (1961). *Industrial dynamics*. Cambridge, MA: MIT Press.
Fountain, J. (2001). *Building the virtual state*. Washington, DC: Brookings.
Fudenburg, D., & Tirole, J. (1986). A "Signal-Jamming" theory of predation. *Rand Journal of Economics, 17*, 366-376.
Galbraith, J. K. (1956). *American capitalism: The concept of countervailing power*. Boston: Houghton Mifflin.
Galbraith, J. K. (1967). *The new industrial state*. Boston: Houghton Mifflin.
Ganley, J., & Cubbin, J. (1992). *Public sector efficiency measurement*. New York: Elsevier Science.
Garson, G. D., & Overman, E. S. (1983). *Public management research in the United States*. New York: Praeger.
Garvin, D. A. (1988). *Managing quality*. New York: The Free Press.
Gibbons, R. (2003). Team theory, garbage cans and real organizations: Some history and prospects of economic research on decision-making in organizations. *Industrial and Corporate Change, 12*(4), 753-787.
Gill, D. (2001). New Zealand experience with public management reform. In L. R. Jones, J. Guthrie, & P. Steane, (Eds.), *Learning from international public management reform* (Vol. 11A, pp. 143-160). Oxford, England: JAI Press.
Go, M. (2005, August 1). A new order. *Newsbreak*, p. 8.
Godfrey, B. (1994). Can large government learn? In P. Senge, N. Cambron-McCabe, T. Lucas, B. Smith, J. Dutton, & A. Kleiner (Eds.), *The fifth discipline fieldbook* (pp. 87-107). New York: Doubleday.
Goldin, K. D. (1977, Spring). Equal access vs. selective access: A critique of public goods theory. *Public Choice, 29*, 53-71.
Gooptu, S. (2005). Achieving fiscal sustainability. In *East Asia decentralizes: Making local government work* (pp. 53-66). Washington, DC: World Bank. Retrieved

from http://siteresources.worldbank.org/INTEAPDECEN/Resources/dc-full-report.pdf

Gore, A. (1993). *The Gore report on reinventing government: From red tape to results, creating a government that works better and costs less, report of the National Performance Review.* New York: Times Books.

Gray, A., & Jenkins, B. (1995, Spring). From public administration to public management: Reassessing a revolution? *Public Administration, 73*, 75-99.

Green, M., Jones, L. R., & Thompson, F. (1999). Local heroes? Reinvention laboratories in the department of defense. In H. Rainey et al. (Eds.), *Public sector management* (pp. 46-74). New York: Marcel Dekker.

Gregory, R. (2001). Getting better but feeling worse? Public sector reform in New Zealand. In L. R. Jones, J. Guthrie, & P. Steane (Eds.), *Learning from international public management reform* (Vol. 11A, pp. 211-231). Oxford, England: JAI Press.

Gulick, L. H., & Urwick, L. (Eds.). (1937). *Papers on the science of administration.* New York: Institute of Public Administration, Columbia University.

Guthrie, J., Humphrey, C., Jones, L. R., & Olson, O. (Eds.). (2005). *Debating public sector financial management reforms: An international study.* Greenwich. CT: Information Age.

Guthrie, J., Humphrey, C., & Olson, O. (1997). Public financial management changes in OECD nations. In L. R. Jones & K. Schedler (Eds), *International perspectives on the new public management* (pp. 255-269). Stamford, CT: JAI Press.

Guthrie, J., Olson, O., & Humphrey, C. (1999). Debating developments in new public financial management: The limits of global theorising and some new ways forward. *Financial Accountability and Management, 15*(3/4), 209-228.

Guthrie, J., & Parker, L. (1998). "Managerialism" and "Marketisation." Financial management change in Australia. In O. Olson, J. Guthrie, & C. Humphrey (Eds.)., *Global warning—debating international developments in new public financial management* (pp. 49-75). Bergen, Norway: Cappelen Akademisk Forlag.

Hamel, G., & Prahalad, C. K. (1889). Strategic intent. *Harvard Business Review, 67*(3), 63-76.

Hamel, G., & Prahalad, C. K. (1990). The core competence of the corporation. *Harvard Business Review, 68*(3), 79-91.

Hamel, G., & Prahalad, C. K. (1993). Strategy as stretch and leverage. *Harvard Business Review, 71*(2), 75-84.

Hamel, G., & Prahalad, C. K. (1994). *Competing for the future.* New York: Free Press.

Hammer, M. (1990, July-August). Reengineering work: Don't automate, obliterate. *Harvard Business Review,* 104-112.

Hammer, M. (1996). *Beyond reengineering: How the process-centered organization is changing our work and our lives.* New York: Harper Business.

Hammer, M., & Champy, J. (1993). *Reengineering the corporation: A manifesto for business revolution.* New York: Harper Business.

Hammer, M., & Stanton, S. A. (1995). *The reengineering revolution: A handbook.* New York: Harper Business.

Hardin, G. (1968, December 13). The tragedy of the commons. *Science, 162,* 1243-1248.

Harr, D. J. (1989, Summer). Productive unit resourcing: A business perspective on government financial management. *Government Accountants Journal*, 51-57.

Harr, D. J. (1990, September). How activity accounting works in government. *Management Accounting*, 72, 36-40.

Harr, D. J., & Godfrey, J. T. (1991). *Private sector financial performance measures and their applicability to government operations*. Montvale, NJ: National Association of Accountants.

Harr, D. J., & Godfrey, J. T. (1992, Winter). The total unit cost approach to government financial management. *Government Accountants Journal*, 15-24.

Heifetz, R. A. (1993). *Leadership without easy answers*. Cambridge, MA: Harvard University Press.

Hemingway, A. W. (1993). Cost center financial management: Training OPTAR managers. *Navy Comptroller*, 3(3), 2-26.

Hilderbrand M. E., & Grindle, M. S. (1995). Building sustainable capacity in the public sector: what can be done? *Public Administration and Development*, 15(5), 441-464.

Hood, C. (1991). A public management for all seasons. *Public Administration*, 69(1), 3-20.

Hood, C. (1995, Spring). Emerging issues in public administration. *Public Administration*, 73, 165-183.

Hood, C. (2000). Paradoxes of public sector managerialism, old public management and public service bargains. *International Public Management Journal*, 3(1), 1-20.

Hood, C., & Peters, G. (2004). The middle aging of NPM: Into the age of paradoxes? *Journal of Public Administration Research and Theory*, 14(3), 267-282.

Horngren, C. T., & Foster, G. (1991). *Cost accounting: A managerial emphasis* (7th ed.). Englewood Cliffs, NJ: Prentice-Hall.

House, R., Prichard, R., & Trebilcock, M. (1990). Smaller or smarter government? *University of Toronto Law Journal*, 40, 498-541.

Hughes, T. P. (1998). *Rescuing prometheus: Four monumental projects that changed the world*. New York: Pantheon Books.

Hughes, O., & O'Neill, D. (2001). Public Sector Management in the State of Victoria: 1992-1999: Genesis of the transformation. In L. R. Jones, J. Guthrie, & P. Steane (Eds.), *Learning From international public management reform* (Vol. 11A, pp. 61-76). Oxford, England: JAI Press.

Hyde, A. (1997). Cornerstones of quality: Special section. *Government Executive*, 29(7), 47-68.

Ichniowski, C., & Shaw, K. (2003). Beyond incentive pay: Insiders' estimates of the value of complementary human resource management. *Journal of Economic Perspectives*, 17(1), 155-180.

IMF raises world growth outlook. (2006a, September 15). *International Herald Tribune*, 13.Ingraham, P. W., Selden, S. C., & Moynihan, D. P. (2000). People and performance: Challenges for the future public service. *Public Administration Review*, 60(1), 54-60.

In Japan, quality problems wound nation's pride. (2006b). *International Herald Tribune*, pp. 1, 14.

Jensen, M., & Meckling, W. (1976). Theory of the firm: Managerial behavior, agency costs, and capital structure. *Journal of Financial Economics, 3,* 305-360.

Jin J., & Zou, H. (2003). Soft-budget constraints and local government in China. In Rodden, J. A., Eskeland, G. S., & Litvack, J. (Eds.), *Fiscal decentralization and the challenge of hard budget constraints.* Cambridge, MA: MIT Press.

Johansen, C., Jones, L. R., & Thompson, F. (1997). Management and control of budget execution. In R. Golembiewski & J. Rabin (Eds.), *Public budgeting and finance* (4th ed., 577-584). New York: Marcel Dekker.

Jones, L. R. (1984). Phases of recognition and management of financial crisis in public organizations. *Canadian Public Administration, 27*(1), 52-68.

Jones, L. R. (1985). *University budgeting for critical mass and competition.* New York City: Praeger.

Jones, L. R. (2005). Understanding public management as an international academic field. *International Public Management Review, 6*(1), 1-17. Retrieved from http://www.ipmr.net

Jones, L. R., & Bixler, G. (1992). *Mission financing to realign national defense.* Greenwich, CT: JAI Press.

Jones, L. R., & Kettl, D. F. (2003). Assessing public management reform in an international context. *International Public Management Review, 4*(1), 1-19.

Jones, L. R., & McCaffery, J. (1989). *Government response to financial constraints.* Westport CT.: Greenwood Press.

Jones, L. R., & McCaffery, J. L., (2005). Reform of PPBS and management control in the U.S. department of defense: Insights from budget theory. *Public Budgeting and Finance, 25*(3), 1-19.

Jones, L. R., & Mussari, R. (2001). Management control reform within a responsibility framework in the U.S. and Italy. In L. R. Jones, J. Guthrie, & P. Steane (Eds.), *Learning from international public management reform* (Vol 11b, pp. 499-530). Oxford, England: JAI Press.

Jones, L. R., & Schedler, K. (Eds.). (1997). *International perspectives on the New Public Management.* Stamford, CT: JAI Press.

Jones, L. R., & Thompson, F. (1999). *Public management: Institutional renewal for the 21st century.* Oxford, England: JAI Press.

Junsheng, L. (2006). *Performance budgeting reform in China* (Issue Brief No. ?). Beijing, China: Central University of Finance and Economics.

Juola, P. (1993). Unit cost resourcing: A conceptual framework for financial management. *Navy Comptroller, 3*(3), 42-48.

Juran, J. M. (1944). *Bureaucracy, a challenge to better management: A constructive analysis of management effectiveness in the federal government.* New York: Harper & Brothers.

Kaplan, R. S. (1992, November). In defense of activity-based cost management. *Management Accounting,* 58-63.

Kaplan, R. S., & Cooper, R. (1998). *Cost and effect: Using integrated cost systems to drive profitability and performance.* Cambridge, MA: Harvard Business School Press.

Katz, M. L., & Shapiro, C. (1986). Technology adoption in the presence of network externalities. *Journal of Political Economy, 94*(4), 822-841.

Kelman, S. (1987a). *Making public policy a hopeful view of American Government.* New York: Basic Books.
Kelman, S. (1987b, Spring). Public choice and public spirit. *Public Interest, 87,* 80-94.
Keohoe, J., Dodson, W., Reeve, R., & Plato, G. (1995). *Activity-based management in government.* Washington, DC: Coopers & Lybrand.
Kerkvliet, B. T., & Porter, D. (1995). Rural Vietnam in rural Asia. In B. T. Kerkvliet & D. Porter (Eds.), *Vietnam's rural transformation* (pp. 1-37). Boulder, CO: Westview.
Kettl, D. (2000a). *The global public management revolution: A report on the transformation of governance.* Washington, DC: The Brookings Institution.
Kettl, D. (2000b, November/December). The transformation of governance: Globalization, devolution, and the role of government. *Public Administration Review,* 488-497.
Kettl, D., Ingraham, P. W., Sanders, R., & Horner, C. (1996). *Civil service reform: Building a government that works.* Washington, DC: The Brookings Institution.
Keynes, J. M. (1936). *The general theory of employment, interest and money.* London: Macmillan, .
Kibblewhite, A. (2001). Effectiveness: The next frontier in New Zealand. In L. R. Jones, J. Guthrie, & P. Steane (Eds.), *Learning from international public management reform* (Vol. 11A, pp. 177-192). Oxford, England: JAI Press.
Kickert, W., Klijn, J., & Koppenjan, J., (Eds.). (1997). *Managing complex networks: Strategies for the public sector.* London: Sage.
Klein, J. (1998). *The constitution of the Kingdom of Thailand, 1997: A blueprint for participatory democracy.* Bangkok, Thailand: Asia Foundation.
Klitgaard, R., & Light, P. C. (2005). *High performance government: Structure, leadership, incentives.* Santa Monica, CA: Rand Corporation.
Knechtenhofer, B., & Schedler, K. (2003). Switzerland. Reforming governmental accounting and budgeting in Europe. In K. Lüder & R. Jones (Eds.), *Reforming governmental accounting and budgeting in Europe* (pp. 853-940). Frankfurt A. M: Moderne Wirtschaf.
Kolb, D. (1984). *Experiential learning: Experience as the source of learning and development.* Englewood Cliffs, NJ: Prentice-Hall.
Laking, R. (2001). Reflections on public sector reform in New Zealand. In L. R. Jones, J. Guthrie, & P. Steane (Eds.), *Learning from international public management reform* (Vol. 11A, pp. 133-142). Oxford, England: JAI Press.
Lao-Araya, K. (2001). *Economics and politics of fiscal decentralization: The effect of decentralization strategy on macroeconomic stability in Thailand.* Unpublished manuscript.
Lapsley, I. (1994). Responsibility accounting revived? Market reforms and budgetary control. *Management Accounting Research, 5*(3), 337-352.
Lazear, E. P. (2000). Performance pay and productivity. *American Economic Review, 90*(5), 1346-1361.
Lewis, B., & Umum, D. A. (2001, March). *Description, analysis and recommendations.* Paper presented at the 3rd IRSA International Conference, Indonesia's Sustainable Development in a Decentralization Era, Singapore.

Lin, J. Y., & Zhiqiang, L. (2000). *Fiscal decentralization and economic growth in China.* Paper prepared for workshop on the PRC's long-term economic prospects and challenges, ADB, Manila.

Lynn, L. E. (1996). *Public management as art, science, and profession.* Chatham NJ: Chatham House.

Malone, T., & Rockart, J. (1995). Computers, networks and the corporation. *Scientific American, 6*(21), 140-147.

Malone, T., Yates, J., & Benjamin, R. (1987). Electronic markets and electronic hierarchies. *Communications of the ACM, 30*(6), 484-497.

March, J. G., & Olsen, J. P. (1995). *Democratic governance.* New York: The Free Press.

Masten, S. E. (1984). The organization of production. *The Journal of Law and Economics, 27*(3), 403-417.

McCaffery, J., & Jones, L. R. (2001). *Budgeting and financial management in the federal government.* Greenwich, CT: Information Age.

Meyer, C. (1993). *Fast cycle time: How to align purpose, strategy, and structure for speed.* New York: The Free Press.

Milgrom, P., & Roberts, J. (1992). *Economics, organization, and management.* Englewood Cliffs, NJ: Prentice Hall.

Milward, H. B. (1994). Nonprofit contracting and the hollow state. *Public Administration Review, 54*(1), 73-77.

Ministry of Home Affairs. (2001). *Decentralization policy for poverty reduction.* Policy paper presented at the CGI meeting, Jakarta, Indonesia. Retrieved from http://www.gtzsfdm.or.id/public/diverses/MoHA_PreCGI_Paper2001.pdf

Mintzberg, H. (1994). *The rise and fall of strategic planning.* New York: Free Press.

Moe, T. M. (1984). The new economics of organization. *American Journal of Political Science, 28*(4), 739-777.

Monteverde, K., &. Teece, D. (1982). Appropriate rents and quasi-vertical integration. *The Journal of Law and Economics, 25*(3), 403-418.

Moore, M. H. (1995). *Creating public value: Strategic management in government.* Cambridge, MA: Harvard University Press.

Moynihan, D., & Ingraham, P. (2003). Look for the silver lining: Managing for Results in State Governments. *Journal of Public Administration and Theory, 13*(4), 469-490.

Nelson, M. H. (2000). *Local government reform in Thailand: With some comparative perspectives.* Nonthaburi, Thailand: Center for the Study of Thai Politics and Democracy, King Prajadhipok Institute.

Newberry, S. (2001). Network structures, consumers and accountability in New Zealand. In L. R. Jones, J. Guthrie, & P. Steane (Eds.), *Learning from international public management reform* (Vol. 11A, pp. 257-278). Oxford, England: JAI Press.

Newberry, S. (2003). Book review: Graham Scott, 2001. Public sector management in New Zealand: Lessons and challenges. *International Public Management Review, 4*(2), 96-103.

Newberry, S. (Ed.). (2006). *The legacy of June Pallot.* Greenwich, CT: Information Age.

Newberry, S., & Pallot, J. (2003). Fiscal (ir)responsibility: Privileging PPPs in New Zealand. *Accounting, Auditing & Accountability Journal, 16*(3), 467-492.

Newberry, S., & Pallot, J. (2005). A wolf in sheep's clothing? Wider consequences of the financial management system of the New Zealand central government. *Financial Accountability & Management, Financial Accountability & Management, 21*(3), 263-276.

New Zealand Treasury. (1987). *Government management: Brief to the incoming government 1987*. Wellington, New Zealand. Government Printing Office.

Niskanen, W. (1971). *Bureaucracy and representative government*. Chicago: Aldine-Atherton.

Nissen, M. E. (2006). *Harnessing knowledge dynamics: Principled organizational knowing and learning*. New York: Idea Group.

Nonaka, I. (1990). Redundant, overlapping organization: A Japanese approach to managing the innovation process. *California Management Review, 32*(2), 26-41.

Nooteboom, B. (2000). Learning by interaction: Absorptive capacity, cognitive distance and governance. *Journal of Management and Governance, 4*, 69-92.

O'Donnell, M. (2000). Creating a performance culture? Performance-based pay in the Australian public service. *Australian Journal of Public Administration, 57*(3), 28-40.

O'Faircheallaigh, C., Wanna, J., & Weller, P. (1999). *Public sector management in Australia: New challenges, new directions*. Australia: Macmillan.

Olsen, J. P., & Peters, G. (1996). *Lessons from experience: Experiential learning in administrative reforms in eight democracies*. Oslo: Scandinavian University Press.

Olson, O., Guthrie, J., & Humphrey, C. (Eds.). (1998). *Global warning—Debating international developments in new public financial m*anagement. Bergen, Norway: Cappelen Akademisk Forlag.

Olson, O., Guthrie, J., & Humphrey, C. (1998). International experiences with financial management reforms in the world of public services: new world? small worlds? In O. Olson, J. Guthrie, & C. Humphrey (Eds.), *Global warning: Debating new public financial management* (pp. 17-48). Bergen, Norway: Capelen Akademisk Forlag.

Organisation for Economic Co-operation and Development. (1995). *Budgeting for results: Perspectives on public expenditure management*. Paris: Author.

Organisation for Economic Co-operation and Development. (1997). *In Search of Results: Performance management practices*. Paris: Author.

Organisation for Economic Co-operation and Development. (1999). *PUMA. Performance contracting: Lessons from performance contracting case studies*. Paris: Author.

Organisation for Economic Co-operation and Development. (2005). *Working party on aid effectiveness and donor practices, Paris declaration on aid effectiveness*. Paris: Author.

Osborne, D., & Gaebler, T. (1992). *Reinventing government: How the entrepreneurial spirit is transforming the public sector from schoolhouse to statehouse, city hall to the Pentagon*. Reading, MA: Addison Wesley,

Otley, D. (1994). Management Control in Contemporary Organizations: Towards a Wider Framework. *Management Accounting Research, 5*(3), 289-299.

Otley, D., Broadbent, J., & Berry, A. (1995). Research in management control, An overview of its development. *British Journal of Management, 6*(Special Issue), 31-44.

O'Toole, L., & Meier, K. (2004). Public management in intergovernmental networks: Matching structural networks and managerial networking. *Journal of Public Administration Research and Theory, 14*(4), 469-494.

Pallot, J. (1998). The New Zealand revolution. In O. Olson, J. Guthrie, & C. Humphrey (eds.), *global Warning—Debating international developments in new public financial management* (pp. 156-184). Bergen, Norway: Cappelen Akademisk Forlag.

Pallot, J. (2001, November). A decade in review: New Zealand's experience with resource accounting and budgeting. *Financial Accountability and Management, 17*(4), 383.

Pascale, R. T. (1984). Perspectives on strategy. *California Management Review, 26*(3), 46-64.

Perrow C. (1986a). *Economic theories of organization.* New York: Springer.

Perrow, C. (1986b). *Complex organizations.* New York: Random House.

Peters, T. (1986, April 1). *What gets measured gets done.* New York: Tribune Media Service. Retrieved from http://www.tompeters.com/col_entries.php?note=005143&year=1986

Peters, T. (1987). *Thriving on chaos: Handbook for a management revolution.* London: Macmillan.

Peters, T. J., & Waterman, R. H., Jr. (1982). *In search of excellence.* New York: Harper & Row.

Pfeffer, J. (1998). *The human equation: Building profits by putting people first.* Boston: Harvard Business School Press.

Polanyi, K. (1944). *The great transformation.* New York: Rinehart.

Pollitt, C. (1993). *Managerialism and the public services: Cuts or cultural change in the 1990s?* (2nd ed.). Cambridge, MA: Basil Blackwell.

Pollitt, C. (2003). *The essential public manager.* London: Open University Press.

Pollitt, C., & Bouckaert, G. (2000). *Public management reform: A comparative analysis* (1st ed.). Oxford, England: University Press.

Pollitt, C., & Bouckaert, G. (2004). *Public management reform: A comparative analysis* (2nd ed.). Oxford, England: University Press.

Porter, D. (1995). Economic liberalisation, marginality, and the local state. In Kerkvliet, B., & Porter, D. (Eds.), *Vietnam's rural transformation* (pp. 215-246). Boulder, CO: Westview.

Porter, M. E. (1980). *Competitive strategy: Techniques for analyzing industries and competitors.* New York: The Free Press.

Pusey, M. (1991). *Economics rationalism in Canberra: A nation-building state changes its mind.* London: Cambridge University Press.

Putterill, M., & Speer, D. (2001). Information policy in New Zealand. In L. R. Jones, J. Guthrie, & P. Steane (Eds.), *Learning from international public management reform* (Vol. 11A, pp. 279-290). Oxford, England: JAI Press.

Quibria, M. (2002, February). Growth and poverty: Lessons from the East Asian miracle revisited. *ADB Institute Research Paper, 33*.

Quinn, J. B. (1992). *Intelligent enterprise: A knowledge and service based paradigm for industry.* New York: Free Press.
Rao, G. (2001). *Challenges of fiscal decentralization in transitional economies: An Asian perspective.* Paper prepared for public finance in Developing and Transition Countries: A conference in honor of Richard Bird, Georgia State University, Atlanta.Ramnath, R., & Landsbergen, D. (2005). IT-enabled sense-and-respond strategies in complex public organizations. *Communicatuons of the ACM, 48*(5), 58-64.
Rauch, J. E. (1995). Bureaucracy, infrastructure, and economic growth: Evidence from U.S. cities during the Progressive Era. *American Economic Review, 85*(4), 968-979.
Reich, R. (1991). *The work of nations.* New York: Knopf.
Reschenthaler, G. B., & Thompson, F. (1996). The information revolution and the new public management. *Journal of Public Administration Research and Theory, 6*(1), 125-144.
Rhodes, R. A. W. (1991). The New Public Management. *Public Administration, 69*(1), 27-43.
Rieder, S., & Lehmann, L. (2002). Evaluation of new public management reforms in Switzerland. Empirical results and reflections on methodology. *International Public Management Review, 3*(2), 25-43.
Riley, K., & Watling, R. (1999, July-September). Education action zones: An Initiative in the making. *Public Money and Management,* 51-58.
Ritz, R. (Ed.). (2005). 10 Jahre Verwaltungsreform in den Schweizer Kantonen, and 10 Jahre New Public Management in der Schweiz. Bilanz, Irrtümer und Erfolgsfaktoren. In A. Lienhard, A. Ritz, R. Steiner, & A. Ladner (Eds.), *Bern, Stuttgart, Wien* (pp. 47-68). Paul Haupt.
Roberts, A. (1997). Performance based organizations: Assessing the Gore plan. *Public Administration Review, 57*(6), 465-481.
Roberts, C., Smith, B., & Ross R. (1994). Opening moves: How to find an appropriate path through the five disciplines. In P. Senge et al. (Ed.), *The fifth discipline fieldbook* (pp. 77-83). New York: Doubleday.
Roberts, N. (2001). Coping with wicked problems: The case of Afghanistan. In L. R. Jones, J, Guthrie, & P. Steane (Eds.), *Learning from international public management reform* (Vol. 11B, pp. 353-376). Oxford, England: JAI Press.
Rodden, J. A., Eskeland, G. S., & Litvack, J. (Eds.). (2003). *Fiscal decentralization and the challenge of hard budget constraints.* Cambridge, MA: MIT Press.
Rosenberg, N., & Birdsall, L.E. (1986). *How the West grew rich: The economic transformation of the industrial world.* New York: Basic Book.
Savoie, D. J. (1995, Spring). Just another voice from the pulpit. *Canadian Public Administration,* 133-136.
Scavo, C., & Shi, Y. H. (2000). Public administration—The role of information technology in the reinventing government paradigm—Normative predicates and practical challenges. *Social Science Computer Review, 18*(2), 166-178.
Schedler, K. (1995). *Ansätze einer Wirkungsorientirten Verwaltungsführung: Von der Idee des New Public Managements (NPM) zum konkreten Gestaltungsmodell.* Bern, Switzerland: Verlag Paul Haupt.

Schedler, K. (2001). Performance budgeting in Switzerland: Implications for political control. In L. R. Jones, J. Guthrie, & P. Steane (Eds.), *Learning from international public management reform* (pp. 455-478). Oxford, England: JAI Press.

Schedler, K. (2003). Local and regional public management reforms in Switzerland. *Public Administration, 81*(2), 325-344.

Schedler, K., & Proeller, I. (2006). *New public management* (3rd ed.). Bern, Switzerland: Paul Haupt.

Schiavo-Campo, S., & Tommasi, D. (1999). Strengthening "Performance" in public expenditure management. In S. Schiavo-Campo & D. Tommasi (Eds.), Schick, A. (1998, February). Why most developing countries should not try New Zealand reforms. *The World Bank Research Observer*, 123-131.

Schwartz, H. (1994). Small states in big trouble. *World Politics, 46*(4), 527-555. *Managing government expenditure* (pp. 97-127). Manila: ADB.

Scott, G. (1996). Changing concepts of decentralization: Old public administration and new public management in the Asian context. *Asian Journal of Public Administration, 18*(1), 3-21.

Scott, G. (2001). Public management reform and lessons from experience in New Zealand. In L. R. Jones, J. Guthrie, & P. Steane (Eds.), *Learning from international public management reform* (Vol. 11A, pp. 133-142). Oxford, England: JAI Press.

Scott, G. (2001). *Public sector management in New Zealand: Lessons and challenges.* Wellington: Australian National University.

Scott, G., Bushnell, P., & Sallee, N. (1990). Reform of the core public sector: The New Zealand experience. *Public Sector, 13*(3), 11-24.

Shand, D. (2001). The World Bank and Public Sector Management Reform. In L. R. Jones, J. Guthrie, & P. Steane (Eds.), *Learning from international public management reform* (Vol. 11B, pp. 377-390). Oxford, England: JAI Press.

Shewhart, W. A., & Deming, W. E. (1945). *Statistical method from the viewpoint of quality control.* Washington DC: The Graduate School, U.S. Department of Agriculture.

Senge, P. (1990). *The fifth discipline: The art & practice of the learning organization.* New York: Doubleday/Currency.

Senge, P., Cambron-McCabe, N., Lucas, T., Smith, B., Dutton, J., & Kleiner, A. (1994). *The fifth discipline fieldbook.* New York: Doubleday.

Sergiovanni, T. J. (1992). *Moral leadership.* San Francisco: Jossey-Bass.

Simons, R. (1995). *Levers of control: how Managers use innovative control systems to drive strategic renewal.* Boston: Harvard Business School Press.

Smith, D. (1985). The roots and future of modern-day military reform. *Air University Review, 16*, 33-40.

Smoke, P. (2005). The rules of the intergovernmental game in East Asia: Decentralization frameworks and processes. In *East Asia decentralizes: Making local government work* (pp. 25-53). Washington DC: World Bank.

Soden, D. (1988). *The tragedy of the commons: Twenty Years of Policy Literature, 1968-1988.* Monticello, IL: Vance Bibliographies.

Software engineering: Made to measure. (1993, January 23). *The Economist*, p. 79.

Stalk, G., & Hout, T. M. (1990). *Competing against time: How time-based competition is reshaping global markets.* New York: The Free Press.

Steiner, R. (2000). New public management in Swiss municipalities. *International Public Management Journal, 3*(2), 169-190.
Takeuchi, H., & Ikujiro Nonaka, I. (1989). The new new product development game. In *Managing projects and programs*. Boston: Harvard Business School Press.
Tani, T. (1995). Interactive control in target cost management. *Management Accounting Research, 6*(4), 401-414.
Teece, D. J. (1993). The dynamics of industrial Capitalism. *Journal of Economic Literature, 31*(1), 199-225.
Thomas, P. R. (1990). *Competitiveness through total cycle time*. New York: McGraw-Hill.
Thompson, F. (1997). Capital budgeting. In *the International Encyclopedia of Public Policy and Administration* (pp. 330-337). Boulder, CO: Westview Press.
Thompson, F. (1998). Cost measurement and analysis. In R. Meyers (Ed.), *Handbook of public budgeting* (pp. 112-139). San Francisco: Jossey-Bass.
Thompson, F. (2003). "Cost analysis": Handbook of public budgeting. In A. Schick & R. Meyers (Eds.), San Francisco: Jossey-Bass.
Thompson, F. (2004). "Capital Budgeting." In *International Encyclopedia of Public Policy and Administration*. Boulder, CO: Westview Press.
Thompson, F. (2006). Evolution or revolution? E-government in the U.S. In S. Borins et al. (Eds.), *Digital state at the leading edge*. Toronto, Canada: University of Toronto Press.
Thompson, F., & Jones, L. R. (1986). Controllership in the public sector. *Journal of Policy Analysis and Management, 5*(3), 547-571.
Thompson, F., & Jones, L. R. (1994). *Reinventing the Pentagon: How the New Public Management can promote institutional renewal*. San Francisco: Jossey-Bass.
Thompson, J. D. (1967). *Organizations in action*. New York: McGraw-Hill.
Tooley, S. (2001). Observations on the imposition of new public management in the New Zealand state education system. In L. R. Jones, J. Guthrie, & P. Steane (Eds.), *Learning from international public management reform* (Vol. 11A, pp. 233-255). Oxford, England: JAI Press.
Trebilcock, M. J. (1994). *The prospects for reinventing government*. Toronto, Canada: C. D. Howe Institute.
United Nations Development Programme. (2001). *United Nations development programme. Human development report 2001*. New York: Oxford University Press,
Vesey, J. T. (1991). The new competitors: They think in terms of "Speed-to-Market." *Academy of Management Executive, 5*(2), 22-31.
Vining, A. R., & Weimer, D. (1998, March-April). Government supply and government production failure: A framework based on contestability. *Journal of Public Policy, 10*, 54-90.
Wanna, J. (2004). Introduction—the changing role of central budget agencies. In J. Wanna, L. Jensen, & J. de Vries (Eds.), *Controlling public expenditure and the changing role of central budget agencies—Better guardians?* (pp. 1-28). Sydney, Autralia: Macmillan.
Web plays wild card in U.S. election. (2004, October 19). *Toronto Star*, p. 27.
Weick, K. E., & Sutcliffe, K. M. (2001). *Managing the unexpected: Assuring high performance in an age of complexity*. San Francisco: Jossey-Wiley.

Welch, J. (2001). *Straight from the gut*. New York: Warner Business Books.
Wescott, C. (2001). Measuring governance in developing Asia. In L. R. Jones, J. Guthrie, & P. Steane (Eds.), *Learning From International Public Management Reform* (Vol. 11B, pp. 295-310). Oxford, England: JAI Press.
Wescott, C. (2003). Hierarchies, networks and local government in Viet Nam. *International Public Management Review, 4*(2), 33-47.
Wescott, C. (2004a). E-government in the Asia-Pacific region: Progress and Challenges. In J. V. Carrasquero et al. (Eds.), *Proceedings of international conference on politics and information systems: Technologies and applications* (Vol. 2, pp. 116-121). Orlando, FL: International Institute of Informatics and Systemics.
Wescott, C. (2004b). Improving public administration in the Asia-Pacific region: Lessons, approaches and reform priorities. *International Public Management Review, 5*(2), 78-102.
Wescott, C., & Jones L. R. (2005, October). *Fiscal devolution in East Asia, Asian Development Bank*. Working paper presented at the training workshop on optimizing local revenue generation for local governments and development, Makati City, Philippines, Manila.
Wescott, C., & Jones L. R. (2006). *Improving the performance of management in Asia*. Manila, Philippines: Asian Development Bank.
Wescott, C., & Porter, D. (2002). Fiscal decentralization and citizen participation in East Asia. In I. Lichaed (Ed.), *Citizens in charge: Managing local budgets in East Asia and Latin America*. Washington, DC: Inter-American Development Bank. Retrieved DATE?, from http://www.adb.org/Governance/fiscal_decentralization.pdf
Whyte, G. (1989). Groupthink reconsidered. *Academy of Management Review, 14*(1), 40-56.
Wildavsky, A. (1964). *The politics of the budgetary process*. Boston: Little-Brown.
Wildavsky, A. (1966). Toward a radical incrementalism. In A. De Grazia (Ed.), *Congress: The first branch of government* (pp. 27-45). Washington, DC: American Enterprise Institute.
Wildavsky, A. (1988). *The new politics of the budgetary process*. Glenview, IL: Scott, Foresman.
Wildavsky, A., & Hammond, A. (1965). Comprehensive vs. Incremental Budgeting in the Department of Agriculture. *Administrative Sciences Quarterly, 10*, 321-346.
Williamson, O. E. (1975). *Markets and hierarchies*. New York: Free Press.
Williamson, O. E. (1985). *The economic institutions of capitalism*. New York: Free Press.
Womack, J. P., Jones, D. T., & Roos, D. (1990). *The machine that changed the world: Based on the Massachusetts Institute of Technology 5-million dollar 5-year study on the future of the automobile*. New York: Rawson Associates.
Wong C. (2005). *Public sector budget management issues in China*. Paris: Organisation for Economic Co-operation and Development. Retrieved from www.oecd.org/gov/budget
Wong, C., & Mountfield, E. (2005). Public expenditure on the frontline: Toward effective management by subnational governments. In *World Bank, East Asia*

decentralizes: Making local government work (pp. 85-106). Washington DC: World Bank.

World Bank. (2001). *Global economic prospects.* Washington, DC: Author.

World Bank. (2002). *Global economic prospects.* Washington, DC: Author.

World Bank. (2003a). *Decentralizing Indonesia.* Jakarta, Indonesia: Author. Retrived DATE?, from http://www.gdsonline.org/resources/pdf/keyreading/1%20decentralizing_indonesia.pdf

World Bank. (2003b). *Public expenditure review.* Washington, DC: Author.

World Bank. (2005). *Global economic prospects* (Table 1.1, p. 25). Washington, DC: Author.

Xiang, H., & Lou J. (Eds.). (2004). *Five years of budget reform in China, 1998-2003 (in Chinese).* Beijing: China Financial Economics Press.

Yuk-fai Au, K., Vertinsky, I., & Yu-long Wang, D. (2001). New Public Management in Hong Kong: The long march toward reform. In L. R. Jones, J. Guthrie, & P. Steane (Eds.), *Learning from international public management reform* (Vol. 11B, pp. 311-336). Oxford, England: JAI Press.

Yu-Ying, K. (2001). New public management in Taiwan: Government reinvention. In L. R. Jones, J. Guthrie, & P. Steane (Eds.), *Learning from international public management reform* (Vol. 11B, pp. 337-351). Oxford, England: JAI Press.

Zahra, S. A., & George, G. (2002). Absorptive capacity: A review, reconceptualization, and extension. *Academy of Management Review, 27*(2), 185-203.

Zhang, T., & Zou, H. (1998). Fiscal decentralization, public spending and economic growth in China. *Journal of Public Economics, 67,* 221-240.

Zimmerman, J. L. (1995). *Accounting for decision making and control.* Chicago: Irwin

Zuboff, S. (1988). *In the age of the smart machine: The future of work and power.* New York: Basic Books.

Printed in the United States
71832LV00001B/193-225